THE BUZZ ON

FINANCE

John Craddock

LF LEBHAR-FRIEDMAN BOOKS
NEW YORK • CHICAGO • LOS ANGELES • LONDON • PARIS • TOKYO

The Buzz On Finance

Lebhar-Friedman Books
425 Park Avenue
New York, NY 10022

Copyright © 2000 Lebhar-Friedman Books
The Buzz On™ is a trademark of Lebhar-Friedman Books.

All rights reserved. No part of this work covered by the copyright hereon may be reproduced or used in any form or by any means—graphic, electronic, or mechanical, including photocopying, recording, taping, or information storage and retrieval systems—without the written permission of the publisher.

Published by Lebhar-Friedman Books
Lebhar-Friedman Books is a company of Lebhar-Friedman, Inc.

Printed in the United States of America

Library of Congress Cataloging-in-Publication Data on file at the Library of Congress

ISBN: 0-86730-818-4

Produced by Progressive Publishing
Editor: John Craddock; Creative Director: Nancy Lycan; Art Director: Peter Royland
Editorial Contributors: Rusty Fischer, Martha Richard, Justin Misik, Gordon Theisen
Designers: Angela Connolly, Vivian Torres, Bill Payne, Rena Bracey

Visit our Web site at lfbooks.com

Volume Discounts
This book makes a great gift and incentive. Call (212) 756-5248 for information on volume discounts

THE BUZZ ON FINANCE

ACKNOWLEDGMENTS

The author dutifully wishes to thank the following for their contributions to this book:

Chris White, several of whose Top-5 lists appear in this book and who was a countless inspiration for those that don't! Chris is owner of TopFive.com, at http://www.topfive.com.

Haythum Raafat Khalid, who has graciously allowed us to use the quotes found in this book, which also appear on his website, Famous Quotations Network: http://www.famous-quotations.com.

The staff at Lycomm and especially Nancy Lycan and her assistant, Sissy.

THE BUZZ ON™ FINANCE

CONTENTS

INTRO: CRACKING THE CODE 1
Take Stock of Hollywood 2
But That Was Then 4

CHAPTER 1: THE ABSOLUTE BASICS:
YOUR FINANCIAL FUTURE (OR TOTAL LACK THEREOF) 5
This Could Be You 6
    What it Takes to Invest? Savings & Strategy 7
    However, Before You Invest, Meet Your Finances 7
    Getting Started: Your Income and Expenses 9
    Keeping Records 10
A Word or Two About Savings: How to Start 10
    Just Save It 11
    Save in a Special Kind of Mutual Fund 13
    Plusses of Money Market Funds 14
    Negatives of Money Market Funds 14
What Savings Aren't & Your Credit 14
    There Must be Some Kinda Way Out of Here 15
The R Word 16
    I'm a Member of the IRA 17
    Roth IRA 17
    Glad You Asked 18
    Mini-Glossary 20
Finance Diaries: Budget Blues 24

CHAPTER 2: HOW THE WORLD WORKS:
RISK AND REWARD, FEAR AND GREED 27
The Big Picture 28
    Rate of Return 29
What's Your Risk Tolerance? 32
    What Investments to Choose? 32
    You Own It 33
    You Lend It 34
    Other Things 34
Setting Strategy 35
    Is There a Formula? 35
    Are There Really New Fundamentals? 37

> The Dot Com Bears 38
> One Dozen Facts, Questions, and Almost No Answers 39
> The History of Economics 41
> Theoryland 42

CHAPTER 3: INVESTING 43
> The Old Way 43
> The New Way 43

Blue Light Brokers, Or: They Don't Call Them "Discount" for Nothing .. 44
> Cheap, Cheaper, Cheapest 44
> Read the Fine Print 44
> Ante Up 45
> It's a Bank! 45
> Mutual Funds 45
> Selection 45
> Research 45
> It's Free! 45

Picking an Online Firm: Your Priorities Will Change 46
> When Old Is New 47
> How to Open an Account 47
> Online Brokerages: A Sampling 48
> What Else? 49
> Placing an Order 49

Pot Holes on the Internet 50
> Keep This in Mind (Beware) 50

The New Account Agreement 52
Selecting Your Broker (If He/She Is a Human Being or a Variation Thereof) .. 54
Basic Investing 55
> Places to Invest, Or: Are You Sure "Red 17" Is Safe? 56

Regionals 57
> Philadelphia Stock Exchange 57
> Chicago Stock Exchange 58
> Market Maker 58
> Electronic Communications Network (ECN) 59

Getting Started: Research 59
Finance Diaries: Get Rich Quick! 61

CHAPTER 4: STOCKS:
HOW TO ENTER THE MARKET (CAREFULLY) 65

Does Anyone Understand the Stock Market? 66
> A Closer Look 66
> Investment Categories 67
> Profits Matter 68
> Is the P/E Still Useful? 69
> Are There Other Ratios? 70

Learning the Ropes Without Being Hung 72
> Annual Reports 73
> Government Reports 74
> Third Party 75
> Sites That Can Help 76

How Do You Build Your Portfolio? 80
> Baby Steps 81
> Stock Screeners on the Web 81
> Day Tripper 82
> Then There's Gina 82
> Other Ways 84
> Know the Product 84
> Keep Your Ears Open 84

Fun, Fun, Fun: Listening to the Experts	86
The Dot Coms	87
No Net	87
Self-fulfilling Prophets	88
Model Investor: In for the Long Term	89
Nervous Wreck	90

CHAPTER 5: MUTUAL FUNDS: "FUN"-DS FOR EVERYONE ... 91

Are Mutual Funds a Good Idea?	92
All Mutual Funds are Not Alike	93
Bond Funds	93
Equity Funds	93
Index Funds	93
Hybrid Funds	94
Money Market Funds	94
Industry Funds	94
Funds of Funds	94
Socially Responsible Funds	94
Where Mutual Funds Invest	95
What Difference Does It Make?	95
How Mutual Funds Earn Money	96
How to Choose a Mutual Fund	97
Fees? What Fees?	98
Historical Performance	100
Finance Diaries	102
Where to Find Out About Mutual Funds	106
Sources	106
The Prospectus	108
After You Invest	108

CHAPTER 6: BONDS AND MORE, FINDING YOUR BEST BETS ... 109

What Gives With the Bond Market?	110
Types of Bonds	113
Other Government Bonds	115
Finance Diaries: Bonding	117
Beyond This Point, There Lie Dragons	121
Chicago Mercantile Exchange	122
MidAmerica Commodity Exchange	123
Chicago Board of Trade	124
Coffee, Sugar, and Cocoa Exchange, Inc.	124

CHAPTER 7: INVESTING AT HOME ... 125

Fear and Desire	126
Is it Worth It?	126
To Buy or Not to Buy	126
A House Is a Home Is an Asset	127
Financing Your Purchase	128
How Much Can You Afford?	128
Lender Fees	129
Yet More Fees	129
Finance Diaries: House (of Blues) Hunting	129
Title Insurance	132
Escrow Fees	132
Legal Fees	133
Mortgages	133
Some Things to Look Out For	135
Shop Around	135
Making an Offer	136
Deposit	137

  Prorated Payments 137
  Personal Property and Property for Sale 137
What to Look for in a House 138
  Location, Baby 138
  Layout 139
  Appliances and Utilities 140
  Building Materials 140
  Some Things to Worry About 141
How to Find a House 142
  Everywhere a Sign 142
  Agents 142
  What to Know About Agents 143
  What Agents Are Good For 143
What to Do Once You've Found a House You Want 144
  After You've Bought Your House 144
  Refinancing 145
Other Kinds of Real Estate Investments 145
  Rentals 146
  Land 146
  Second Homes 146
  Borrowing 146

CHAPTER 8: FRAUDS & SCAMS:
HOW TO SPOT (AND AVOID) INVESTMENT SCHEMES 147
The Internet: Faster, Better Swindles 148
  The "Pump and Dump" Scam 148
  Better Ask the SEC 149
  A Taste of "Spam" 150
  Off-Shore Frauds 152
  Pyramid Power 153
Finance Diaries: SCAM$ 155

CHAPTER 9:
STARTING YOUR OWN BUSINESS, OR INVESTING IN YOURSELF 157
Web Effect 158
Are You the Entrepreneurial Type? 159
  What's Your Business Gonna Be, Exactly? 160
  The Business Plan 161
  Business at Home 164
  An Office of Your Own 166
  Equipment 167
  Financing Your Business 169
Finance Diaries: Business Cents (Or, Risk & Reward, Inc.) 173
  Legal Matters 179
  Payment 181
  Employees 182
  Marketing 184
  Price 184
  Customer Satisfaction 184
  Resources 185
  Franchises & Turnkey Businesses 185

APPENDIX 187

GLOSSARY 193

INDEX 203

intro
CRACKING THE CODE

So you think you're ready to navigate your financial future. Maybe. Sort of. Gulp. But you're confused, and who wouldn't be. Everything is written in code: 401(k), SEC, EBITAD. A CD isn't even a real CD like the hundreds scattered around your apartment. It's actually something to do with savings. Savings? What's that?

But now you've got a job, or you're thinking about taking one, and you have a paycheck, or you're thinking about actually receiving one, and you need to know something about money. What does it mean if your cash isn't flowing? What is the deal with online investing or putting money in retirement accounts? After all, you're nowhere near your parents' age, so why bother? Meanwhile, who are all those people making a fortune trading stocks in dot-com companies? You might not know a stock certificate from a stock car, but when you read that something called Qualcomm increased by 2,600 percent in value in a year, that sounds pretty good. Even Ringo Starr is in on it (in a commercial anyway).

INTRO: CRACKING THE CODE

TAKE STOCK OF HOLLYWOOD

Yes, it's true the crystal ball on your financial future is looking a little cloudy. But it's time to meet your budget face-to-face and come to grips with how to save. You need to learn about the best places to put your money in case you want it fast. Credit is another touchy area. If it's bad, there are ways to fix it.

And whether it's investing in stocks, bonds, mutual funds, commodities, real estate, or even (double gulp) starting a business of your own, there's a way for almost anyone to point his or her financial future in the right direction.

Hey, you may know more than you think. Movies are a great source to learn about finance. Think about the ones you might have seen:

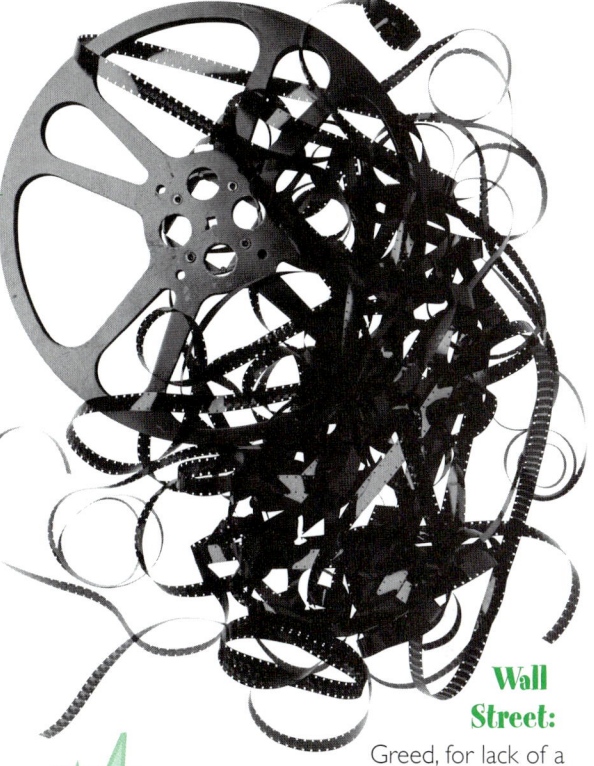

Wall Street: Greed, for lack of a better word, is good. Apparently so is greasy hair. And who can resist another riveting performance by Charlie Sheen as a budding stock market star?

Boiler Room: Sleazy enough to have the characters quote lines from *Wall Street* as their mantra. Great way to learn which scams to avoid.

Trading Places: Can a street crook, a preppy, and a hooker take over the commodities markets and make a fortune? Well, of course they can! So what's stopping you?

Glengarry Glen Ross: Thinking about going into sales as a career move? This is a grifter's guide to sleaze.

Also, you probably have heard somewhere that the business world is changing, with a death-match debate over the old economy versus the new economy.

INTRO: CRACKING THE CODE — 2

What's this about? It's easy to understand this riddle: Just look at *The Godfather* (Old Economy) and *The Matrix* (New Economy).

In *The Godfather*, you hear the line, "You're taking it personal and this is business" so often, you should realize it's a business movie. Okay, an extreme business movie. When you get fired by the Godfather, there's no chance of a rehire. But the entire plot of *The Godfather* is built around solving business problems associated with what is now called the old economy. The Corleone family has been involved in traditional businesses for its industry: prostitution, bookmaking, hijacking. These are essentially mature businesses where they are trying to maintain market share against rival families.

They want to expand to new markets, namely the casinos in Vegas. The Corleones think big-time gambling is a more viable business. Michael keeps saying in five years that the family will be legit, meaning they aspire to be about as respectable as Donald Trump, though they already have better hair. But this is still old economy stuff.

Overall, the movie continually focuses on business issues important to any company, such as employee relationships:

In *The Godfather* a disloyal bodyguard-employee, Paulie, calls in sick the day some gunmen shoot down Don Corleone. The interim Godfather job falls to Sonny Corleone, who steps in and exercises some solid management skills. After learning of the circumstances of the shooting, he calls Paulie in, offers him some brandy for an apparent head cold, then quickly determines that Paulie isn't that sick. He orders that he be "fired." We don't know whether this is done on a Friday, the day consultants say is the best day to fire someone. We do know that the assassin leaves the gun and takes the cannolis.

And so on.

3 — INTRO: CRACKING THE CODE

The basic premise of the movie is, "How do you define what is real?" Now, think a minute about the value of an Internet stock and how that value is determined: What's real? What's not? They are just dots on a computer screen. Hey, that's the entire drift of The Matrix.

One of the first clues in this real/not real issue is when Neo starts to have an inkling that his brain may be tuned in to the wrong channel. He receives telephone calls explaining that someone is watching his every move, as if some giant software system is tracking him. In fact, it is. He comes to find the "truth" by merging with the software system and, in the end, beating the competition. All right, there's some sort of Terminator 2/Messiah riff also going on. But the movie's central point is clear: Reality in electron world is determined by how you view it, and it can be very fluid.

The same way with finance: In the new economy, you have to figure out which are the brightest dots on the computer screen. Or, if you're an old economy type, how to keep those investments you made from sleeping with the fishes. So get started already.

BUT THAT WAS THEN...

The New Economy? Look no further than The Matrix. Yep, even with an "actor" like Keanu Reeves (as Neo), it's a movie that captures the chaos of making a go of it in a world that is all electrons, i.e. the "new" Internet economy.

INTRO: CRACKING THE CODE — 4

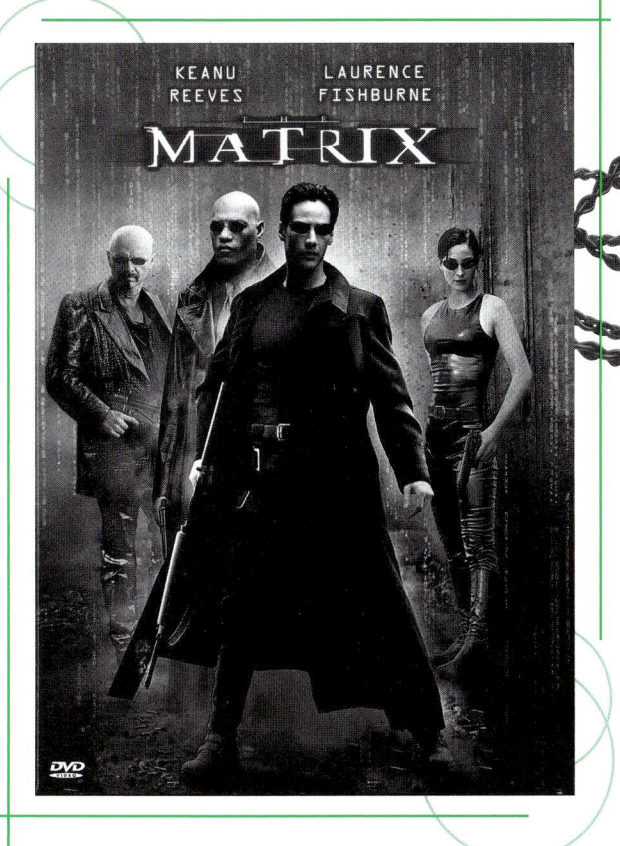

1

THE ABSOLUTE BASICS: YOUR FINANCIAL FUTURE
(OR TOTAL LACK THEREOF)

Finance is a term used in a variety of ways, almost always with the main meaning being "money."

"I can't finance that."
"My finances aren't so hot."
"Who understands finance?"

The answer to the last question is no one, at least in terms of being able to accurately predict what will happen next in the financial world. It has historically been a topic so complex and fluid, it bred the dullest and least useful professional class in history—the economist, who is quickly followed by the accountant, whose job it is to count money, and the banker, who stores the money, and so on down the financial line. That anyone bothers tackling the subject at all befuddles logic except—having money is really useful!

CHAPTER 1: THE ABSOLUTE BASICS: YOUR FINANCIAL FUTURE

THIS COULD BE YOU

Meet Marie and Bill. They have been a couple for two years. She is 24, sports some interesting tattoos, and earns $35,000 a year as a computer programmer. Bill is also 24, opted against tattoos, loves cars, and just finished a graduate course in Web graphic design. He is coming off two internships and soon will enter the work force. He expects to make $30,000 to $40,000 initially, which will give them a combined income of about $70,000. They have some student loan payments, low credit card balances, one car payment, and a Honda with 149,000 miles; they have been sharing an apartment for $800 a month.

They think they'll *maybe* get married—if they have time and their parents keep bitching at them—but more immediately they look forward to a two-income household and more money than they've ever had. And it's theirs. They earned it.

"We were sitting around one Sunday," Marie said, running her hand through her hair, which varies in color, depending on the day. "And wondering what we might want to do with our money in the future. You see all the new technology, and everyone and his brother is a day trader in stocks and everything, and since we're both on the computer most of the time we're awake, we figure, 'How can we get in on this?'"

What makes Marie and Bill typical of their generation is that they are looking to the future with a careful eye. A survey by *American Demographics* magazine examined the savings habits of Americans and revealed that 18- to 34-year-olds "lead the way when it comes to setting aside funds for retirement." Amazingly, according to the survey, "some 64 percent of this group makes a concerted (and consistent) effort to save, with almost half beginning their contributions before the age of 25."

What's fueling this financial fascination among 20- and 30-somethings? One answer, says *American Demographics*, is social security, and the belief that the federal retirement fund will fall far short of what they'll need.

Fear apparently has caused thousands of smart and savvy hipsters like you to squirrel away money with a rodentlike instinct, worried that some wrathful winter will strike with a vengeance, and they won't have enough nuts hoarded. But the question remains: Where to put the nuts?

CHAPTER 1: THE ABSOLUTE BASICS: YOUR FINANCIAL FUTURE

WHAT IT TAKES TO INVEST?
SAVINGS & STRATEGY

To invest you have to save, and the truth is that most people don't save, especially Americans. Compared to other countries, the U.S. savings rate is less than half of what people in other industrialized nations sock away. So if you are one of your generation who is saving, you already are ahead of the game. When you think about investing, you are really thinking about your future: Do you have an age in mind when you might want to stop working? Do you have plans for having a family? Do you just want to sit on a big pile of money like some potentate and enjoy the freedom? Oftentimes the financial planning professionals use the "r" word: Retirement. That usually doesn't strike a resounding note with people who have the bulk of their working careers in front of them. But if having financial freedom at some point in your life is an option in your viewfinder, you'll need one other thing: a strategy.

While it's tempting to go for some big hit—to find the next Microsoft—it's a lot more likely that you'll end up with significant wealth by taking it slow and steady. And the great thing 20- and 30-somethings have going for them is time. You can lay out plans that allow you to achieve your goals over a period of years. Another potential advantage is the ease with which you can make an investment. For years, investing was done by professionals, who from their lofty perch made pronouncements and key decisions about what the right investment choices might be. Some even deserved their good reputation. But there was always an element of mystery involved about their special knowledge.

One of the biggest changes in investing today is the amount of information available to anyone. You can hardly avoid the onslaught of financial info blasting across television, radio, and, of course, the Internet. One of the goals of this book is to show you how to use this information so you can direct your own financial future.

It might not make you a pro, but you can at least make informed decisions. And you'll be smart enough to know when to seek help from a professional.

HOWEVER,
BEFORE YOU INVEST, MEET YOUR FINANCES

As the financial planners like to say, "You can never take a journey without knowing where you're starting from, and a journey to financial security is

Your Net Worth Statement

Assets	Current Value	Liabilities	Amount
Cash	_____	Mortgage balance	_____
Checking account	_____	Credit cards	_____
Savings	_____	Bank loans	_____
Cash value of life insurance	_____	Car loans	_____
Retirement accounts	_____	Personal loans	_____
Real estate	_____	Real estate	_____
Home	_____		
Other	_____		
Investments	_____		
Personal property	_____		
Total	_____	Total	_____
		Net Worth	_____

CHAPTER 1: THE ABSOLUTE BASICS: YOUR FINANCIAL FUTURE

no different." You also have to decide how active you want to be in this journey and what's your speed limit, so to speak. So let's check to see what kind of "vehicle" we're dealing with.

This is called your net worth, and figuring out this number will help start the process of investing. Here are a couple of terms you'll need to know:

Assets: *Possessions you have that have value. As you can see from the list on the previous page, this covers such things as savings, personal items, and real estate.*

Liabilities: *The amount you owe.*

If you subtract your liabilities from your assets, and the assets are larger than your liabilities, you have a "positive" net worth. Good.

If your liabilities are greater than your assets, you have a "negative" net worth. Bad—but at least now you know.

This should be updated every so often, once a year is enough. This should give you some idea of where you stand financially. Don't panic. You're young.

Internet Sources

There are a variety of sources on the Internet that can help you evaluate your financial situation and set some reasonable goals.

A site called **FinanCenter (www.financenter.com)** has easy to understand guidelines to figure how much money you might have to invest.

Also, if you don't seem to have any money to invest, there's even a service to help address the issue. A site developed by **Ohio State University (www.ag.ohio-state.edu/~ames1/page3.htm)** offers a step by step program that can help put you on the right track. Topics include "Where Does Your Money Go?" "Stop Spending Leaks," and "Keeping Records in Order."

CHAPTER 1: THE ABSOLUTE BASICS: YOUR FINANCIAL FUTURE

GETTING STARTED: YOUR INCOME AND EXPENSES

Now, you need to make a record of your income and your expenses for each month.

First write down what you earn (along with what anybody else who might contribute to your financial plight might earn) each month; that's your income. Then calculate your monthly expenses.

Subtract expenses from income, and this should show you if you have money left over to save. It also can alert you to ways to cut some unnecessary expense. For example, if you eat out every night and your food bill is 40 percent of your income, you might try to eat in once in a while. Just a suggestion.

And remember that little things can add up. A couple of packs of Twinkies cost $1. If you spend $1 a day, that adds up to $365 a year. If you saved that $365 for just one year, and put it into a savings account or an investment that earns 5 percent a year, it would grow to $465.84 by the end of five years, and by the end of 30 years, to $1,577.50. It might not seem like a lot of money, but all the little things do add up. If that $365 was $3,650, you'd be looking at a savings of more than $5,000 in five years.

That's the power of compound interest. Over time—your most

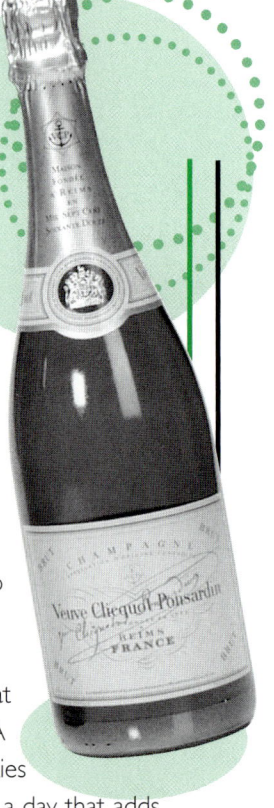

Monthly Income & Expenses
This should show you where you are spending your money.

Income: *(This is what you earn)* $_____

Expenses:

Housing: rent or mortgage	_____
Electricity:	_____
Gas/Oil:	_____
Telephone:	_____
Water/Sewer:	_____
Property tax:	_____
Furniture:	_____
Food:	_____
Transportation:	_____
Loans:	_____
Insurance:	_____
Education:	_____
Recreation:	_____
Health care:	_____
Gifts:	_____
Other:	_____
TOTAL EXPENSES:	$_____

Income - Expenses = Potential Savings

CHAPTER 1: THE ABSOLUTE BASICS: YOUR FINANCIAL FUTURE

valuable asset at this stage—even a small amount saved can add up.

So just tell the waiter: "Bring the Dom Perignon, hold the Twinkies."

In truth, your life probably moves at such a fast pace, you find it hard to keep track of every nickel and dime. You know what you spend on larger items, such as rent, car payments, and champagne, but it's the little ones that may be eating up your funds. "If you take a piece of paper and write down everything you spend, not including the change, you'll be shocked at how much money you go through that you don't realize," says Jim Rhodes, director of education at Metropolitan Financial Management, a Roseville, Minnesota, based non-profit organization that specializes in helping people with consumer debt.

KEEPING RECORDS

If you filled out the two lists mentioned previously, you might have noticed that you had to dig through piles of paper to find the numbers. Keeping a close track of your expenses and your earnings is a necessary part of building a solid financial future. As you invest, you'll quickly realize you need to save the receipts and other scraps of paper to help keep an accurate record for your taxes.

It's, in fact, one of the consequences of investing that your taxes will become more complicated, and you will (if you are successful) be searching all over for ways to minimize your tax bill. Most of the statements you receive of your investment records will break out the interest you earned or other amounts that are necessary to complete your income tax forms. Also, there are a variety of tax deductible and tax-deferred retirement plans you can use to prepare for your future, and these records will be important. Record keeping becomes of paramount importance if you ever are audited by the IRS. Saving paper isn't fun—but then again, neither is being audited by the IRS.

A WORD OR TWO ABOUT SAVINGS: •• HOW TO START

If the word "saving" has entered into your thought process other than as part of a movie title or in relation to empty beer cans or rubber bands, that's good. If you already have some money left over each pay period, you might find it easier to take a set amount from your paycheck and deposit it directly into a savings account or something similar. This is a really good idea. Once you accept the fact that you have the financial discipline of a five-year-old and if the money is in your checking account you'll blow it, the faster you can save. Generally, financial advisers will tell you to keep about six month's of living expenses in an account for emergencies, such as a layoff at work or sickness.

CHAPTER 1: THE ABSOLUTE BASICS: YOUR FINANCIAL FUTURE

JUST SAVE IT

There are plenty of places to put your money, and still have it available if you need it fast. There's the traditional passbook savings account at your bank or savings and loan, often maligned as a step above a tin can buried in the backyard because the interest rate is so paltry. Most banks also have accounts that pay slightly higher interest rates if you keep a minimum balance of a few thousand dollars; the number can vary widely from bank to bank.

Another low-low-risk investment that can easily be converted into cash is the certificate of deposit (CD). A CD is not just something you listen to; it's a special type of deposit account with a bank or savings and loan that typically offers a higher rate of interest than a regular savings account. CDs have an added safety feature most other investments don't: They are, like a savings account, guaranteed by the Federal Deposit Insurance Corporation for up to $100,000. So if you see FDIC insured, that's good.

Here's how CDs work: When you purchase a CD, you invest a fixed sum for a fixed period of time—six months, one year, five years, or more. In exchange, the issuing bank pays you interest, typically at regular intervals. When you cash in or redeem your CD, you receive the money you originally invested plus any other interest you might be due.

Here's the downside: If you redeem your CD before it matures, you probably will have to pay an "early withdrawal" penalty, which can vary depending on where you bought the CD. Basically, you'll forfeit some of the interest.

Usually, people purchase CDs through banks, but now many brokerage firms offer CDs. Sometimes they advertise or send material through the mail. These brokerage firms—known as "deposit brokers"—can usually negotiate a higher rate of interest for a CD. They basically promise to bring a certain amount of deposits to an institution, which gives the brokerage a chance to negotiate a higher rate. The deposit broker can then offer these "brokered CDs" to their customers.

There are some other variations, but here are some questions to ask, all recommended by the U.S. Securities and Exchange Commission:

Find Out When the CD Matures: A lot of people don't ask and then blow a gasket when they learn that they've tied up their money for years. Before you purchase a CD, ask to see the maturity date in writing.

CHAPTER 1: THE ABSOLUTE BASICS: YOUR FINANCIAL FUTURE

Confirm the Interest Rate You'll Receive and How You'll Be Paid: You should receive a disclosure document that tells you the interest rate on your CD and whether the rate is fixed (set in stone) or variable (changes at certain times). Be sure to ask how often the bank pays interest—for example, monthly or semi-annually. And confirm how that interest will be paid to you—for example, by check or by an electronic transfer of funds.

Ask Whether the Interest Rate Ever Changes: If you're considering investing in a variable-rate CD, make sure you understand when and how the rate can change. Some variable-rate CDs feature a "multi-step" or "bonus rate" structure in which interest rates increase or decrease over time according to a pre-set schedule.

Research Any Penalties for Early Withdrawal: Be sure to find out how much you'll have to pay if you cash in your CD before maturity.

For Brokered CDs, Identify the Issuer: Find out where the deposit broker plans to deposit your money. Also be sure to ask what record-keeping procedures the deposit broker has in place to assure your CD will have federal deposit insurance. The broker has to tell you.

At one time, most CDs paid a fixed interest rate until they reached maturity. But, like many other products in today's markets, CDs have become more complicated. Investors may now choose among variable-rate CDs, long-term CDs, and CDs with special redemption features (i.e. in the event the owner dies).

Some long-term, high-yield CDs have "call" features, meaning that the issuing bank may choose to terminate—or call—the CD after only one year or some other fixed period of time. Only the issuing bank may call a CD, not the investor. For example, a bank might decide to call its high-yield CDs if interest rates fall. But if you've invested in a long-term CD and interest rates subsequently rise, you'll be locked in at the lower rate.

Before you consider purchasing a CD from your bank or brokerage firm, make sure you fully understand all of its terms. Carefully read the disclosure statements, including any fine print. And don't be dazzled by high yields. Ask questions and get the answers before you fork over your money.

Investigate Any Call Features: Callable CDs give the issuing bank the right to terminate the CD after a set period of time, but they do not give you that same right. Figures. If the bank calls or redeems your CD, you should receive the full amount of your original deposit plus any unpaid interest.

Understand the Difference Between Call Features and Maturity: Don't assume that a "federally insured one-year non-callable" CD matures in one year. Careful reading shows it could be that there's a no-call provision for the first year. If you have any doubt, ask the sales representative at your bank or brokerage firm to explain the CD's call features and to confirm when it matures.

The bottom-line question you should always ask yourself is: Does this investment make sense for me? A

CHAPTER 1: THE ABSOLUTE BASICS: YOUR FINANCIAL FUTURE — 12

high-yield, long-term CD with a maturity date of 15 to 20 years may make sense for many younger investors who want to diversify their financial holdings, but might not make sense for others.

SAVE IN A SPECIAL KIND OF MUTUAL FUND

You may think a mutual fund is a little more sophisticated than what you're looking for at the moment, but here's another way to put your money in a safe place and get the max out of it.

The three main categories of mutual funds are money market funds, bond funds, and stock funds; and within each category there are countless types. After all, there are more than 10,000 mutual funds. In this section we'll deal with only one type that's designed for savings so you can get your hands on the money fairly fast: the money market mutual funds.

Money market mutual funds have relatively low risk, compared to other mutual funds. The fund managers are limited by law to investing in certain high-quality, short-term investments, such as U.S. government securities. Money market funds try to keep their value at a stable $1 per share, meaning you put a dollar in and when you cash in the share you get a dollar out. The "interest" on your money is paid in a dividend. (Caution: On rare occasion the value may fall below $1 if the fund's investments perform poorly. Investor losses have been very rare, but they are possible.)

Banks now sell mutual funds, some of which carry the bank's name. But mutual funds sold in banks, including money market funds, are not bank deposits. Don't confuse a "money market mutual fund" with a "money market deposit account." The names are similar, but they are completely different:

A **money market fund** is a type of mutual fund. It is not guaranteed, and comes with a prospectus.

A **money market deposit account** is a bank deposit. It is really just a bank account. It is guaranteed by federal deposit insurance, and comes with a form explaining the guarantee.

CHAPTER 1: THE ABSOLUTE BASICS: YOUR FINANCIAL FUTURE

PLUSSES OF MONEY MARKET FUNDS

Pretty Safe: Cash investments are viewed as safe because your money generally is invested with reliable borrowers for only a brief period. In addition, the Securities and Exchange Commission requires that all taxable money market funds invest at least 95% of their assets in securities of the highest grade.

Current Income: Dividends, distributed monthly by the funds, typically are higher than the equivalent interest rate paid by a bank savings account or CD.

Cashing In: Most of the funds offer free check writing privileges, and you can redeem your money at any time.

NEGATIVES OF MONEY MARKET FUNDS

Inflation Eats It: From 1926 through 1998, cash investments returned an average of 3.9 percent per year while inflation averaged 3.1 percent, leaving a return after inflation of only 0.8 percent per year.

Risk: A money market fund is neither insured nor guaranteed by the Federal Deposit Insurance Corporation or any other government agency. The funds seek to maintain a stable $1 net asset value, but there is no assurance that they will do so.

WHAT SAVINGS AREN'T & YOUR CREDIT

Contrary to popular belief, it's important to note that "savings" are not the difference between the limit on your credit card and your current balance.

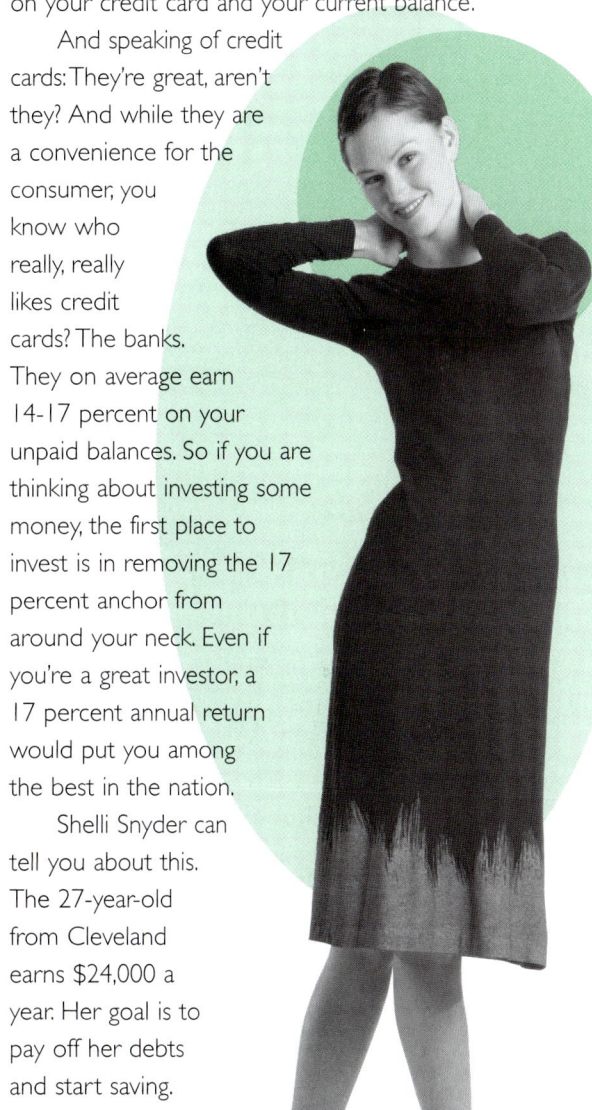

And speaking of credit cards: They're great, aren't they? And while they are a convenience for the consumer, you know who really, really likes credit cards? The banks. They on average earn 14-17 percent on your unpaid balances. So if you are thinking about investing some money, the first place to invest is in removing the 17 percent anchor from around your neck. Even if you're a great investor, a 17 percent annual return would put you among the best in the nation.

Shelli Snyder can tell you about this. The 27-year-old from Cleveland earns $24,000 a year. Her goal is to pay off her debts and start saving.

Although she says she's very good at telling other people how to manage their money, Shelli hasn't

CHAPTER 1: THE ABSOLUTE BASICS: YOUR FINANCIAL FUTURE — 14

been able to put that financial savvy to work for herself just yet. Her problem is debt. An aspiring systems administrator and Internet Web-design entrepreneur, Shelli works as a network technician at the "computer help" desk of a local university. It's a stopover job to keep the creditors away and lay the groundwork for her soon-to-be company, called WebInks.

With credit card debt, loan debt, and a self-admitted "ruined" credit rating, Shelli says she'd file for bankruptcy if it would take her school loans away, but she doesn't think it will. (She's right.) For now, she lives paycheck to paycheck, with a few certificates of deposit serving as saving accounts, and only a small basic retirement fund provided by her employer.

"Hopefully, I should be able to start saving in a few years, maybe a couple," she says.

Shelli's debt began in college where she spent freely on credit, believing that she would be able to make decent money after graduation. But that didn't happen right away. Her education was financed with loans and grants, and a large part of her woes came from the struggle of trying to pay off Perkins and Stafford loans. "I deferred my loans by taking classes at the school I work for," she says, "but now my deferment is over, and they have been coming after me, bugging my parents, my grandma. The credit cards were the main drain, though. You name it, I charged it: rent, food, books, clothing, frivolous things."

Shelli's not overly worried about her situation because she has a few tricks up her sleeve: She's managing her debt through free consumer credit counseling services and is about to start up a side-business tutoring people who are new to computers and the Internet. Keeping a positive outlook comes naturally for Shelli, and though she's under stress, it's easier for her to laugh about her situation. "Money doesn't grow on trees," she says, "but if it did, I probably would have bought one on credit."

THERE MUST BE SOME KINDA WAY OUT OF HERE

Just when you thought you were getting away from report cards, there's this one that follows you around like a bad relationship that won't go away. It's your credit report. Remember that rug shampooer you rented but forgot to return the "super brush" attachment that your dog hid with his secret bone collection? The company sent a bill, and you said, I'm moving anyway. Well, there's another kind of collection looming. That's the notice sent to your credit report that you stiffed the rug shampoo company. To get the report you need to contact: Equifax (800-685-1111), Experian (800-682-7654), or Trans Union (800-888-4213). You will be charged about $8. It will show how good or bad your record is for paying your bills.

As Shelli Snyder knows, in some cases these complaints about your payment record are true and the only way to make it right is to pay your bills promptly. If you are falsely accused of being a deadbeat, you call the credit agencies and tell them they are wrong. However, if you win the dispute, occasionally the error will reappear. There is a regulation that prevents

CHAPTER 1: THE ABSOLUTE BASICS: YOUR FINANCIAL FUTURE

this from happening, but you know that computers can't read regulations.

Also, the report might be true but you've turned over a new leaf (again). If you once were delinquent on an account but now pay on time, it's possible to contact the creditor and ask that the old information be deleted. If you can offer a convincing explanation of both your delinquency and your improved credit behavior, you may be able to get them to drop the thing.

To build new credit, you'll have to prove you are a good risk. If you still have a credit card—Visa, MasterCard, or Discover—use it modestly, pay it off each month, and check to be sure that the credit bureaus are notified. But if all your accounts were closed, there's still a way to get back on track—with a secured bank card. These cards offer people who can't get a standard Visa or MasterCard the chance to start over. Secured cards typically have higher annual fees and interest charges than unsecured cards and require you to deposit reserve funds in a savings account as collateral.

> **"WE CAN LOAN YOU ENOUGH MONEY TO GET YOU COMPLETELY OUT OF DEBT."**
> —RANDOM BANK SIGN

A free booklet published by the Federal Trade Commission, "Getting Back in the Black," explains credit repair. You can get a copy by writing to the Commission's Public Reference Branch, Room 130, Sixth Street and Pennsylvania Avenue, N.W., Washington, D.C. 20580.

As a last resort, you can do what more than 1.3 million cash-strapped consumers have done in the past year—file for bankruptcy. Under Chapter 7, or straight bankruptcy, you fill out a form and file it with a fee of about $160.

A judge then decides how to divide your assets among your creditors. But some debts can't be erased by Chapter 7, including most student loans, child-support obligations, and back taxes. While bankruptcy has lost some of its stigma, you'll live with it as a black mark on your credit report for a decade to come.

THE R WORD

This is related to savings, but not quite the same because we're talking about putting your money in a place that's going to be a little more difficult to retrieve it if you have to. Basically it is a way to save some money and dodge some taxes. We're talking about retirement options here.

Congress passed a bill called the Taxpayers Relief Act back in 1997; it went into effect January 1, 1998. It's a law that's burdened with a name that should normally send you running for cover, but it has some advantages you need to know about, and the sooner the better.

These options can be extremely useful at that period we will call "the time when you decide you want to stop working." Maybe that's age 65; maybe that's age 25. For example, if you ever visit Key West, Florida you'll see in bars, especially open-air bars, a class of young people who do not seem to have jobs but also seem to have enough money to sit around and drink all day. They often have blond mustaches, wear funny vests, sport great tans, and never look in a hurry. Where their

CHAPTER 1: THE ABSOLUTE BASICS: YOUR FINANCIAL FUTURE — 16

money is coming from, we won't speculate. Perhaps a well-invested retirement account? But there's no question about one thing: They're retired.

If you're not at that point yet, the topics we'll touch on here are important. These are called retirement accounts because, generally, if you wait until you're older, you can withdraw the money and get a tax break. But some are more flexible than others.

You may already be participating in a 401(k) account. About 27 million Americans have entered that fold. There are some real plusses: an immediate tax savings, the possibility of an additional contribution from your employer, and tax-deferred growth on your savings.

Your employer sets the maximum contribution as a percentage of your salary (usually 6-8 percent), with a ceiling of $10,000. You don't pay taxes on what you contribute to the fund. Some employers also match a portion of what you save each year, typically 50 cents on each dollar of the first 6% you put in. The money in your 401(k) grows free of income taxes, until you withdraw it. But if you withdraw money before age 59.5, you pay the taxman the income tax and an additional 10 percent. Ouch. This penalty is waived for certain early withdrawals, such as those made to pay medical expenses in excess of 7.5 percent of your income.

You'll read a lot more about 401(k)s later in the book. Following are some accounts you could open on your own tomorrow that will start working for you today.

I'M A MEMBER OF THE IRA

If you have no retirement plan at work, you can invest in a traditional Individual Retirement Account. Basically, you can deduct all of your contributions to a traditional IRA off your federal income taxes. Straight out. Say you owe $2,001 in taxes; you throw $2,000 in your IRA. You now owe $1 in taxes. But $2,000 is the limit you can add each year. The interest you earn on the money and the value of the investment in the IRA can accumulate each year without you paying taxes now. But this is a tax-deferred account, like the 401(k). Withdrawals are subject to ordinary income tax (about 25 to 30 percent in your bracket) and generally if you take out the money before you are a lot older, you pay a penalty of 10% on top of that. There's also a nondeductible IRA, but they are not as popular.

ROTH IRA

Contributions to a Roth IRA do not qualify for an up-front tax deduction. But the growth of the account is sheltered from taxes, and there are ways you can tap this fund to make it a good deal. It allows you to put up to $2,000 (non-deductible from your taxes) per year of your money into the account. While in the plan, the dividends, interest, and growth are not taxable, and money withdrawn from the plan is tax free under certain conditions.

17 — CHAPTER 1: THE ABSOLUTE BASICS: YOUR FINANCIAL FUTURE

GLAD YOU ASKED

A Few FAQs:

Can everyone have a Roth IRA?
Answer: A Roth IRA can be established by anyone with an income, even if you participate in various company retirement plans, such as 401(k)s.

What income levels define eligibility?
Answer: Probably nothing for you to worry about. It's roughly up to $110,000 for singles and $160,000 if you're married.

Is the contribution to the Roth IRA deductible from current taxes?
Answer: No.

Since the contribution to the Roth IRA is not deductible from current taxes, then what's the big deal?
Answer: There are a number of advantages, to wit: Most people can have a Roth IRA even though they have another company retirement plan. Dividends, interest, and capital gain growth within a Roth IRA are not taxable and monies eventually removed are tax free if the account is owned at least 5 years and the owner is over 59.5, which you're not going to be for a while. After the account is opened five years you can withdraw a maximum of $10,000 (contributions and earnings) without taxes or penalties for a first time home purchase. At any age, for any reason, you can withdraw the equivalent of the amount contributed (not the earnings) without tax or penalties.

How do I start one?
Go to a bank or a brokerage, which basically act as IRA custodians. It's just a matter of coming up with the money and filling out a form.

Which is better?
Roth Rules! For younger people, Roth is better, a lot of financial advisers say. It's more flexible.

A Walk in the Park

This is a quiz from the American Savings Education Council, modified for the 20- to 30-something reader, to help you figure out what you might need to save before you "stop working" (also known as retirement). Just something to get your attention. It's called the ballpark estimate.

1. How much annual income will you want in retirement? (Figure 70 percent of your current annual income just to maintain your current standard of living. Really.) So if you're earning $30,000, that's $21,000.

2. Subtract the income you expect to receive annually from:

Social Security: If you make under $25,000, enter $8,000; between $25,000-$40,000, enter $12,000; over $40,000, enter $14,500

In your income bracket that's $12,000 you would receive. So, $21,000 minus $12,000 equals $9,000, the amount you need to cover.

CHAPTER 1: THE ABSOLUTE BASICS: YOUR FINANCIAL FUTURE

There are some other sources to consider:

Traditional Employer Pension—a plan that pays a set dollar amount for life, where the dollar amount depends on salary and years of service.

Part-time income

Other

(We don't know what the other amounts for pension, etc., would be, but you can figure that out for yourself. Let's figure zero for this equation.)

3. To determine the amount you'll need to save to maintain your lifestyle, make a guess at how old you'll be when you retire. Let's say 65. Multiply the shortfall you need to make up ($9,000) by the factor below.

Age you expect to retire:	Your factor:
55	21.0
60	18.9
65	16.4
70	13.6

You expect to retire at 65: $9,000 × 16.4 = $147,600.

4. Multiply your savings to date by the factor below (include money accumulated in a 401(k), IRA, Roth IRA, or similar account):

If you want to retire in:
10 years	1.3
15 years	1.6
20 years	1.8
25 years	2.1
30 years	2.4
35 years	2.8
40 years	3.3

Let's say you have $2,000, and you'll retire in 40 years. That's $2,000 × 3.3 = $6,600

Subtract that from the amount needed, and you have: $147,600-$6,600 = $141,000, for the total additional savings needed at retirement.

5. To determine the amount you'll need to save each year, multiply the total amount by the factor below.

If you want to retire in:
10 yrs.	.085
15 yrs.	.052
20 yrs.	.036
25 yrs.	.027
30 yrs.	.020
35 yrs.	.016
40 yrs.	.013

Let's say you'll retire in 40 years, that's $147,600 × .013 = $1,918.80. That's the amount you'll need to save each year.

See? It's not impossible. It just takes planning. And the sooner you start, the better off you'll be.

CHAPTER 1: THE ABSOLUTE BASICS: YOUR FINANCIAL FUTURE

MINI-GLOSSARY

While most finance books use a glossary at the end to define terms (we have one of those, too, along with some other resources), we thought the most useful place to have key terms is at the front of the book, thereby increasing the chances dramatically that you'll have a clue what we're writing about.

Bank

(n.) A place to keep money.
(v.) Used in the lie spoken by every stockbroker, "You can bank on it!"

Book Value

Unless you checked out this copy from the library, it's about $16.95. Actually, book value is one way to measure how much a company is worth. You take the tangible assets, which are mainly the things a company owns that have value, less some accounting hocus pocus called depreciation, which only means something to tax collectors and other nerds. Subtract liabilities (money owed). It's as if the company sold everything it owned and paid off its debt. What's left is the book value of the company. Sometimes you figure the book value per share, which means you simply divide book value by the number of shares in circulation. It's just another theoretical measurement of a company's worth.

Bear

A period when prices fall and fall and fall and… Comes from the idea that a bear pulls its opponent down. (See Bull)

Bull

Opposite of bear. Term used to describe a market that is growing or moving up. Comes from the quaint idea that when a bull attacks it throws its opponent upward. Think of a bull's horns pointing up.

Bull & Bear

Often used as the name of a restaurant or bar where market types go to get soused.

TOP 5 ACCOUNT NAMES AT THE NEW "PO' FOLKS SAVINGS & LOAN"

5 The cookie jar account.

4 The coffee can CD.

3 The sock drawer trust.

2 The "Your Mom's Purse" fund.

1 The "Your Dad's Wallet" IRA.

Debt to equity ratio

When you're in college your debt to equity ratio is about a zillion (debt) to one (equity or the net value of what you own). For example, your 1986 Honda, the only thing you own, has a value of $1,000 when it runs; you owe at least $20,000 in student loans and another $5,000 for that goofy credit card some annoying bank sent you. That makes your debt to equity ratio 25:1. In olden days, that would send you straight to debtor's prison where you could meet a cast of Dickensian characters and end up being thankful for a turkey dinner. For companies, to determine the debt to equity ratio, divide the company's total amount of long-term debt by the total amount of equity. This ratio measures

CHAPTER 1: THE ABSOLUTE BASICS: YOUR FINANCIAL FUTURE

the percentage of debt the company is carrying. Many firms average a debt level of 50 percent or 1:2. Debt to equity ratios greater than 50 percent may indicate trouble.

Dividends

Dividends are usually little checks you get in the mail as a reminder that you still own a stock Aunt Ethel gave you when you graduated from high school. It's usually paid quarterly. New companies or high-growth companies reinvest earnings and don't bug you with those pesky little checks.

Dividend yield

Dividend yield is the sort of thing you see mentioned in commercials with some football players or rock stars reciting a script they clearly don't understand. They probably think a dividend yield is where you veer off to head to the town of Dividend. It is actually the amount of the dividend divided by the most current stock price—kind of like interest on a savings account and about as lucrative. Companies that don't pay a dividend have a dividend yield of zero.

Earnings per share (EPS)

Earnings per share (EPS) is just one letter switch away from being ESP. Think how useful that would be in picking a winner in the market!

It is simply the amount of profit (net income) divided by the number of shares in circulation. A company that has 10 million shares and earned $10 million has an EPS of $1.

Economic Indicators

Big picture information released by the federal government showing what the economy is up to. People who spend their careers worrying about inflation, unemployment, etc., instead of whether they can find a seat at the latest movie or get into new club openings, talk about these indicators all the time. Some new one is released every week, and since these people get paid to react, they do. Much like talking about the weather. If there were an economic version of The Weather Channel, this is what they'd be discussing.

Leveraged Buyout

Used to be the means du jour of making a fortune, then going to jail. Michael Milken was a bright bulb in this area, which is simply taking a public company private by borrowing money and paying off the shareholders. Mike overdid it and went to the federal pen. Paul Bilzerian pulled his trick on Singer Co., hired his wife to head a subsidiary, built a mansion no one could touch, did his pokey time, and walked away clean. Some of the early big players were just greedy, not crooked. They stripped the companies and sold them for parts.

CHAPTER 1: THE ABSOLUTE BASICS: YOUR FINANCIAL FUTURE

point worth more than Sears, Kmart, J.C. Penney, Saks, and Neiman Marcus Group combined.

Net Income

"Michael Jordan from 20-feet—nothing but net." That sweet feeling when the ball swishes through is the equivalent of net income. It's the profit, the honey pot, the nectar, or more mundanely, revenues minus expenses.

Outstanding Shares

The term outstanding shares refers to the total number of shares held by shareholders. In essence, they are in circulation. Some shares, called treasury stock, are issued but not outstanding by virtue of being held by the company.

P/E Ratio

Another term batted around by tennis stars and others in commercials. It's another way to judge a company's profitability and how the stock market views its profit potential. You divide the price of the stock by the current earnings per share. For example, the stock price is $12, and the EPS is $1. That's a P/E ratio of 12:1. If the stock were $1 and the EPS $1, the ratio would be 1:1. A low P/E ratio is something around 5 to 10, and might indicate that the company is undervalued. A high P/E ratio can mean almost anything. An Internet company called VeriSign intrigued one investor until he noticed it was trading for 6,779 times its earnings, or 6,779:1. Said the investor, "I couldn't pull the trigger." Welcome to the Internet.

Revenues

The money a company rakes in through sales and about any other way its employees can dream up to keep the dollars or yen or whatever coming in so they can get paid and improve the company's value, thereby increasing the stock price and allowing them to quit the first chance they get.

Market capitalization

Market capitalization is also called market cap by those irritating TV commentators who blather on all afternoon about the stock market. Example:

TV Moron: Wow! That increase in price today really pushed up their market cap.

Other TV Moron: Yeah!

Market capitalization is calculated by multiplying the number of outstanding shares times the current stock price of those shares. People often cite the high-tech stocks with huge caps far surpassing traditional industries. For example, America Online's market capitalization was worth more than General Motors, Ford, and the entire American steel industry—combined.

Amazon.com in terms of market value was at one

CHAPTER 1: THE ABSOLUTE BASICS: YOUR FINANCIAL FUTURE — 22

Securities

Nothing but paper and a promise. Includes stocks, bonds, notes, etc.

Stock Exchange

A place where securities are bought and sold, such as the New York Stock Exchange. Nothing like the closed clubs they used to be.

Stock Split

Let's say a stock is selling for $100 a share. Pricey if you want to buy 100 shares, the usual minimum. So to attract more people to buy the stock, the company declares a split at a ratio, very often at 2:1. Suddenly, there are twice as many shares out there and the stock price reflects that dilution and falls to about $50. The cost of 100 shares drops to a more manageable $5,000, and you buy. If you were just holding the stock, you own twice as many shares by doing nothing, but the lower price means you didn't really make any money. The company hopes the price will keep rising and everyone wins. Sound Zenish? It is.

Street Name

You may be known as Harold at home but your street name, Rwanda (Bon-Bon) Jobbie, strikes fear whenever it's mentioned. In finance the street name is used by a brokerage firm to hold a stock for you so it can be sold more quickly. If the stock was registered in your name, you would have the physical certificates transferred, a costly and time-consuming process.

> "An economist is an expert who will know tomorrow why the things he predicted yesterday didn't happen today."
>
> —Laurence J. Peter

23 — CHAPTER 1: THE ABSOLUTE BASICS: YOUR FINANCIAL FUTURE

FINANCE DIARIES

BUDGET BLUES

Marie was going through the checkbook one night when she noticed a slight inconsistency: All of the handwriting was hers! Why was this an inconsistency? Well, wasn't that Bill who had come home with a stack of new techno-dance-rave CDs the other day? And hadn't Bill just done the grocery shopping that weekend while she was busy meeting a rush deadline at work? And she was pretty sure Bill had used the check card to pay for that sumptuous four-course Chinese extravaganza they had had earlier in the week to celebrate his first job interview. (Even though he didn't get the job.) Since she had taken away his one credit card ever since he ran it up to the limit on that extra laptop he just had to have, not to mention the software, CD-ROMs, and that ultra-deluxe edition of cyber poker to load onto it, she knew he wasn't using that. Besides, she knew that his cash flow was severely limited because he didn't have a job yet. Therefore, there was only one solution: Bill wasn't updating the checkbook!

TOP 5 SIGNS YOU'RE NOT READY FOR A SAVINGS ACCOUNT

5 "Savings account? That's what cookie jars are for."

4 "What do you mean you don't take Monopoly money?"

3 You set your alarm for the 4 a.m. QVC *Star Wars* spectacular!

2 "I can't be out of money. There are still checks left in my checkbook!"

1 Credit card. ATM card. There's a difference?

CHAPTER 1: THE ABSOLUTE BASICS: YOUR FINANCIAL FUTURE

sitting him down at the kitchen table.

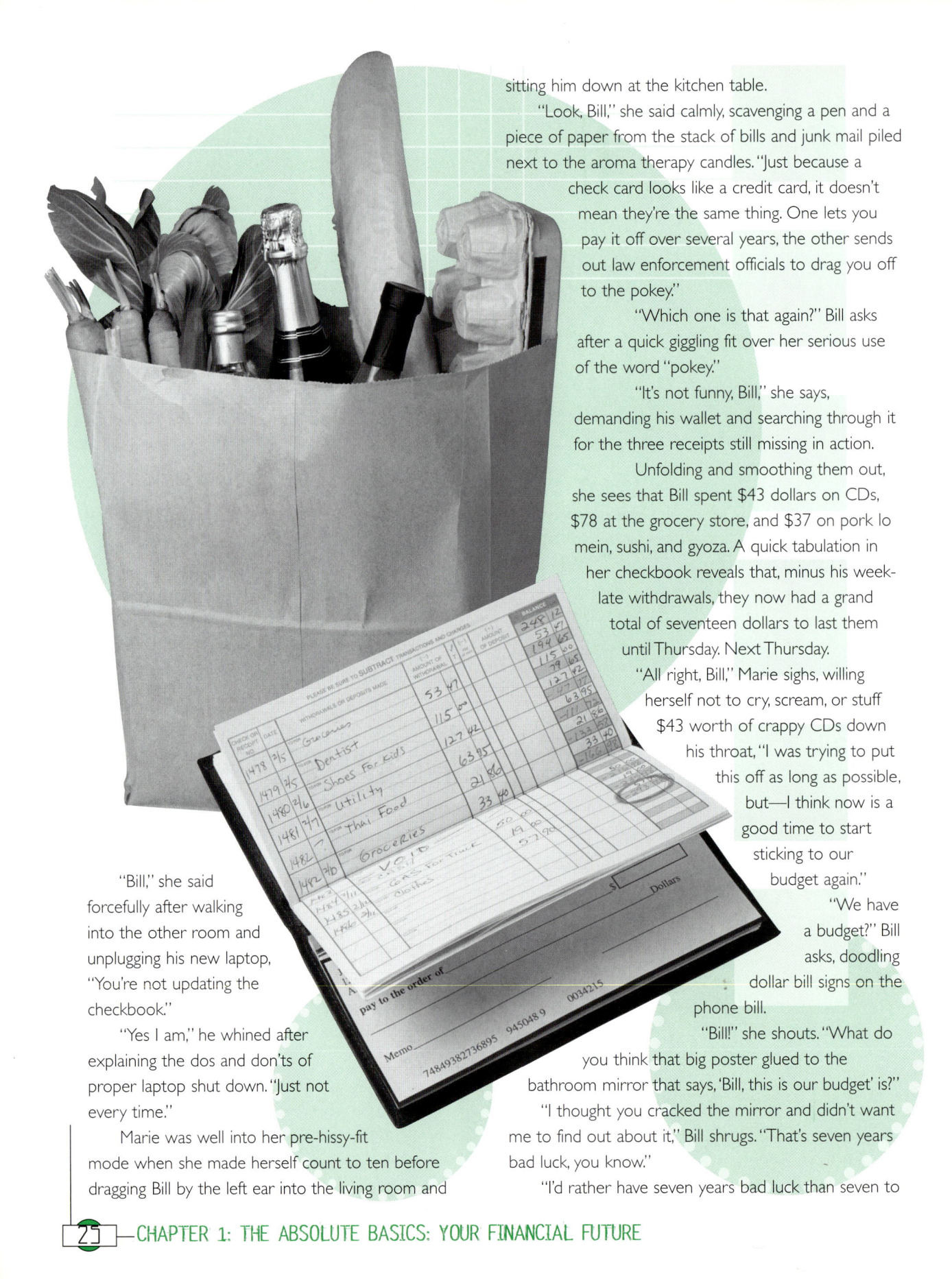

"Look, Bill," she said calmly, scavenging a pen and a piece of paper from the stack of bills and junk mail piled next to the aroma therapy candles. "Just because a check card looks like a credit card, it doesn't mean they're the same thing. One lets you pay it off over several years, the other sends out law enforcement officials to drag you off to the pokey."

"Which one is that again?" Bill asks after a quick giggling fit over her serious use of the word "pokey."

"It's not funny, Bill," she says, demanding his wallet and searching through it for the three receipts still missing in action.

Unfolding and smoothing them out, she sees that Bill spent $43 dollars on CDs, $78 at the grocery store, and $37 on pork lo mein, sushi, and gyoza. A quick tabulation in her checkbook reveals that, minus his week-late withdrawals, they now had a grand total of seventeen dollars to last them until Thursday. Next Thursday.

"All right, Bill," Marie sighs, willing herself not to cry, scream, or stuff $43 worth of crappy CDs down his throat, "I was trying to put this off as long as possible, but—I think now is a good time to start sticking to our budget again."

"Bill," she said forcefully after walking into the other room and unplugging his new laptop, "You're not updating the checkbook."

"Yes I am," he whined after explaining the dos and don'ts of proper laptop shut down. "Just not every time."

Marie was well into her pre-hissy-fit mode when she made herself count to ten before dragging Bill by the left ear into the living room and

"We have a budget?" Bill asks, doodling dollar bill signs on the phone bill.

"Bill!" she shouts. "What do you think that big poster glued to the bathroom mirror that says, 'Bill, this is our budget' is?"

"I thought you cracked the mirror and didn't want me to find out about it," Bill shrugs. "That's seven years bad luck, you know."

"I'd rather have seven years bad luck than seven to

25 — CHAPTER 1: THE ABSOLUTE BASICS: YOUR FINANCIAL FUTURE

life for bouncing checks at every record shop, grocery store, and Chinese restaurant in town," Marie announces. "There's rent, there's the car payment, and then there's the utilities. Those have to be paid first. Phone, electric, sewer, cable. Okay, now we'll estimate how much we spend a week on groceries—"

"Fifty bucks?" shouts Bill, watching her pen in a paltry number on her bare bones budget. "Is that enough to live on? I mean, will I still be able to get my Yoo Hoo?"

"Yes, Bill," says Marie.

something else. Well, we can't do without electric—"

"Right," nods Bill. "Otherwise, how would we cool off all that Yoo Hoo."

"Exactly," agrees Marie, just glad that Bill is finally paying attention. "Okay, so that leaves cable. Bye-bye HBO. Sayonara Cinemax. So long Showtime—"

"No way," pouts Bill. "There's a real cliffhanger on *Arli$$* this season. I can't just quit watching now."

Marie puts down her pen and looks Bill in the eye. The poor kid. Between his high hopes for his burgeoning cyber career, his doubling up on internships at prestigious start-up companies, and his good intentions by at least doing the grocery shopping, wasn't he entitled to a few sips of Yoo Hoo and a little Cinemax After Dark once in a while?

"Okay, Bill," she sighs, sliding aside her budget and reaching into his wallet for his check-card. "You can keep your damn Yoo Hoo and your damn cable. But I'm keeping your check card. When you're ready to start updating the check book, I'll be ready to give it back to you. I promise. And as a reward, we'll hold off on the budget for another few months until we see how your job prospects go. Deal?"

"Deal," he says, snatching the *TV Guide* off of the coffee table on his way to his darkened den and buzzing laptop.

Breathing a sigh of relief, Marie sidles over to the couch and picks up the remote. Thank goodness she didn't get rid of the cable. After all, *Sex and the City* was just about ready to start.

> "A budget is just a method of worrying before you spend money as well as afterward."
>
> —Anonymous

"You can still get your stupid Yoo Hoos. You just can't get a six-pack for every day of the week like you used to. From now on, we're going to have to start cutting back on some of the luxuries."

"Yoo Hoo isn't a luxury, Marie," says Bill. "It's a necessity. I need it to live. Like air or the Internet."

"Okay, fine," says Marie, moving back up her budget. "If you insist on seventy-two full ounces of Yoo Hoo a day, then we're going to have to give up

CHAPTER 1: THE ABSOLUTE BASICS: YOUR FINANCIAL FUTURE

2
HOW THE WORLD WORKS:
RISK AND REWARD, FEAR AND GREED

Some fundamentals are easier to grasp than others: keep your eye on the ball; when in London look to the right for the car most likely to kill you; never buy a Kathie Lee Gifford album. Ever.

Similarly, grasping fundamental economics doesn't require a deep knowledge of obtuse theories or mathematical formulas about supply and demand. If you can add and subtract, that's enough. And most of the questions you need to answer require little more than common sense and reliable information. It helps, however, to have an idea of How the World Works, as one economic theorist titled his book. This understanding will enable you to come to grips with a very important, but sometimes difficult, concept: the relationship of risk and reward.

27 — CHAPTER 2: HOW THE WORLD WORKS: RISK AND REWARD, FEAR AND GREED

THE BIG PICTURE

While economics is sometimes called the dismal science, it actually is entertaining, in an offbeat sort of way. Here are a few key points to keep in mind:

There have always been cycles in the economy, and they will determine in large part how your investments will fare. The down cycle known as the Dark Ages in Europe (also featuring the bubonic plague) lasted about one thousand years.

Fortunately, most downturns don't last that long. But they still occur. The U.S. stock market has had its own versions of the Dark Ages, the worst being the years 1929-1932. Stocks lost almost 90 percent of their value in what came to be described as a panic. Driven by fear, investors sold their stocks and bonds because they believed they would be worth even less the next day. The downward spiral ushered in the Great Depression.

There is still plenty of risk in the financial markets, and for investors, the rules over the years remain unchanged: The higher the rate of return, the riskier the investment. You're taking a chance (risk) with your money, and in some cases you could lose it all. Every nickel. Remember that it was the whopping returns, also known as greed, that lured investors into the stock market in the 1920s. So how exactly do you figure your return? Easy. Turn the page.

"The economy of the next century will not be dramatically different from the economy of this century."

— economist Paul Romer, Stanford 1999

CHAPTER 2: HOW THE WORLD WORKS: RISK AND REWARD, FEAR AND GREED — 28

RATE OF RETURN

Let's look at stocks first. Stocks are shares of ownership in a business. Say you bought $5,000 worth of ABC Corp. The purchase was for 1,000 shares at $5 per share. Over the course of a year, the stock has increased to $6. Your return for the year is 20 percent. Here's how you figure it:

Take the current value of your investment, in this case $6,000, and subtract what you originally paid, or $5,000. The difference is $1,000. Divide that by the original amount you paid ($5,000) and the return is .20 or 20 percent.

$$\frac{\$6,000 \text{ (current value)} - \$5,000 \text{ (purchase price)}}{\$5,000 \text{ (original purchase price)}} = .20$$

Your next question might very well be: How does that stack up with other stocks and other investments?

Stocks overall have had an annual return on average of 8.4 percent since way back in the 1800s when they started to keep track of this stuff. The inflation rate over this same broad period has been about 1.3 percent, meaning the "real" return has been about 7.1 percent. (8.4-1.3=7.1) Over the years bonds have fared somewhat worse—roughly in the three to four percent range.

Let's delve a little deeper into the risks of the stock market. For the last decade, the real question might be: What risk? Between 1990 and 1999 the stock market has more than tripled in value. Stocks on average produced a dazzling 18.1 percent annual rate of return for that time period.

But let's say you needed to pull your money out in a hurry. And the day you needed it happened to be October 28, 1997. The Dow Jones average (a good measuring gauge of how the market is performing) dropped 554 points—a 7.2 percent loss on that day. Chances are that you did not realize a very good return on your investment if you were forced to sell when

CHAPTER 2: HOW THE WORLD WORKS: RISK AND REWARD, FEAR AND GREED

the stock was plummeting in price.

(By the way, the Dow Jones Industrial Average is a market index that tracks the performance of thirty large U.S. companies. The companies tend to be from a variety of industries, so the "average" offers a broad overview of how the market is performing, as well as the economy. It's not a measure of every stock. Also, the companies on the DJIA change as they merge, become less important in business, whatever.)

There are other market drops worth pondering. In 1987, the market lost 36 percent of its value in a brief period in October. In 1973-74, stocks fell 44 percent. And if you had bought the stocks in the Dow Jones Industrial Average at their peak in early 1966, you wouldn't have made much of a profit until mid-1983—more than 17 years later.

If all this gives you a queasy feeling, you are beginning to understand risk.

To spread the risk, most financial advisors recommend a strategy of maintaining a diversified investment portfolio consisting of stocks, bonds, and cash in varying percentages, depending upon your objectives.

Now take a look at bonds. They are just a paper promise that obligates a government or a company to pay you back the money you invest, plus interest. The return historically is not as high as stocks, but you probably won't have the kind of panic attacks usually associated with a pilot saying in midair, "Ladies and gentlemen, we have mechanical problems." Consider 1994, a tough year for bonds. A medium maturity U.S. Treasury bond, a very safe investment, fell 1.8 percent in value. The next year the bonds (which were due in seven to ten years) made a comeback, and were up 14.4 percent. In other words, with bonds the highs aren't as high, but the lows aren't as low.

In one way, the rate of return for bonds is the easiest number to calculate. The interest rate (also called the coupon rate) is determined before you buy. That's your return. If you decide to sell the bond before it is due, the price can

CHAPTER 2: HOW THE WORLD WORKS: RISK AND REWARD, FEAR AND GREED

fluctuate, either up or down depending on the current rate of interest rates and the financial condition of the entity that issued the bond. There is a number called the current yield that you can find in the newspaper where bonds are listed, just like stocks. (We discuss bonds in more depth in Chapter 6.)

Also remember that bonds don't behave like stocks. They seem to have their own set of rules, but the key to watch is interest rates. When they rise, bond prices fall. Why? Because bond buyers won't pay as much for an existing bond with a fixed interest rate of seven percent as they will for a new one that is paying, say, eight percent or more. But when interest rates fall, bond prices go up. That eight percent bond is worth more than a new seven percent bond.

Real estate, too, has its ups and downs. Every market sooner or later will suffer through some sort of downturn. For example, in New York City the commercial real estate values plummeted in the early 1990s, in some cases 20-40 percent. Essentially the prices had been ratcheted higher and higher as people overpaid for properties with a business use. The crash flattened many investors, who couldn't keep up the payments during the recession of the early 1990s. But in only a few years the cycle turned up, and investors who held on not only survived, but thrived. However, very few markets are exactly alike. Real estate can be as lucrative as the stock market with double-digit annual returns, but it's a lot easier to sell a share of stock than an office complex.

And in truth there is some risk in every investment. Whether you recognize this risk is another matter. For example, leaving money in a bank savings account seems to be risk free. But after several years of earning a low interest rate, the money you have saved is robbed of its purchasing power by the tendency of prices to rise, an erosive process called inflation. (It is defined as the rate at which the general level of prices for goods and services increases.) Over recent years inflation has been about three percent annually in the United States. (Historically over the last 100-plus years, the rate has been 1.3 percent.) So, in terms of purchasing power, your savings account is losing ground. Your interest payments, less the taxes you pay, don't really cover the increase in prices. In effect, you lost money. That's not much of a reward.

"I figure you have the same chance of winning the lottery whether you play or not."

—Fran Lebowitz

CHAPTER 2: HOW THE WORLD WORKS: RISK AND REWARD, FEAR AND GREED

WHAT'S YOUR RISK TOLERANCE?

Your risk tolerance, or intolerance, is your ability to ride the markets and not panic. But people respond to pressure in a variety of ways. Some investors can handle drops in their investment and never blink; others see the value fall and become catatonic. It's sort of like lactose intolerance: It affects everyone differently, for it's not only the relationship of risk and reward but also that of fear and greed.

The Wall Street Journal ran a "risk quiz" that posed eight questions, such as: Would you put $5,000 of your assets into an investment where you have a 70 percent chance of doubling your money (to $10,000) and a 30 percent chance of losing the entire $5,000? Yes received five points, no received zero. The cumulative points determined whether you as an investor should: "Avoid risk! Open a money market account—or buy a bigger mattress." Or: "Viva Las Vegas, baby! Place your bets on 'Net stocks and new-tech issues. Risks are high, but so are the payoffs."

Your emotional makeup will in fact play a significant role in how you set your investment strategy. For instance, if you are saving for the future, and you have 35 years before you retire, you may want to invest in riskier investment products, knowing that if you stick to only the "savings" products or to less risky investment products, your money will grow too slowly—or given inflation or taxes, you may lose the purchasing power of your money. A frequent mistake people make is putting money they will not need for a very long time in investments that pay a low amount of interest.

A financial planner in Atlanta, sees one client after another who errs on the side of caution when it comes to retirement planning. "My typical clients are too conservative with their investments," she says.

"They think of it as safe money, as sacred money. They forget that it's long-term money. It's a good place to take a little risk."

On the other hand, if you are saving for a short-term goal, you don't want to choose risky investments, because when it's time to sell, you may have to take a loss. Since investments often move up and down in value rapidly, you want to make sure that you can wait and sell at the best possible time.

Consider how you would react to a 20 to 25 percent decline in the value of a stock investment—a typical "bear market" move. Feel okay?

WHAT INVESTMENTS TO CHOOSE?

All right, you paid off your credit cards and cleaned up your credit record, your expenses are under control, and you have savings, plus a pretty good idea of whether you'll throw up every time you hear the least bit of bad financial news. The next step: Where do you invest your money?

Bill Frazier, a broker with A.G. Edwards, says that most of the young clients he sees typically are not planning for their retirement yet. He tries to get them to see the advantage of early planning. He tells them to open an IRA or a 401(k) as soon as they can. The sooner they do it, the more they stand to benefit.

"After that, we look at (insurance), then stock and mutual funds," he says.

We've touched on some of the various investment options you could

CHAPTER 2: HOW THE WORLD WORKS: RISK AND REWARD, FEAR AND GREED — 32

choose: Stocks, bonds, mutual funds, real estate. But there's a near endless stream of choices, including gold, silver, and, yes, Beanie Babies. How do you decide what's right for you? It might help simplify your choices if you consider that there are really only two kinds of investing, so here are the basic categories to consider as you start to think about your financial future.

YOU OWN IT

Buying stock means becoming an owner. You own a share of General Electric, which in turn owns NBC; so, by God, Jay Leno works for you! Of course, one share will not give you a lot of clout, since at this point GE has millions of shares in circulation.

Owning stock is a great way to share in the growth of companies and increase your wealth. There are the classic stories of people who bought Microsoft early and have profited wildly as the company has prospered. That's the stock market, which rewards companies that show such phenomenal growth in profits over a period of time. The market also has its tales of woe, as companies once considered high fliers crash and burn.

Remember that the biggest single determiner of stock prices is earnings. Over the short term, stock prices fluctuate based on just about anything—news about global warming to the latest report on retail clothing sales. But over time, profit matters. If a company's profits rise substantially over the course of ten years, so will its share price.

Real estate is also an ownership stake. Obviously, you can purchase a house and live in it, thus investing in your own financial future by building equity in the house. (Equity is the difference between what the property is worth on the market and what you owe.) You can also purchase property and rent it out, giving you the chance to build equity as the property appreciates in value and the size of your mortgage decreases. That usually requires a substantial time commitment.

Owning your own business is another way to invest: It essentially is an investment in yourself. Again, this is another area where the landscape has changed dramatically from years past. Computers and other innovative communication devices have opened up low cost options to help start a business, especially a business in the service sector of the economy, meaning you perform a task for someone else.

Some business owners eschew making investments in almost anything else other than their business. They think it is the arena where they have the most control over their financial future.

One hazard of owning a business is that it can have some severe ups and downs. If the pressure of performing on deadline and juggling several tasks at once doesn't fit your personality type, then owning your own business probably isn't a good idea. The truth is, most small businesses don't make it.

—CHAPTER 2: HOW THE WORLD WORKS: RISK AND REWARD, FEAR AND GREED

YOU LEND IT

Another way to add to your wealth is through lending, but that doesn't mean loan-sharking to your friends. For example, if you have money in a savings account, you are lending the bank money. Unfortunately the return on your account isn't that great, probably in the three to four percent range. On the other hand, your money is safe; you can't lose your savings, even if the bank goes broke. (Virtually every account in a U.S. banking or savings institution is insured by the federal government for up to $100,000 per account.)

There are other types of lending that pay higher returns. Money market funds are not insured but they are often invested in government-backed securities and are considered extremely safe. Their interest rates are always a few percentage points above the bank rate, and thus can generate more income.

Bonds are another form of lending. If you purchase bonds, you are loaning money to a government or a corporation, which promises to pay you back with interest. Some of these bonds have next to no risk; U.S. Treasury bonds are as close to a sure thing as an investor can get.

As a result, the interest rate of Treasuries is considered a risk-free rate, but some corporate bonds are so risky, they're called junk and pay very high rates of return. The downside is that the company could default and your investment would be worthless.

OTHER THINGS

Whether they are Beanie Babies, gold, silver, or heating oil, there are a variety of ways to invest that depend tremendously on perceived value. This is "ownership," but it is off the screen for most people. Again, whether you invest in these commodities depends on your stomach for risk. Most of these are considered outside the mainstream of investments and tend to be more unpredictable.

Futures markets, where people buy and sell everything from cotton to frozen OJ, have been described as continuous auction markets. This is where

CHAPTER 2: HOW THE WORLD WORKS: RISK AND REWARD, FEAR AND GREED — 34

buyers and sellers of commodities meet to set the price for agricultural products, petroleum, precious metals, foreign currencies, and much more. Their primary purpose remains the same as it has been for nearly a century and a half in the U.S. By buying or selling futures contracts—contracts that establish a price level now for items to be delivered later—individuals and businesses seek to achieve what amounts to insurance against price changes. This is called hedging. Volume has increased from 14 million futures contracts traded in 1970 to hundreds of millions of futures and options traded today.

Besides the companies and people who really have a need for oil or OJ at stable prices, the other players in these markets are speculative investors. That could be you. Most speculators have no intention of making or taking delivery of the commodity but, rather seek to profit from a change in the price. That is, they buy when they anticipate rising prices and sell when they anticipate declining prices.

Sounds risky? It is. Sometimes it is described as a type of portfolio diversification. Speculation in futures contracts, however, is clearly not for everyone. Just as it is possible to realize substantial profits in a short period of time, it is also possible to incur substantial losses almost overnight.

Oftentimes as traditional markets, such as stocks or bonds, go through periods of fluctuation, these "other" investments surface as alternatives. You'll even see "get acquainted" offers on late night television. Potential investors may be searching for the high returns they reaped before but can't find as easily anymore. Usually, that's asking for trouble.

"An economic forecaster is like a cross-eyed javelin thrower: they don't win many accuracy contests, but they keep the crowd's attention."

— Anonymous

SETTING STRATEGY

IS THERE A FORMULA?

You know the investment categories (own or lend), you understand that the payout potential is higher in a risky investment than it is on one that is less risky. But the question remains: How much should you own of each?

Naturally, there are plenty of answers. In fact, you can find so many pie charts to help you allocate your investment dollar, you could open a financial bakery. But a lot of the advice tends to dwell on the product the company drawing the chart sells: mutual funds tout mutual funds as the dominant element in your portfolio, and so on.

In truth, history shows that the ownership route usually means more potential for growth. These investments (stocks, real estate, etc.) have consistently been the category that posts the biggest gains over time. Of course, you can feel the impact of downturns; the 17-year drought that hit the stock market in the 1960s and 1970s could be repeated. But you're in this for the long haul, right?

$$100 - \text{YOUR AGE} = \% \text{ OF ASSETS IN RISKIER INVESTMENTS}$$

CHAPTER 2: HOW THE WORLD WORKS: RISK AND REWARD, FEAR AND GREED

There are a couple of rules to keep in mind that might help as you navigate your way into the financial unknown.

One rule is to subtract your age from 100 and put that percentage of your assets in growth investments. (100 minus your age, say 25, equals 75 percent.) This is a long-term strategy for your money. As mentioned in Chapter One, if you are going to need the money in a couple of years, the less risky investments are better.

There's also the pyramid approach. Hey, it worked for the pharaohs. Build a base with a balanced personal budget, savings for six months of living expenses, insurance, and a home mortgage. Move up from there to the retirement plans such as a 401(k) or IRA and make the maximum contribution there. Then at the top are the investment in stocks, real estate, bonds, mutual funds, and whatever else suits your fancy.

You also should keep in mind a strategy that is as old as the chicken: Don't put all your eggs in one basket. This is a smart way of tacitly admitting some of your investment decisions could be wrong.

Lastly remember that this can be a bumpy process. Stocks have historically provided a solid investment over time, but few smart portfolio managers put all their money in stocks. If stocks return about eight percent annually and bonds around three to four percent, a return of a little better than five percent is what you might guess would be the realistic number you could expect from your investment treasury.

TOP 5 WAYS TO PICK YOUR INVESTMENTS (UN)WISELY

5 "Honey, what do you think? Heads or tails?"

4 When E. F. Mutton, the local butcher, talks, people really listen . . .

3 What's that old saying about falling stars?

2 Now, does *paper* beat rocks? Or is that *scissors*?

1 Hmm, is that a four-leaf clover? What's Leprechaun.com stock at these days?

CHAPTER 2: HOW THE WORLD WORKS: RISK AND REWARD, FEAR AND GREED

ARE THERE REALLY NEW FUNDAMENTALS?

Unless you've been visiting Mars, you'll note the impact of technology, and in particular the Internet, on investing. Whether it is the ready access to information, the ease of executing a stock purchase from your den, or the spectacular rise in value (or drop) of dot-com companies, the business world today seems far different from the way it looked 10 years ago.

Still, people disagree on whether investing has changed in any significant way. The basic questions remain the same: Where is the economy heading? Where should your money be? What types of investments will be the most secure but have some real potential for gaining in value? They are the same old questions raised about the financial future from yesteryear on.

Historical perspective provides some insights. For example, there were hundreds of auto manufacturers in the United States at the first part of the last century, and no one knew that Ford and General Motors would be the big winners.

Just substitute names like Amazon.com or Buy.com and you can see the similarity. What companies will eventually succeed and how you can profit are exactly the same questions asked 100 years ago. But there are some very important differences.

You can't discount the extraordinary wealth of information. The information barrage puts 20- and 30-something people in a position unique in economic history. They are relatively new to the world of work, and if they started their careers after 1992, they've never experienced a recession, much less a depression. While they look forward to an earnings potential that looks very positive, they are subject to bombardments of the latest news via the Web or broadcast. No event of even the slightest magnitude goes unnoticed, but at the same time advisors keep saying that long-term investing is the better way to go. Weighing this information and making choices leave most investors perplexed.

"Who wouldn't be?" says one financial adviser. "There's never been anything like this. But it's important to remember the truth about long-term investing. The basics aren't going to change."

Really? Spyridon Ganas is a teenager in Massachusetts who invests not just in technology stocks but in options—a bet on future stock prices. He told *The New York Times* that for him, to hold a long-term investment is two to three days.

The gap between what people see and hear and what the professional investment counselors say seems to be growing. How does investing long-term stand up to a stock that gains 1000% in value in two days? And that news is broadcast via Web and TV, nonstop.

37 — CHAPTER 2: HOW THE WORLD WORKS: RISK AND REWARD, FEAR AND GREED

The Dot-Com Bears

Many of the best-known gurus about matters financial have inadvertently become stand-up comedians. They do their best imitations of pretzels as markets keep doing things they can't predict. If you were born with a personality defect and fight vainly the old ennui, you'll definitely enjoy watching these guys several days in a row trying to explain a world they no longer understand. It's not that they are wrong, they eventually may be right, but many of their long-held beliefs have been pounded, and they have to respond to today's questions with answers that reflect their portfolio picks losing 5 percent of their value every minute. They are almost praying for some retribution.

This column appeared in early 2000, written by Dr. Irwin Kellner for CBS's *Market Watch*:

"On Jan. 7, discussing a tale of two markets, I found a faint glimmer of sanity. The Nasdaq had shed 8-1/2 percent in this year's first week, while the Dow Jones Industrial Average went down only two percent. Of course, a lot has happened since then, but I am pleased to report that sanity, indeed, appears to be returning to the stock market. Investing is in, gambling is out."

Oh, well said. But by mid-year the markets, though well below where they were at the beginning of the year, had stayed steady.

Or this from the Jerome Levy Economics Institute of Bard College in New York:

"Those who believe this economy has sound underpinnings without recognizing the stock market's extraordinary influence risk leaving themselves vulnerable to severe business and investment losses."

After which the market gained 200 points and the U.S. economy posted one of its best quarters of growth. The market continues to chug along.

But still, every Cassandra has her day.

"It was during the glory years (of IBM), its years of greatest profit and greatest admiration, that it was making the mistakes that sowed the billions of dollars of losses that came later."

— Bill Gates

CHAPTER 2: HOW THE WORLD WORKS: RISK AND REWARD, FEAR AND GREED

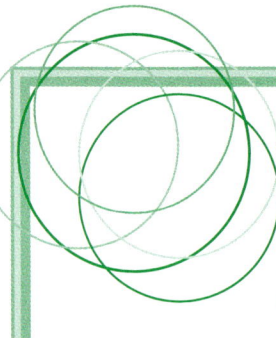

One Dozen Facts, Questions, and Almost No Answers

1. Many of the highly touted companies of today don't turn a profit. They have to eventually make money. When is eventually?

2. The number of places to invest and the ease with which to invest have changed dramatically. Mutual funds have become like toothpaste, each with its own special flavor. With extra fluoride or global growth stocks—what's the difference? Brands become important. Investment is retail, retail, retail.

3. The world of investing has turned upside down? Gurus such as Warren Buffett, for years the platinum standard for investing, saw his fortunes turn south when his portfolio stocked with familiar names, such as Gillette, The Washington Post Co., Coca-Cola, and American Express, all were down significantly from their top prices over a twelve month period: Gillette was down 51 percent and Coca-Cola down 47 percent. He sold his stake in the once-invincible Disney Co. Meanwhile, a company agreeing to service Microsoft saw its stock increase in 2000 by 463 percent—in a week.

4. What goes up must come down, but what if the world is upside down? Buffett (no relation to Jimmy of "Cheeseburger in Paradise" fame) wrote his shareholders in 1999 that the only explanation he could give for the poor results was an answer they were probably tired of hearing. "We are in a momentum market and value stocks, no matter how cheap they become, are out of vogue." The inference here is that they will be back in fashion. Then in 2000, Buffett lamented again, "We had the worst absolute performance of my tenure...even Inspector Clouseau could find last year's guilty party: your Chairman." That Buffett, a man well acquainted with his own worth, could mention himself in the same sentence with Inspector Clouseau says a lot.

5. John Templeton, the man called the wise old owl of Wall Street, once said that investing in many ways is easy. He named a stock, Alcoa Aluminum, and noted that it always seemed to fall to less than $5 a share. The fall was prompted by drops in demand for aluminum and increases in the cost of electricity, which is needed in megawatts to manufacture the stuff. He would buy the stock. Then, a few months later, it would rise to more than $25 and he would sell it. Alcoa closed in a 2000 blue chip revival at $68. Some things are different, but then...

6. People feel more like taking a financial risk in a good economy. They figure they can recover if they make a poor investment choice.

7. Many brokers and analysts on Wall Street today are being flooded with dumb money. It is the same as decades ago when so many individual investors were in the stock market and knew virtually nothing about what they were buying. For example, a 65-year old woman walked into the office of a financial planner in Texas. She told the planner that she wasn't receiving a high enough return on her investment. She was reaping a very healthy 25 percent annual return. She wanted to put it all in "the new economy." However, there is a difference between new places to invest and a new economy. Wal-Mart isn't going out of business soon; Home Depot will still sell plywood; The Gap will cover the spread, so to speak.

8. The year 2000 marked the death of Geoffrey Moore, a real nice old guy who essentially invented watching economic indicators. Whether they are lagging, coincident, or leading, indicators send economic types into talking frenzies about "a remarkable economy that just can't stop growing!" or "they show us that the world, as we know it, will end at 11:01 Eastern, 8:01 Pacific." He was

CHAPTER 2: HOW THE WORLD WORKS: RISK AND REWARD, FEAR AND GREED

86, and had worked at spotting recessions and economic upturns for more than 40 years. To give you an idea of his scope, Fed Chairman Alan Greenspan was one of his students in 1946. However, his ambition as a young man had not been to be an economist and analyst of business cycles, but to be—a chicken farmer. Hey, some choices don't work out.

9. Chat room conversation during a blue-chip rally in the spring of 2000.

Gungho says, "10 more mins and we escape today with gains."
Scouter says, "This sucks. No juice in these oldies"
Tango says, "I'm trying to get out of the dots. Help!"
Gungho, "Come on baby, close, close, close."
Market closes.

10. Out of Here: Tiger Management LLC released the following letter in early 2000, announcing the closure of its funds:

"In May of 1980, Thorpe McKenzie and I started the Tiger funds with total capital of $8.8 million. Eighteen years later, the $8.8 million had grown to $21 billion, an increase of over 259,000%. Our compound rate of return to partners during this period after all fees was 31.7%. No one had a better record.

Since August of 1998, the Tiger funds have stumbled badly and Tiger investors have voted strongly with their pocketbooks, understandably so. During that period, Tiger investors withdrew some $7.7 billion of funds. The result of the demise of value investing and investor withdrawals has been financial erosion, stressful to us all. And there is no real indication that a quick end is in sight.

And what do I mean by, 'there is no quick end in sight?' What is 'end' the end of? 'End' is the end of the bear market in value stocks….

There is a lot of talk now about the New Economy (meaning Internet, technology and telecom). Certainly the Internet is changing the world and the advances from biotechnology will be equally amazing. Technology and telecommunications bring us opportunities none of us have dreamed of. 'Avoid the Old Economy and invest in the New and forget about price,' proclaim the pundits. And in truth, that has been the way to invest over the last eighteen months.

The current technology, Internet and telecom craze, fueled by the performance desires of investors, money managers and even financial buyers, is unwittingly creating a Ponzi pyramid destined for collapse. The tragedy is, however, that the only way to generate short-term performance in the current environment is to buy these stocks. That makes the process self-perpetuating until the pyramid eventually collapses under its own excess….

The difficulty is predicting when this change will occur and in this regard I have no advantage. What I do know is that there is no point in subjecting our investors to risk in a market which I frankly do not understand. Consequently, after thorough consideration, I have decided to return all capital to our investors, effectively bringing down the curtain on the Tiger funds…."

—Julian Robertson

He and his befuddled partners closed the fund and gave back the billions.

There's only one word (okay, two words) for it: amazingly ironic.

11. Watch the Initial Public Offerings, also called IPOs. This is when a company sells stock for the first time to the general public. This has been a ready source of capital for a lot of young companies. As they burn up through this capital, they may find themselves in trouble because their businesses aren't profitable and their credit is shot. By the summer of 2000 some IPOs were being delayed, meaning there wasn't enough interest in investing in the company. Also, there were some pretty famous dot-coms that were on the verge of being delisted from the stock exchange. That's kind of like being thrown off the playing field in Little League. You and your buddy can play catch behind the bleachers, but essentially you're out of the game. Among those on the edge: Value America and Fogdog.

12. Lighten up. You've only seen six year's worth of income go down the drain with your bad investments. It could be worse:

> Baseball bad boy John Rocker told a radio station, regarding his ongoing problems with the media: "There's plenty of things I can do besides deal with the headaches of this garbage every single day. I'd be a stockbroker probably." (See "Top 5," next page)

CHAPTER 2: HOW THE WORLD WORKS: RISK AND REWARD, FEAR AND GREED — 40

TOP 5......
SIGNS JOHN ROCKER IS YOUR STOCKBROKER

5 All your money ends up in NASCAR, not NASDAQ.

4 When Wall Street has a rally, he shows up in a white hood.

3 Since "portfolio" sounds too foreign, he prefers the term "bag o' stocks."

2 Thinks "covering your shorts" is something you do in Greenwich Village.

1 Buys "Yahoo!" because there aren't any stocks called "Stupid Cracker!"

(Courtesy: Topfive.com)

"Ask five economists and you'll get five different answers (six if one went to Harvard."
— R. Fiedler

THE HISTORY OF ECONOMICS

As mentioned at the beginning of this chapter, the Dark Ages were the kind of economic down cycle even an economist couldn't love. It was typified by the phrase "Tu es très screwed-arama" translated loosely as "you are very screwed." Feudalism gave rise to retail commerce in larger towns where goods were traded, and some people other than kings, princes, and others of their ilk made a couple of bucks. On which the kings, princes, and others of their ilk charged a tax. The slogan of these times (translated) was, "You are still screwed but keep a couple of drackles for the effort."

Fast forward as trade developed all over the world.

"I've got guns, you've got butter. Let's trade!"

"I've got salted cod, you've got slaves. Let's trade!"

"I've got beads, you've got Manhattan. Let's trade!"

The trading scheme opened new markets, more jobs, and prompted people to think about doing something other than surviving to an average age of 50 and paying taxes to some fop in ruffles.

41 — CHAPTER 2: HOW THE WORLD WORKS: RISK AND REWARD, FEAR AND GREED

A bunch of factories were built, people moved around, and so on.

Fast forward to today and the trading mechanism of the millennium—the Internet. It is the jet stream of all trade routes and will in some way affect every area of finance.

The Internet, however, is a tool; it doesn't have the power of God, a benevolent alien, or even Courtney Love. It does provide one possibility—more freedom. And thus the ability to make mistakes. Or succeed.

To summarize: The economy is going to have its ups and downs; trade helps keep the world economy healthy; and the Internet keeps screwing with the fundamentals everyday. Easy, huh? So who needs college.

THEORYLAND

There are countless theories today based on the exact impact the Internet and other "new economy" developments will have on your future. And these mindless sallies into Tomorrowland just won't stop.

For a little perspective you can actually visit Tomorrowland at Disney World. There, tucked in a corner, are a few scenes conceived in the 1950s about what life in 2000 would be like. Infrared cooking for Mom, personal entertainment units for the kids so the parents don't have to listen to that devil music, all set in a sort of "Art Deco meets the Jetsons" lounge environment. In other words, it's a pretty good guess.

Uncle Walt Disney, who had a passion for black cigarillos and a keen eye for what the Amercan public craved, knew the basics of American behavior would stay fairly consistent. So it would seem for the economy, too, but that doesn't keep the theorists from babbling on and on.

One favorite is a myth floating around in, of all places, *The Wall Street Journal*, contending that more and more people will take a break in their 30s or 40s.

They'll go live on an island for a few years (can you say *Survivor*?), then return to the work force refreshed and fully ready to continue in their careers until age 99, this ripe old age being achieved through biotech breakthroughs that allow you to live longer.

There are some historic holes in this scenario. To wit: Americans don't save and are heavily in debt on their credit cards. If a person doesn't have savings, a midlife time-out will be difficult unless aluminum can collecting is part of the plan.

Then, upon returning to the work force after the hiatus, a well-rested person likely will find that whatever skills and knowledge he or she had before they entered the "vacation force" have now become sadly outdated. The lazy days will continue as they collect welfare because there are no jobs to match their over-the-hill skills.

CHAPTER 2: HOW THE WORLD WORKS: RISK AND REWARD, FEAR AND GREED — 42

3 INVESTING

Before we get into actual investing, let's talk about brokers—those stuffed shirts that allow you to invest your money in the first place.

The OLD Way

It's important to understand how brokerages used to make a lot of their money.

A mainline Wall Street brokerage firm routinely would take a commission of about five percent on every transaction that passed through its hands. Whether you, the client, made a profit or absorbed a loss, the broker earned a fee. In the immortal words of Eddie Murphy in the movie Trading Places, "You guys are . . . bookies." And the advice of olden days varied very little, and most of it could be summarized in a couple of sentences.

"Buy low, sell high."

"Hey, it's not my fault you lost money!"

But if you want to enter the investing world, you will need a brokerage firm for buying stocks, bonds, and (sometimes) mutual funds, though the latter usually offer direct purchase options.

The NEW Way

Ten years ago, 97 percent of the stock trades made in the U.S. were through traditional brokers. That percentage is now 40 percent, according to the U.S. Securities and Exchange Commission. Everyday investors have access to much of the same information brokers once relied on to sway clients, thanks to the Internet and online brokers. Almost anyone can make a trade for less than 1,000 shares for a fee of less than $20. The speed of the Internet allows instant access to prices and enables an investor to hop on an investment that's a rocket or bail out of one that looks ready to crash.

CHAPTER 3: INVESTING

BLUE LIGHT BROKERS
OR: THEY DON'T CALL THEM "DISCOUNT" FOR NOTHING

So you want to, maybe, look into finding a brokerage firm and wade a little deeper into the world of investing. As explained in Chapter 1 and Chapter 2, your strategy for investing, based on age, income, financial goals, and risk tolerance, will play a big part in what course you take in making investments and also in hiring a brokerage firm.

If you are simply going to buy stocks, bonds, and mutual funds and put them in a closet for several years, you don't need to fret much about what brokerage you choose. Stock trading at the speed of light and catching the right price per share at the right instant aren't paramount to your financial life. So here's a tip: Most of the discount brokerage firms—which are about the equivalent of the self service lane at the gas station—are all pretty much the same.

However, if you fancy yourself a stock predator, downing plates of steak tartare, railing against the tax laws, and roaring with laughter as the stock you sold just in time falls to the depths of Hades, well that's a different matter. The mundane matters of costs per trade and other fees can make a difference. And many brokerage firms now seek out the active trader, meaning there's some price competition from which you can chose.

CHEAP, CHEAPER, CHEAPEST

Okay, you're right. The discount brokers can't all be exactly the same, especially if you plan to be watching your stocks like they're the last hand in a high stakes poker game, which they kind of are. Basically they fall into three categories:

El cheapo—brokers that charge from $4 to $12 per trade. If you're making a thousand trades a day, these are your guys.

Middle range—at $12 and $20 per trade, these brokers tend to be a little better known and offer some conveniences that el cheapos don't. The mid-range firms are more likely to have a better customer service department than the lowest priced ones. This can be useful when you have a question and don't want to wait on hold for 20 minutes. (Stories of these delays are rampant.)

High-priced—brokers that charge more than $20 per trade behave more like big-name firms and in many cases are the discount arm of a well-known company, such as Merrill Lynch. You'll find some research available and a full menu of investment options.

READ THE FINE PRINT

The biggest pitfalls to watch out for when choosing a brokerage are the nickel and dime fees the firm may sneak in on your statement. Obviously you pay for buying or selling a stock, but there are other fees, including ones for asset transfers from one account to another, fees for closing an account, IRA custodian fees, wire transfer fees, account inactivity fees, annual fees, and fees for not maintaining a minimum balance. That's how they make up for the commission they don't earn on the trades.

CHAPTER 3: INVESTING

ANTE UP

Minimum amounts to start an account can vary tremendously. If it's a trading account for stocks, there are at least a dozen companies that have no minimums; others, usually the better-known firms, have $1,000 and $2,000 minimums. If you are opening an IRA, it usually has a low or no minimum.

IT'S A BANK!

Brokerages also offer other financial services, much like a bank. Many include ATM cards, credit cards, checkwriting, and money market accounts. The downside here is that the firm may not have an office within 500 miles of you. So, unless you like spending a lot of time in your car, forget this option.

MUTUAL FUNDS

As the operators that don't offer the frills, discount brokerages used to not deal in mutual funds; after all, there were other cheap ways to buy the funds directly from the mutual fund company. Now the discount brokers do offer mutual funds. In fact, there are mutual fund companies that offer discount brokerage service online. Naturally their family of funds is available as well as others. (We explore mutual funds in Chapter 5.)

SELECTION

Some discount brokerages just concentrate on stocks and might not offer certain kinds of bond investments. Be sure to ask, if bonds are in your financial future.

reSEARCH

The amount of research available for free on the Internet makes the offer of "free" research fairly meaningless. However, if you find a brokerage that has done some good research, and you invested in a company and made money based on the research, then this obviously is a factor in choosing your brokerage.

IT'S FREE!

Some brokerages will offer inducements to lure you in as a customer, sort of like the credit card offers that give you frequent flier miles. In fact, some brokerages offer frequent flier miles. Some even add money to your initial account as an incentive. These offers change every week.

CHAPTER 3: INVESTING

PICKING AN ONLINE FIRM: YOUR PRIORITIES WILL CHANGE

The Internet makes it easy to play the markets and that's part of the appeal: Click your mouse and you can buy and sell stocks from more than 100 online brokers. Some trades are as low as $10 per transaction for up to 1,000 shares of stock.

And while online investors say that low cost is the chief reason they open an online brokerage account, their priorities actually change once they become customers.

Online investors said that their checklist of priorities (after price) were items such as: keeping personal information and portfolio data secure, offering uninterrupted access under normal conditions and speedy execution, and having credibility, according to a survey by Spectrem Group and NFO Interactive of Greenwich, Connecticut. The survey, titled *Online Brokerage Market: Consumers, Web Sites & Competition, Third Edition*, compared investors' opinions regarding the Web sites for a number of firms, including Ameritrade, Charles Schwab, DATEK, DLJ Direct, E*TRADE, Fidelity, Waterhouse, and others. Customers were asked to rate the firms in more than twenty categories; Fidelity had the highest overall customer satisfaction rating in the survey, with Waterhouse in second place, and Schwab in third place.

As for other Web site attributes, DLJ Direct was rated best overall in the "speed or performance of its site," DATEK had the best rating for "general ease of site navigation," and online investors said Schwab was number one in "the ability to access all required investing information at one site."

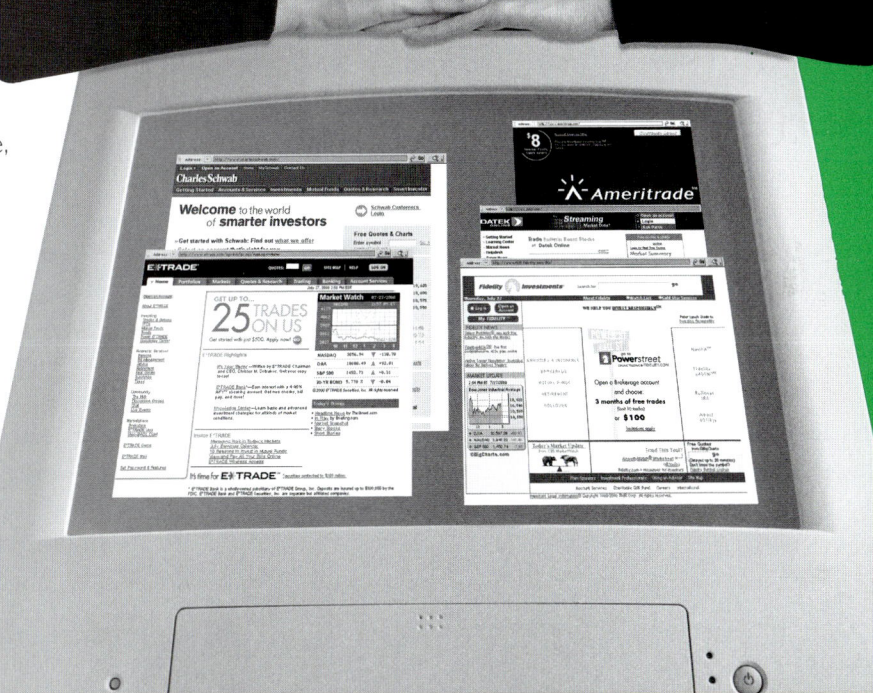

CHAPTER 3: INVESTING 46

WHEN OLD IS NEW

Discount firms usually don't give investment advice; full service firms do. And the new companies that made online trading popular are now feeling competition from the old-line firms that finally decided to trade their cap-toe oxfords for a pair of Nikes.

Once eschewing online trading as somehow untrustworthy, and even running ads to that effect, companies like Wall Street giant Merrill Lynch have entered full bore into the online competition. Merrill Lynch wasn't the first of the major full-service firms to get into online discount brokerage. Morgan Stanley Dean Witter did so through its discount unit Discover, as well as Prudential and PaineWebber, which had online trading sites up and running before Merrill's. But Merrill's entry was a milestone in the industry's development. Merrill's capitulation signaled that the online brokerage business had arrived: It was something that every retail broker would have to offer.

But so far, the old line brokers have not grabbed a huge market share. The top ten online brokers still held 96 percent of the market.

Merrill and Morgan Stanley Dean Witter ranked near the bottom in TheStreet.com's "OnLine Broker 2000 Survey." That means that fewer than 312 of the more than 10,000 readers who participated identified these firms as their primary broker.

David Holmgren, who teaches high school math and physics in Williamstown, Massachusetts, wrote in his survey that "Schwab was excellent. I moved to Merrill Lynch because it offered online trading with broker help, plus expanded financial offerings." But what he has found are accounts that are only updated once daily and a broker who isn't up on hot technology stocks. "I've gone through three [brokers] looking for one that is up on the current trends," he wrote.

HOW TO OPEN AN ACCOUNT

That said, you may want to open an account. Hey, at least you now have some idea what some of the big hurdles might be. Actually opening the account is easy.

Basically, you fill out an application, the way you would open a bank account. There are a couple of ways to secure the application forms: Download the forms, sign them, enclose them in an envelope with a check to fund your account, and receive confirmation of your ability to start

(continued on page 49)

47 — CHAPTER 3: INVESTING

ONLINE BROKERAGES: A SAMPLING

A.B. Watley, Inc. - www.abwatley.com
$9.95 market and limit orders. Add one cent per share on orders over 5,000 shares. By phone, $23.95 up to 5,000 shares, add one cent per share thereafter. Minimum to start: $3,000 and account cannot fall below $1,000.

Accutrade - www.accutrade.com
$29.95 up to 1,000 shares. Beyond that, add two cents per share to the rate. Phone trading: $28.00 plus 2 cents per share flat rate. Minimum to start: $5,000.

American Express Brokerage - www.americanexpress.com
Commissions are based on asset balance in your account. Three levels: below $25,000, $25k-100k, over $100k. Level 1: $14.95 per buy or sell up to 3,000 shares. After that, additional 3 cents per share. Level 2: buys are free, sells are $14.95, 3 cent rule applies here too. Level 3: buys and sells are free. 3 cent rule applies here again on any order over 3,000 shares. No minimum to start.

Ameritrade - www.ameritrade.com
$8 trades online, $12 by phone. Flat rates. Minimum to start: $2,000.

Bidwell & Company - www.bidwell.com
$12 per trade up to 1,500 shares. Add one cent per share above 1,500 to the rate. No minimum to start.

Brown & Co. - www.brownco.com
$5.00 up to 5,000 shares. Over 5,000 shares = $5.00 plus 1 cent per share retroactive all the way to the first share. E.g. 6,000 shares = $65.00 commission. Minimum to start: 5 years minimum of investment experience, net income of at least $40,000 per year from all sources, net worth of at least $50,000 (exclusive of family residence), $15,000 in cash and/or securities to open the account.

Bull & Bear Securities - www.bullbear.com
$19.95 up to 5,000 shares. Over 5,000, add one cent per additional share. No minimum to start.

Charles Schwab - www.schwab.com
$29.95/1st 1,000 shares, $.03 per share thereafter: up to 30 trades this way. At 31 trades, it becomes $19.95/1st 1,000 shares, $.03 per share thereafter. At 61 trades, it becomes $14.95/1st 1,000 shares, $.03 per share thereafter. Minimum to start: $5,000.

Datek - www.datek.com
$9.99 per trade up to 5,000 shares. Anything above 5,000 shares is considered the next trade and incurs another $9.99. Minimum to start: no minimum, but $2,000 to open a margin account.

DLJ Direct - www.dljdirect.com
$20 per trade up to 1,000 shares, plus $.02 per share thereafter. No minimum to start.

Dreyfus - www.tradepbs.com
Flat $15 on Internet orders, unlimited volume. Phone orders: $25 flat up to 5,000, penny on each share beyond. Minimum to start: no minimum, but $2,000 is required to open a margin account.

E*Trade - www.etrade.com
$14.95/first 29 trades. $9.95/trades 30-74, $4.95 trades 75+. For NASDAQ and limit/stop orders, following the same format as above, the rates are: $19.95, $14.95, $9.95. No minimum to start.

Fidelity Power Street - www.personal300.fidelity.com
Initially, online trade commissions are $25 and phone trades are $38.95. After you have traded with them at least 12 transactions per year, the rates shift to...online: $14.95, phone: $38.35 (a very weird reduction for the phone rate, but true). Minimum to start: $5,000.

JB Oxford - www.jboxford.com
$14.50 up to 1,000 shares. One cent additional on every share over 1,000. Minimum to start: $2,000 cash and/or securities.

Morgan Stanley Dean Witter - www.online.msdw.com
$29.95 up to 1,000 shares. Anything over 1,000 shares, rate shifts to 3 cents per share for the entire order. Purchasing stocks valued at less than $1 per share: there is a $25 minimum purchase. Add to that 2.75% of this principal amount. (2,000 shares at .25 per share = $500. Commission = 500 x 2.75% = $13.75. Add $13.75 to the $25 purchase for a commission of $38.75.) Minimum to start: $2,000.

CHAPTER 3: INVESTING

(from page 47)
trading in pretty short order. Or the firm can send you a form through the mail and you can return it.

It gets a little more complicated if you want to open a margin account. A margin account is an account with your brokerage that allows you to buy stocks or other securities with money you borrow from the broker. Naturally, you pay interest, so the big profit you make on a stock you bought on margin is sliced somewhat by the interest you have to pay to your broker. There are regulations on these accounts set by the federal government, but like any borrowed money, you're going to have to pay it back. And if you borrowed money to buy a stock that plummets in value, you are going to feel a cash pinch that could really hurt. The firm will definitely check your credit record.

Other types of accounts for the beginning investor:

- **Cash account:** You put up the money, and then you buy whatever kind of investment you choose—stocks, bonds, mutual funds, whatever.

- **IRA account:** Allows you to control the investment of your IRA. Usually there is a low minimum investment for these accounts.

WHAT ELSE?

You'll need a computer and access to the Internet. If you want to keep track of the market while you're at work (and your boss doesn't catch you) make sure your system at home and work are compatible. And remember that if you send an order in off-hours to your firm, it will execute the order the next day when trading opens. Also, there are after-hours markets where you can trade.

PLACING AN ORDER

There are several different ways to designate your order. The way you tag it could determine whether it even takes place, so understanding the different kinds of orders is important. However, it isn't complicated:

- **Market order:** An order, either buy or sell, for immediate execution at the best price available. The most common type of order, a market order has the advantage of nearly always being filled, since no price is specified.

- **Limit order:** Any order in which the seller or buyer specifies the price he or she will accept. For the seller the limit is the minimum amount acceptable; for the buyer it is the maximum he or she will pay.

- **Day Order:** An order that terminates automatically at the end of the business day if it has not been filled.

49 — CHAPTER 3: INVESTING

• **Stop Order:** A market order that is entered after a specified price level has been reached. Say you want to sell XYZ Corp. shares if the price falls to $6. Or say you want to buy shares of XYZ if they hit $5. However, while the broker will enter the order based on your instructions, the exact price isn't guaranteed.

• **GTC (Good Till Canceled):** An order either to buy or to sell a security that remains in effect until it is canceled by the customer or until it is executed by the broker.

• **Fill-or-Kill:** An order that is sent for immediate execution. If it cannot be filled immediately, it is automatically canceled.

• **All or None (AON):** A limit order either to buy or to sell a security in which the broker is directed to attempt to fill the entire amount of the order or none of it. An all-or-none order differs from a fill-or-kill order in that with an all-or-none order immediate execution is not required.

The online firms often hire other firms to actually make the trade for securities. For example, you want to sell 500 shares of Earwig Inc., the new earwax cleaning company. You send the sell order and your online broker looks for a buyer. But the online broker is also looking out for his/her own pocketbook. Since another firm actually executes the trade, at up to one to two cents a share, the online broker likely will take the cheaper cost, but that might not be the best deal for you. Even if it is just a one-sixteenth difference, that's $31.25 you don't get on 500 shares. The practice is considered widespread and there's no real way for the customer to know.

Also, the GAO noted that online firms don't do a very good job of letting customers know the kind of hole they can fall in if they open a margin account. In short, it's a new experimental industry, and you're the lab rat.

POT HOLES ON THE INTERNET

NOT SO CHEAP

The General Accounting Office (GAO), which tackles topics like defense spending for hammers and congressional budget whoppers, took a look at online stock trading and came up with some serious questions about trading with online firms.

KEEP THIS IN MIND (BEWARE)

Here are some other issues that the Securities and Exchange Commission has raised:

Online trading is not always instantaneous. Investors may find that technological "choke points" can slow or prevent their orders from reaching an online firm. Speed can count in a hot market. If the

CHAPTER 3: INVESTING

prices are escalating or falling, you might not get the price you want if there are problems with you or your broker's modem, computer, or the Internet service provider. Also, if traffic on the Internet is heavy, it can delay the deal.

Know your options for placing a trade if you are unable to access your account online.
Most online trading firms offer alternatives for placing trades. These alternatives may include touch-tone telephone trades, faxing your order, or doing it the low-tech way by talking to a broker over the phone. Make sure you know whether using these different options may increase your costs. And remember, if you experience delays getting online, you may experience similar delays when you turn to one of these alternatives.

If you place an order, don't assume it didn't go through.
Some investors have mistakenly assumed that their orders have not been executed and place another order. They end up either owning twice as much stock as they could afford or wanted, or with sell orders, selling stock they do not own. Talk with your firm about how you should handle a situation where you are unsure if your original order was executed.

If you cancel an order, make sure the cancellation worked before placing another trade.
When you cancel an online trade, it is important to make sure that your original transaction was not executed. Although you may receive an electronic receipt for the cancellation, don't assume that that means the trade was canceled. Orders can only be canceled if they have not been executed. Ask your firm about how you should check to see if a cancellation order actually worked.

If you trade on margin, your broker can sell your securities without giving you a margin call.
Now is the time to reread your margin agreement and pay attention to the fine print. If your account has fallen below the firm's maintenance margin requirement, your broker has the legal right to sell your securities at any time without consulting you first.

CHAPTER 3: INVESTING

Some investors have been rudely surprised that "margin calls" are a courtesy, not a requirement. Brokers are not required to make margin calls to their customers.

Even when your broker offers you time to put more cash or securities into your account to meet a margin call, the broker can act without waiting for you to meet the call. In a rapidly declining market your broker can sell your entire margin account at a substantial loss to you, because the securities in the account have declined in value.

No regulations require a trade to be executed within a certain period of time.

There are no Securities and Exchange Commission regulations that require a trade to be executed within a set period of time. But if firms advertise their speed of execution, they must not exaggerate or fail to tell investors about the possibility of significant delays.

Set your price limits on fast-moving stocks: market orders vs. limit orders.

To avoid buying or selling a stock at a price higher or lower than you wanted, you need to place a limit order rather than a market order. A limit order is an order to buy or sell a security at a specific price. A buy limit order can only be executed at the limit price or lower, and a sell limit order can only be executed at the limit price or higher. When you place a market order, you can't control the price at which your order will be filled.

For example, if you want to buy the stock of a "hot" IPO that was initially offered at $9, but don't want to end up paying more than $20 for the stock, you can place a limit order to buy the stock at any price up to $20. By entering a limit order rather than a market order, you will not be caught buying the stock at $90 and then suffering immediate losses as the stock drops later in the day or the weeks ahead.

Remember that your limit order may never be executed because the market price may quickly surpass your limit before your order can be filled. But by using a limit order you also protect yourself from buying the stock at too high a price.

THE NEW ACCOUNT AGREEMENT

Here's a little cautionary tale whether you pick an online firm or a traditional broker:

A woman in Sarasota, Florida, signed up with a brokerage firm because she was disappointed with the returns she was receiving elsewhere. She knew the broker from a committee she served on and felt comfortable with him.

The account, which was marketed as the passport plan, was to be a flat-fee account. That means instead of charging commissions for each transaction, the broker received a percentage of the total assets, in this case one percent. If the assets grew, the broker would be rewarded.

Unfortunately the only place this "passport" account was taking her was to the cleaners. Her accounts showed almost no profit in the bull market of the 1990s, and her broker was making out like a bandit. That's because there was a fine print clause, which gave the broker leeway to deal in securities in a category called "fee exempt." These are essentially new stocks just

CHAPTER 3: INVESTING

coming onto the market and for these the broker can earn a commission. In this case the broker loaded up her account with an electric company that the broker's company was taking public. The stock plunged and the woman lost a lot. Overall, the broker earned about 4-5 percent, which is exactly what the old fee used to be for brokers for commissions. Coincidence? We think not.

Lesson: *Read the fine print.*

The SEC recommends that you ask to see any account documentation prepared for you by the sales representative. Completion of the new account agreement requires that you make three critical decisions:

1. Who will control decision-making in your account? You will control the investment decisions made in your account unless you decide to give discretionary authority to your broker to make investment decisions for you. Discretionary authority allows a broker to make investment decisions based on what the broker believes to be best—*without consulting* you about the price, the type of security, the amount, and when to buy or sell. Do not give discretionary authority to your sales representative without seriously considering whether this arrangement is appropriate for you.

2. How will you pay for your investment? Most investors maintain a cash account that requires payment in full for each security purchase. An alternative type of account is a margin account. Buying securities through a margin account means that you can borrow money from the brokerage firm to buy securities and requires that you pay interest on that loan. You will be required to sign a margin agreement disclosing interest terms.

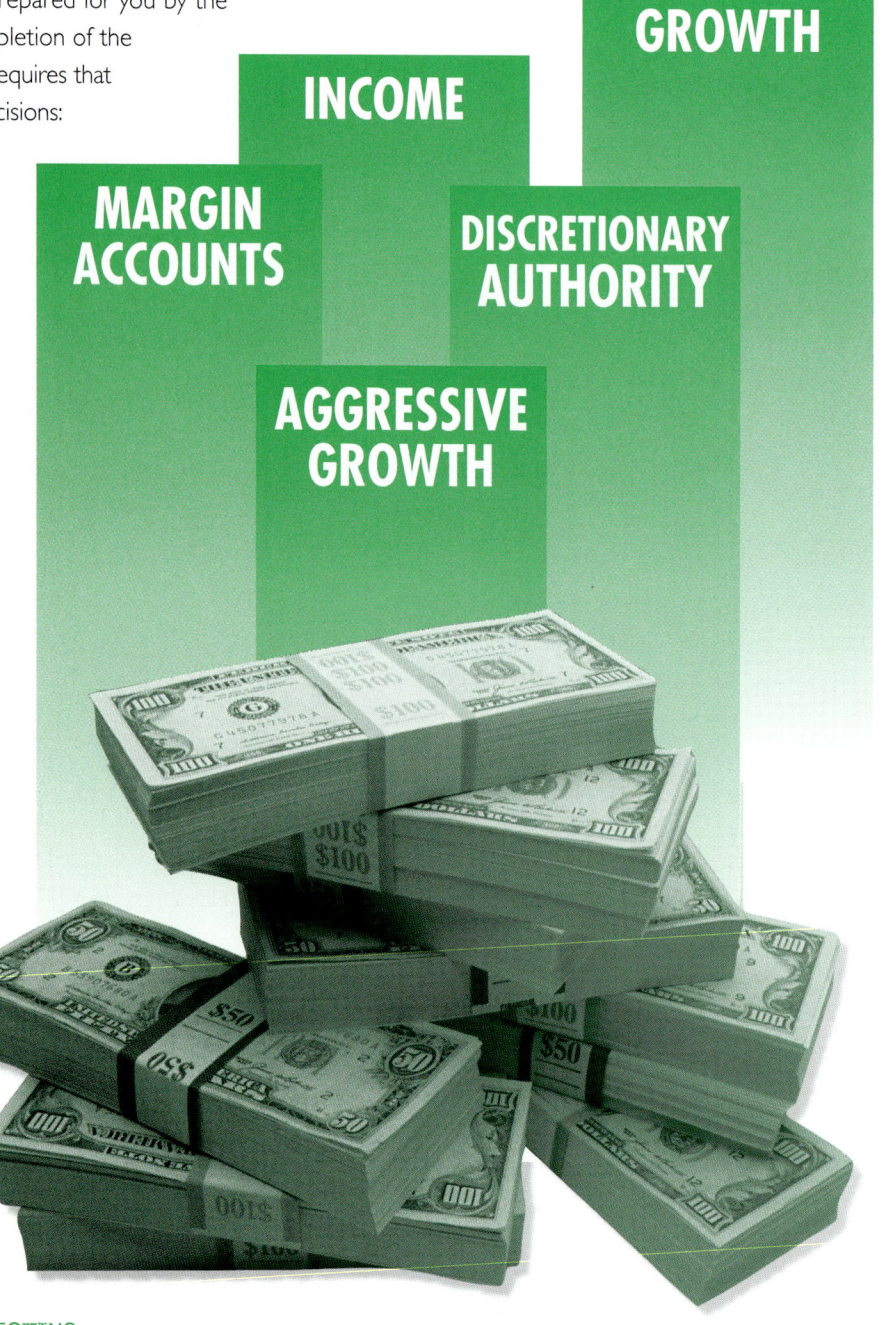

GROWTH

INCOME

MARGIN ACCOUNTS

DISCRETIONARY AUTHORITY

AGGRESSIVE GROWTH

CHAPTER 3: INVESTING

SELECTING YOUR BROKER
(IF HE/SHE IS A HUMAN BEING OR A VARIATION THEREOF)

If you purchase securities on margin (by borrowing money from the brokerage firm), *the firm has authority to immediately sell any security in your account, without notice to you, to cover any shortfall resulting from a decline in the value of your securities.* If the value of your account is less than the amount of the outstanding loan—even due to a one day market drop—*you are liable* for the balance. This may be a substantial amount of money even after your securities are sold. The margin account agreement generally provides that the securities in your margin account may be lent out by the brokerage firm at any time without notice or compensation to you.

3. How much risk should you assume? In a new account agreement, you must specify your overall investment objective in terms of risk. Categories of risk may have labels such as income, growth, or aggressive growth. Be careful you understand the distinctions between these terms, and be certain that the risk level you choose accurately reflects your investment goals. Be sure that the investment products recommended to you reflect the category of risk you have selected.

When opening a new account, the brokerage firm may ask you to sign a *legally binding contract* to arbitrate any future dispute between you and the firm or your sales representative. This may be part of another document, such as a margin agreement. The federal securities laws do not require that you sign such an agreement. You may choose later to arbitrate a dispute for damages even if you do not sign the agreement. Signing such an agreement means that you give up the right to sue your broker and firm in court.

You may have your securities registered either in your name or in the name of your brokerage firm. Ask your sales representative about the relative advantages and disadvantages of each arrangement. If you plan to trade securities regularly, you may prefer to have the securities registered in the name of your brokerage firm to facilitate clearance, settlement, and dividend payment.

First decide whether you need the services of a full service or a discount brokerage firm. A full service firm typically provides execution services (buying and selling), recommendations, investment advice, and research support. A discount broker generally provides execution services and does not make recommendations regarding which securities you should buy or sell. The charges you pay may differ depending upon what services are provided by the firm.

Find out if the brokerage firm is a member of the Securities Investor Protection Corporation (SIPC). SIPC

CHAPTER 3: INVESTING

provides limited customer protection if a brokerage firm becomes insolvent. Ask if the firm has other insurance that provides coverage beyond the SIPC limits. SIPC does not insure against losses attributable to a decline in the market value of your securities. For further information, contact SIPC at 805 Fifteenth Street, N.W., Suite 800, Washington, D.C. 20005-2207; or call (202) 371-8300.

Research the disciplinary history of any brokerage firm and sales representative by calling 1-800-289-9999, a toll-free hot line operated by the National Association of Securities Dealers, Inc. (NASD). The NASD will provide information on disciplinary actions taken by securities regulators and criminal authorities. State securities regulators also can tell you if a sales representative is licensed to do business in your state.

Ask for a copy of the firm's commission schedule. Firms generally pay sales staff based on the amount of money invested by a customer and the number of transactions done in a customer's account. More compensation may be paid to a sales representative for selling a firm's own investment products. Ask what fees or charges you will be required to pay when opening, maintaining, and closing an account.

BASIC INVESTING

So, let's talk to a broker.
Name: Brice Bernard
Age: 31
Occupation: Stockbroker
Income: $65,000 plus
Marital Status: Single
City: New York
Goal: Retire early and live off of investments

A stockbroker by trade, Brice Bernard takes advantage of every investment opportunity that comes his way. (The "legal" ones, that is.) In fact, he's been investing so much for so long, he's still not quite sure of his net worth.

"I totally expect to show up on *Oprah* one of these days," he explains with a smirk. "You know, on one of those shows where she presents some factory worker with a check for $17,000 because he invested in some penny stock when he started work and has forgotten all about it. I've got so many stocks, I can't keep track."

Brice naturally is a close market watcher. But not in the way one might think. "I'm more like a talent scout," he explains. "Once I've invested in something, I let it sit and watch it periodically, say every quarter. But in my daily life, I'm on the look out for 'the next big thing.' Not so much particular companies, but specific sectors of the business community."

For instance, Brice admits that Internet stocks haven't made

TOP 5 SONGS WITH "STOCK" IN THEIR TITLE

5 Riou "Stock"

4 Bobs "(First I Was a Hippie, Then I Was a Stockbroker) Now I Am a Hippie"

3 Dean Evenson "Future Stock"

2 Fall "Choc-Stock"

1 Urban Dance Squad "Bank Stock 6 Zeros"

CHAPTER 3: INVESTING

him rich, but that he slyly invested in a few of the "top" movers and shakers and is quite proud of the way it has turned out. Along with the NASDAQ numbers, Brice explains that he also follows industries such as genetics, cloning, pharmaceuticals, and waste management.

"You have to always be thinking of the future," Brice insists. "People who invested in nylon stocking makers and light bulb manufacturers back in their day are set for life by now. You just have to always be on the lookout for the next stocking or light bulb. That's all."

While not exactly frowning on the current trend in online investing, Brice insists that there's still nothing like financial advice from a paid professional. "Our job is to make you money," he boasts. "And we take our job very seriously."

Brice admits that being a stockbroker isn't for everyone. "I don't even know if it's for *me* anymore," he admits. "Why do you think I want to retire early?"

Gee, that's reassuring.

PLACES TO INVEST, OR: ARE YOU SURE 'RED 17' IS SAFE?

The Markets—Welcome to Vegas!

Financial markets have a variety of locations, much like casinos, where people place their bets and pray. Some of these are stately institutions, with big columns and storied histories; others are really no more than a wired synapse where some electrons intermingle and take off.

In its stripped down form, it's the place to trade what you have (money) for what they have, be it stocks, bonds, cotton, electricity, heating oil, or orange juice.

Look, I'm Exchanging

An exchange is a marketplace where traders can buy or sell stocks, bonds, and other financial instruments. For a stock that's listed on an exchange, such as the New York Stock Exchange (NYSE), your broker may direct the order to that exchange, to another exchange (such as a regional exchange), or to a firm called a "third market maker."

NASDAQ.COM

NASDAQ's Webster is the source for information on this particular market. The home page is thick with news stories on the NASDAQ and has links to other financial news as well. If it's quotes you're looking for, this page provides an unusual multi-quote feature that lets you select up to ten stocks. You're then provided with all the relevant statistics, including company news stories, analyst firm recommendations on buying and selling, and a link to the company's Web site. The info for the companies you've selected is arranged on a single Web browser page for easy comparison and analysis.

If you know what you're looking for but not exactly what you want, you can screen stocks by criteria that you select by using a multi-field form. The site then searches out stocks that meet your specifics, allowing you to scout out your next ideal buy. It's an easy matter to set up a custom ticker, too, on which you can receive quotes, net changes and percentages for NASDAQ, Amex, and NYSE stocks. The ticker updates every three minutes and provides links to news headlines regarding the chosen stocks. You can track your portfolio with the ticker or by setting up an account in the portfolio section, and you can read up on investment strategies and basics in the "Investor's Resource Guide."

CHAPTER 3: INVESTING

NYSE—Big Daddy

The New York Stock Exchange had a very humble beginning. In May of 1792 a group of twenty-four brokers met under a buttonwood tree at 68 Wall Street and agreed to trade with each other—this gathering was the conception of The Big Board.

It took twenty-five years to formally establish the organization as the New York Stock and Exchange Board (the name was shortened to the New York Stock Exchange in 1863). In 1817, they rented a room at 40 Wall Street, appointed a president, and adopted formal rules for conducting business.

In 1865, the Exchange moved to a five-story building at 10 Broad Street that was witness to the first million-share day in December of 1886. In 1901 this building was demolished to make room for a new building. The neo-classical eight-story building at 18 Broad Street is still in use today, along with two other buildings on Broad and Wall Street.

Within these three buildings, there are four trading areas where brokers represent buyers and sellers in a frenzy of daily auctions. The trading begins at 9:30 and ends at 4:00; openings and closings are signaled by ringing brass bells. It is considered an honor to be invited to ring the opening or closing bell; however, this privilege is usually only granted to members celebrating a special event and visiting dignitaries.

REGIONALS

PHILADELPHIA STOCK EXCHANGE

As the first securities exchange in the United States, the Philadelphia Stock Exchange has one of the more fascinating histories among the stock exchanges. It began trading in the year 1790, in this historic city, which was then the financial heart of the nation. The coastal city of New York was the first to receive economic news as ships arrived from Europe and from it dashed speculators and people with inside information that could move the market. These people made fortunes at the expense of Philadelphia merchants, and it wasn't long before a system of signal stations was set up along the high points of New Jersey. Signalmen watched through telescopes, passing along coded signals with lights and mirrors, cutting the advantage of New York speculators. The signal often reached Philadelphia in under ten minutes. Today, the exchange still prides itself on its innovative spirit. It was the first U.S. exchange to erect a Web site (phlx.com), and the first to offer an evening trading session.

The PHLX is many things, among them a smaller mirror exchange of the NYSE. It trades stocks, equity options, index options, and currency options. One of its most important innovations has been the customization of its currency options; you now have your choice of expiration date, strike (exercise) price, and premium payment, so it's a good place to go if you want control over your specifics. Another interesting offer at PHLX is TheStreet.com Internet Sector, which is the most actively traded Internet index option. It offers investors a way to ride the volatile technology sectors without having to select individual stocks.

The Web site is linked to Zack's investment

CHAPTER 3: INVESTING

research site, allowing you necessary tools to monitor your portfolio. You can order brochures through PHLX, and there is a suggested reading list done in conjunction with Amazon.com that will get you on the road to understanding. Phlx.com also offers a somewhat technical guide to currency option investing, but it is a good place to start asking questions.

CHICAGO STOCK EXCHANGE

The Chicago Stock Exchange opened its doors in 1882 with a focus on trading local securities, but didn't stay that way for long. By 1959, it had merged with exchanges in St. Louis, Cleveland, Minneapolis-St. Paul, and New Orleans and changed its name to the Midwest Stock Exchange before having a change of heart and going back to the original. The financial communities of those cities are still vital to the Chicago Exchange. It's now the fastest growing exchange in the U.S.

The Chicago exchange trades NYSE, AMEX, NASDAQ, and CHX stocks on its floor and is the only brick-and-mortar market where investors can shop the big three markets in the same place. The CHX is highly boastful of its technology and fills 90 percent of its orders electronically and automatically through its MAX order routing system, often in seconds. Unlike some other exchanges, the brokers are right on the floor, which gives them access to the exchange's systems and specialists, helping to make the transaction a speedy one.

CHX also claims to be the only exchange where you can trade after hours (but that's a bit misleading; the NYSE will soon follow, and many online companies now offer extended-hours trading over the Internet). The exchange uses e-sessions, which are extended-hours trades that go on until 5:30 Central Time—a full two and a half hours after the markets close in New York. The Web site (Chicagostockex.com) is loaded with information about the exchange, which it hypes up considerably.

MARKET MAKER

A "market maker" is a firm that will buy or sell a stock at publicly-quoted prices. Market makers in exchange-listed stocks are known as "third market makers." Market makers in stocks that trade in over-the-counter (OTC) markets, such as the NASDAQ, are known as "NASDAQ market makers" or simply "market makers."

CHAPTER 3: INVESTING

ELECTRONIC COMMUNICATIONS NETWORK (ECN)

An electronic communications network (ECN) is an electronic trading system that automatically matches buy and sell orders at specified prices.

In truth, there is always a stock market open somewhere in the world. And the established exchanges have been looking at ways to expand their trading hours. Traders with programs like RealTick III, connected directly to services like Reuters' Instinet, are trading before and after exchange hours every day. Many brokerages already offer Instinet trading service through the live broker, so it is to be expected that the exchanges and brokerages will compete with the demand for longer trading hours.

Another good site is the one the New York Stock Exchange (www.nyse.com) runs. In its "Getting Started" section, it offers these words of wisdom that sound like a good old Dutch Uncle:

"Before you invest your first dollar in the stock market, you must understand that there are risks involved. Every investment strategy involves risk, which means that for every dollar that you invest, part or all of it can be lost."

GETTING STARTED: RESEARCH

If you have gotten this far, we'll assume you're serious enough to want to do some of your own research.

A decent place to begin is at a site called Cyberinvest (www.cyberinvest.com). It offers the full line-up of ways to invest, mainly through listings, which seem to consist of prominent names, such as DLJ Direct, Merrill Lynch Direct, and lesser known names, such as Scottrade, which is also an advertiser. In fact, what you find with most of these sites is that the advertisers show up on lists and other compilations.

The value of examining this site is its scope: It has buckets full of access to stocks, bonds, mutual funds, tons of reports, and links to other sources to determine whether your investment hunch is a winner or a stinker. And it is straightforward: A recent story on bonds started with the line, "If you don't know beans about bonds."

CHAPTER 3: INVESTING

Here are some other sites and portals that are good for overall information:

Dow Jones
Dowjones.com

Dowjones.com, from the publishers of *The Wall Street Journal*, specializes in fundamental investment education, but includes full-service financial tools and portfolio monitoring, available for use once you complete the free registration.

If you have specific financial questions, try clicking the link to "ask smartmoney.com" where you'll be able to e-mail professional advisers or browse through the archives. There's a useful international business locator, plus white and yellow pages, local maps, and city guides for the traveler. Get involved with the discussion forums and read up on industry news after you register. There's extensive information at Dowjones.com on all sorts of financial topics. It will take a while to become familiar with all the options, but hey, it takes time to absorb the libraries of knowledge built by the top financial publication in the nation's history.

Yahoo! Finance
finance.yahoo.com

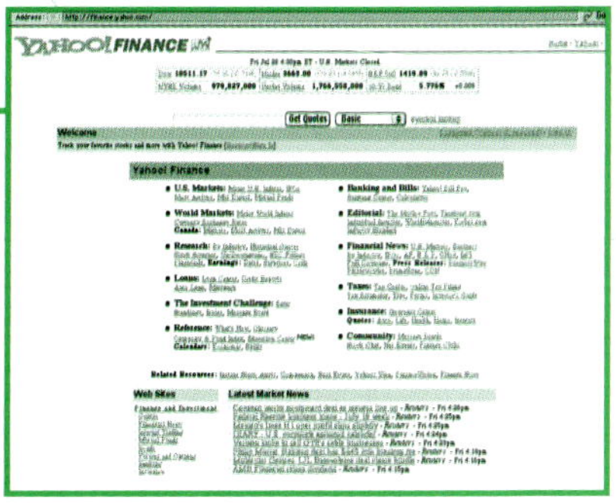

Yahoo! is probably the most popular financial portal on the Web, and with good reason. It offers a wide variety of resources and customizable features. You can create multiple portfolios here and monitor the stocks you hold in any of over forty world markets from Indonesia to Japan, France, Chile, and many more. You can view on your own page, where you're automatically shown recent headlines for each stock in your portfolio, and every stock symbol is hyperlinked to a snapshot of the company, complete with chart and headlines.

There are easily accessible research tools, plus links to company homepages. Make your symbols flash to attract your attention if they move past certain set price points, and leaf through a load of news stories from such diverse news and editorial sources such as Reuters, Businesswire, The Motley Fool, On-line Investor, and the AP Business and Finance wires. Customize the whole thing: Choose colors and edit the informational content you receive. Yahoo! Finance is easy to appreciate.

Excite Finance
Excite.com/money

Don't be fooled. At first glance, it looks like Excite.com is an absolutely second-rate financial portal. In itself, it doesn't hold its own, until you realize that it is linked to Excite's Quicken.com, a powerhouse investment site. Excite itself offers some rudimentary tools, including a news archive and single-quote, chart, and analyst estimate look-up. One misleading link takes you to the Schwab Web site, where you are led to believe you'll be getting free, detailed reports and analyses on your stocks. You will, but only if you pay; only the first three are free. Through Excite you can access message boards, investment clubs, and chatrooms, but if you move forward to Quicken, you'll be treated to one of the best of the best. Quicken has solid information on insider trading, which are behind-the-scenes trades by members of the corporations themselves. Quicken also helps you make sense of all the numbers, by walking you through the research process and explaining the significance of the numbers, helping with inter-company comparisons, and pointing out problems that may arise down the line.

CHAPTER 3: INVESTING

Finance Diaries

"Lottery: A tax on people who are bad at math."

—Random bumper sticker

GET RICH QUICK

Bill hadn't been having very much luck with the job search lately, so he'd been doing a little research into what he liked to call "easy money." Marie, on the other hand, called his brilliant ideas "get-rich quick" schemes (i.e. searching for that ever-elusive pot of gold). He disagreed with her wholeheartedly. Number one, he wasn't getting rich at all. And number two, there was nothing quick about it. (Although he did have to agree with her about the "scheme" part.)

First there was the "work at home," idea. He saw signs for the "job" all over town, posted prominently on telephone poles and down every highway and back road he traveled in search of the coolest bottle of Yoo Hoo in town. And so, one day, stopped at a red light and sipping his favorite chocolate drink, Bill wrote down the local number and put it away for safe keeping. A few days later, frustrated with yet another Internet job search and a Sunday classifieds section full of jobs he was either over- or under-qualified for, he pulled out the number and gave it a call.

"HomeWorkers, Incorporated," answered a pleasant female voice on the other end. "Where the work comes to you! How can I help you today?"

"Uh, yeah," said Bill winningly. (He was shocked that someone answered the phone instead of just hearing another automated phone message.) "I was just looking to inquire about the job opportunity you're endorsing."

"Spectacular," said the voice. "Well, first of all, I'd like to inform you that this is your lucky day. As our first caller of the hour, you receive the introductory offer discount. This means we'll

61 — CHAPTER 3: INVESTING

knock a total of $79.95 off of the start-up fee for your envelope stuffers, lickers, and stampers party pack!"

Bill listened politely as the pleasant voice on the other end of the line droned on about "unlimited potential" and "your attitude determines your altitude," but he had mentally hung up on her the minute he heard the words "start-up" fee. After all, if they were knocking eighty bucks off of it, what must the actual fee be?

Then there was the Internet newsletter brainstorm tossed out by his friend Scully one day at the local coffee shop after another dismal interview.

"Hey, Bill," said Scully after yet another free refill of vanilla cappuccino, "You've got your own computer at home, right? Why not start up an e-mail newsletter and start selling something online?"

"Like what, Scully?" asked Bill, warming up to the idea of yet another "work at home" opportunity. (And hoping it wouldn't be as misleading as the first.)

"Well," said Scully, dumping an endless stream of sugar into his fourth cup of coffee. "Let's say you've got some gadget that you want to sell—"

"But I don't," countered Bill. "I couldn't even build a paper airplane at this point, let alone a gadget or a wadget or whatever."

"That's beside the point, Bill," disagreed Scully. "It's not the gadget you're selling, anyway, it's yourself. Now get this, you throw up a free Web site on the Net, find a free hosting service to send out your newsletter, you claim to be an expert on something like, say, light bulb repair, and then you offer your newsletter for free to subscribers who can't help but miss the several ads you include for whatever your widget or gadget is. Like a light bulb mitten, or something."

"A light bulb mitten?" asked Bill, sipping his lukewarm coffee but really jonesing for a Yoo Hoo. "What the hell is that?"

"You know?" urged Scully. "It's like a potholder for light bulbs."

"Who goes around touching hot light bulbs?" asked Bill.

"I dunno," said Scully. "But picture this scenario, you're reading this really good mystery or something, and it's just getting to the 'whodunit' part, you know, and you're on the edge of your seat, and suddenly the light bulb in your reading lamp goes out. Bang, right at the dénouement. So, you stumble around in the hall closet, grab a fresh light bulb, and rush to replace it. But you don't have time to wait for the old light bulb to cool off, so you use your light bulb mitten to unscrew it ASAP! See, we'll make a mint."

"Or," countered Bill. "I could just get up and move to another room while the light bulb cools."

"No way, Bill," says Scully around a mouthful of hot java. "Americans are lazy. They'd rather spend five bucks on our light bulb mitten, that they just happened to

CHAPTER 3: INVESTING — 62

was going to start a light bulb mitten business, I'd just run down to the local dollar store, buy up all the two-for-one pot holders I could find, and *call* them light bulb mittens. You see how that works?"

"Oh," blushes Bill. "Good idea."

And so, hopped up on caffeine and overpriced biscotti, Bill went home, designed an awesome Web site, complete with blinking light bulbs around its border, found a mailing list provider, both for free, and then spent four hours penning his very first "I see the light (bulb)," newsletter. Then he submitted his startlingly simple site to the major search engines and sat back to wait for subscribers to his well-lit newsletter.

Months later, he was still waiting. He supposed the market for "free light bulb e-newsletters," wasn't quite as "huge" as he and Scully had imagined it to be. Unless, that is, his antsy friend had beaten him to the punch and stolen all of his potential subscribers.

"Oh, well," thought Bill, "at least I didn't go out and buy a hundred dollars worth of cheap potholders!"

And so, that was how Bill found himself driving down the road several weeks later, ignoring those taunting "work from home" signs, not to mention the "lose 50 pounds in a week" posters, and stopping in at his favorite convenience store for a fresh injection of bottled, liquid chocolate.

Scrounging around in his lint-filled pocket for change, Bill stared down at the grimy glass of the counter to see the colorful rows of scratch-off Lottery tickets inside. A (real) light bulb of his own went off over his head, and he gave up on his pocket and dug

read about in their free light bulb lover's newsletter, than get up from their easy chair and—"

"But you just said they got up from their easy chair to go get another light bulb," points out Bill.

"Look," sighs Scully. "If you're going to be so narrow minded, don't come to me for financial advice."

"I didn't," counters Bill. "But, just for conversation's sake, if I were to start this newsletter and tout myself as the proud inventor of the light bulb mitten, who am I going to get to sew up these brilliant mittens? Did you think of that one, Einstein?"

"No," admits Scully.

"Thought not," crows Bill.

"I never thought of it," explains Scully, "because, if I

CHAPTER 3: INVESTING

for his wallet instead. Resorting to that "emergency" five dollar bill he'd had stashed there for a month or two, Bill bought his beloved Yoo Hoo and four one dollar scratch offs.

Grinding them feverishly inside his car, all thoughts of Yoo Hoo and professional jobs out the window, Bill won two dollars on the first card, a "free ticket" on each of the next two cards, and a whopping twenty-five dollars on the fourth! Rushing back inside to collect his winnings, Bill took them all out in more lottery tickets, spending the next four hours parked by the side of the convenience store in his seven year old Toyota and scratching feverishly before running back inside to collect on more and more tickets and petty cash.

By the time the sun was getting ready to go down, Bill was forty dollars richer and three pounds lighter from all of that unaccustomed physical activity. Thus began a week-long obsession that found him driving around town endlessly, in between fruitless interviews, scouring the city for fresh scratch-off spots. He was up, he was down. Some days he rolled around flush, downing Yoo Hoos by the bottle and scarfing Twinkies and Devil Dogs to boot. Other days he barely had enough change left in his ashtray to cover one scratch-off ticket to keep his obsession at bay.

By the end of the week, of course, he'd gone through all of his back-up stash, broken his piggy bank, and even spent the weekly allowance Marie provided him with every pay day. He'd gone bust on every ticket since that first, exciting day.

"Beginner's luck," he grumbled over the fresh want-ads that next Sunday, nearly falling over when a symbol for a fresh e-mail appeared in the right-hand corner of his Web browser.

"Dear sir," read the brief e-mail from an address he didn't recognize. "Please be advised that I have held the patent on your so-called 'light bulb mitten' for the past seven years. If you continue to tout this device as your own, I will be forced to acquire a cease and desist order from the Bureau of Patents and Copyright—"

There was more, but Bill had read enough. He terminated his ill-visited Web site, trashed the template for his "illuminating" newsletter, and even changed his e-mail address.

"Wow," he thought, making dinner for Marie that evening and tired from several weeks of working at *not* working. "This unemployment crap is exhausting!"

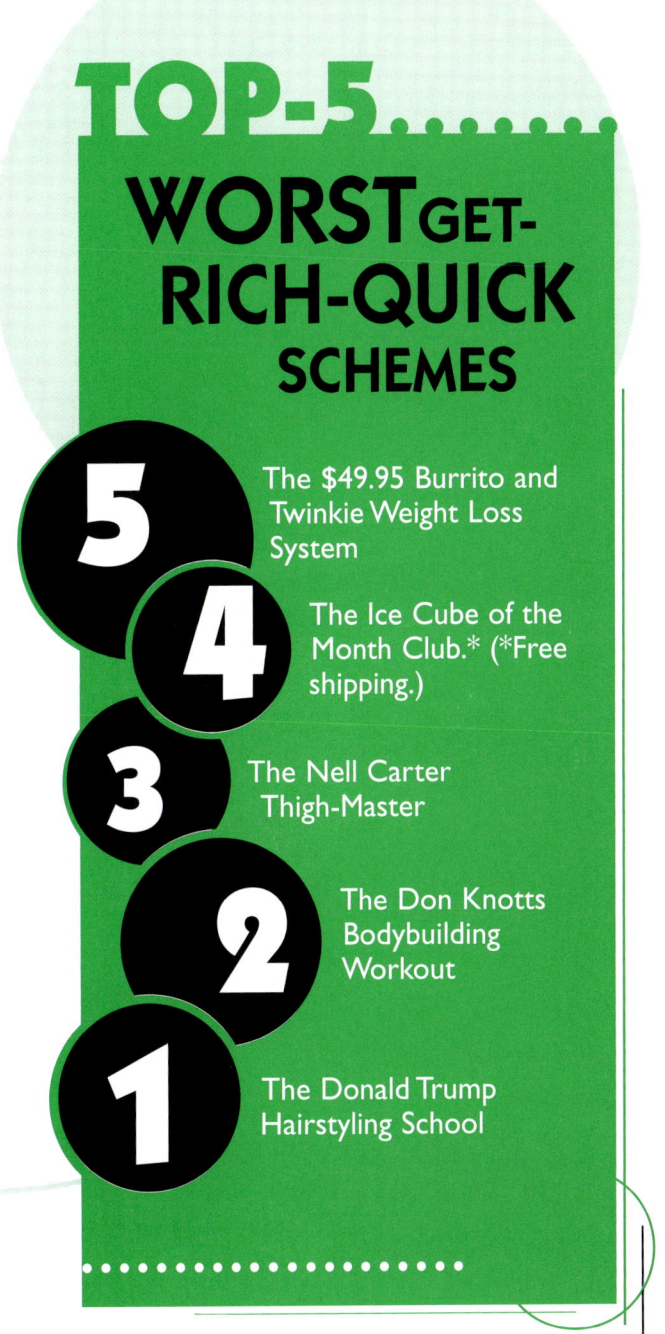

TOP-5........
WORST GET-RICH-QUICK SCHEMES

5 The $49.95 Burrito and Twinkie Weight Loss System

4 The Ice Cube of the Month Club.* (*Free shipping.)

3 The Nell Carter Thigh-Master

2 The Don Knotts Bodybuilding Workout

1 The Donald Trump Hairstyling School

CHAPTER 3: INVESTING — 64

4 STOCKS:
HOW TO ENTER THE MARKET (CAREFULLY)

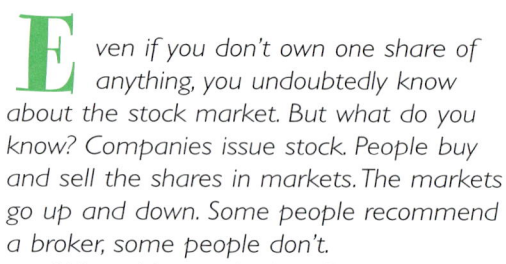

Even if you don't own one share of anything, you undoubtedly know about the stock market. But what do you know? Companies issue stock. People buy and sell the shares in markets. The markets go up and down. Some people recommend a broker, some people don't.

When Marie asked in Chapter 1, "How can we get in on this?" she also might have asked: "Do I want to get in on this?"

CHAPTER 4: STOCKS

DOES ANYONE UNDERSTAND THE STOCK MARKET?

A lot of people look at the stock market and see it as a game they don't fully understand—like Australian rules football or cricket. It's not that there's a lack of coverage of the stock market out there. There's plenty. But how does that translate into your buying a stock, in what company, how many shares, and at the right price?

Legendary stock picker and mutual fund guru John Templeton said that he became interested in stocks while he was in college. He would look at the stock tables and see the daily or weekly changes in price, but there didn't seem to be a ready explanation of *why* they changed. "It fascinated me," he said.

Now retired, he must have figured it out, for his mutual funds were considered among the best performing in the world. So why do the prices change? Think about investors in the stock market as having a vote. There are literally billions of votes cast every day either for or against stocks. The prices can rise or fall, and as in politics, people have a myriad of reasons why they like one candidate more than another.

In truth, there are as many factors influencing these decisions as there are people making them. It is a bromide of finance that no one is smarter than the market. And there seem to be hysterical excesses—wild runs in the market representing billions of dollars. You wonder whether it's like the bumper sticker says: "10,000 lemmings can't be wrong!" But over time, some truths emerge.

52 Weeks Hi	Lo	Stock	Sym	Div	Yld %	PE	Vol 100s	Hi	Lo	Close	Net Chg
3⁵⁄₁₆	1⅜ ♣	GlamisGld	GLG	...	dd	926	1¹⁵⁄₁₆	1⅞	1⅞	– ¹⁄₁₆
16½	9¹³⁄₁₆	Glatfelter	GLT	.70	6.6	10	745	10¹⁵⁄₁₆	10⅝	10⅝	– ⅛
64⁷⁄₁₆	45¼	GlaxoWell	GLX	1.32e	2.3	...	5970	58¾	56½	56⅞	– 2³⁄₁₆
18³⁄₁₆	11⁹⁄₁₆	Glenborough	GLB	1.68	9.5	...	459	17¹³⁄₁₆	17⅝	17¾	– ¹⁄₁₆
20⁹⁄₁₆	13¼	Glenborough pfA		1.94	11.0	...	33	17¾	17⅝	17⅝	– ⅛
16⅝	11¹⁵⁄₁₆	GlimchRlty	GRT	1.92	13.2	17	631	14⅝	14¼	14¼	+ ¹⁄₁₆
21⅝	13¹⁵⁄₁₆	GlimchRlty pfB		2.31	13.2	...	105	17⅝	17	17⁹⁄₁₆	+ ⁹⁄₁₆
13¼	10¹¹⁄₁₆	GlblHilnco	GHI	1.60	12.2	...	349	13⅝	13¹⁄₁₆	13⅛	+ ¹⁄₁₆
30¼	13⅝	GlblMar	GLM			76	16373	28⁵⁄₁₆	27⅛	28¼	+ ⅛
12	9⅝	GlblIncFd	GDF	1.42	12.6	...	214	11⁵⁄₁₆	11⅛	11⁵⁄₁₆	+ ⅛
7¹⁄₁₆	4⁵⁄₁₆	GlblTch	GAI	1.35e	28.1	8	41	4¹³⁄₁₆	4¾	4¹³⁄₁₆	– ¹⁄₁₆
s 39⁹⁄₁₆	9⅝	GlblTelSys	GTS	...		dd	10013	11⁹⁄₁₆	11	11¼	– ⅛
6⅜	2⁷⁄₁₆	GlblVacGp	GVG	...		dd	10	2¹¹⁄₁₆	2¹¹⁄₁₆	2¹¹⁄₁₆	...
8⁹⁄₁₆	4	Goldcp A g	GGA	g	...	...	51	7¾	7⅛	7⅛	– ¹⁄₁₆
10¼	4⅝	Goldcorp B g	GG	g	...	...	4	8⁹⁄₁₆	8⁹⁄₁₆	8⁹⁄₁₆	– ¹⁄₁₆
23¼	12¼	GldnState	GSB			8	2029	19⁵⁄₁₆	18¹⁵⁄₁₆	19¹⁄₁₆	– ³⁄₁₆
s 46¹¹⁄₁₆	26⅞	GldnWstFnl	GDW	21	5	7	3383	42¹⁵⁄₁₆	42	42¼	– ⅞
128	**55³⁄₁₆**	**GoldmanSachs**	**GS**	**.48**	**.5**	**17**	**21773**	**104¼**	**99½**	**104¼**	**+ 2⁵⁄₁₆**
43	21	Goodrich	GR	1.10	3.2	22	3898	35	33⅝	34½	+ ¾
25⅝	21	Goodrich QUIPS		2.08	9.0	...	39	23⅝	23¹⁄₁₆	23⁵⁄₁₆	– ³⁄₁₆
6½	1	GoodrichPet	GDP	...		dd	8	4⅝	4⅝	4⅝	– ⅛
59¹³⁄₁₆	19¾	Goodyear	GT	1.20	5.5	12	5897	22	21⁹⁄₁₆	21⅝	+ ⅛
9¼	4¼ ♣	Gottschks	GOT	...	10	22	5⅞	5¾	5¾	...
21	9	GraceWR	GRA	...		6	2627	12⅜	11⅞	12	...

A CLOSER LOOK

The first thing you see or hear when you notice the market is probably the share price of a stock. Let's remove the mystery from this by looking at a stock table available in newspapers or online.

The first two columns carry the 52-week high and low prices. *Hi* is the highest the stock has been over the last 12 months; *lo* is the lowest.

CHAPTER 4: STOCKS 66

Next is the name of the company. This is an abbreviated form so it can be crammed in a little bit of space. It's alphabetized so you can find it fairly easily.

The stock symbol—those initials you see scrolling on the bottom of the television every time you flip past MSNBC—may or may not have the same letters as the actual name of the company, but essentially it is an even briefer abbreviation. They are not alphabetized; for example, AaronRents' symbol is RNT.

Next is the *div* or dividend, which is a per share payment some companies make to their shareholders. The number is the annual dividend; note that most dividends are paid quarterly. This can include or not include a special dividend.

Yield % is next. It is the amount of the dividend expressed as a percentage of the stock price. For example a $1 annual dividend for a stock priced at $10 would give a yield of 10 percent.

Next is the *P/E ratio* or price/earnings ratio.

We mentioned this in the mini-glossary, and we'll deal with it more in depth in a bit, but for now it's just another way to evaluate the stock.

It is the price of the stock divided by the earnings per share.

Next is *VOL 100s*: That's the number of shares that were traded that day. It is usually shown in hundreds, so add two zeros to the number. The figure 280 is really 28,000 or 28,000 shares that traded that day.

Hi is the high price for the day; *lo* is the low price for the day.

Close is the price when the market closed for the day.

Net Chg. is the change in price from the close of the previous day.

Also remember that the number at the end is dollars and cents, even though it's represented as a fraction. 65 1/4 is $65.25.

The number can be as low as 1/16, a fractional measure that dates back to the way Spanish currency or cheese or something was divided, and yes, you end up with odd cents because 16 won't divide into $1 evenly. Don't ask.

That's it.

Here's the equation:
Say the company earned $1 million last year and it has one million shares in circulation.

$$\frac{\$1,000,000}{1,000,000 \text{ shares}} = \$1 \text{ in earnings per share (EPS)}$$

If its share price is $30 and it earns $1 per share, the ratio of the price (of a share) to earnings (per share) is—30!

$$\frac{\$30.00 \text{ share price}}{\$ 1.00 \text{ EPS}} = 30 \text{ P/E}$$

INVESTMENT CATEGORIES

Stocks—can be classified in many ways, and you may have heard these terms bandied about: blue chips (great with salsa!) or cyclical. There aren't hard and fast rules that determine which categories a stock might fall in; they are just ways people have devised to describe certain stocks and their historical performance.

Blue Chips—AT&T is a blue chip, which comes from the poker term for the most expensive chip you can bet. These companies earn money, pay dividends, and they'll be around tomorrow. You hope.

CHAPTER 4: STOCKS

Cyclical Stocks—They tend to ride the ups and downs of the economy. Good in good times, not so good in bad times. Car companies, building companies, appliance makers, and others that depend on consumer spending are in this group.

Downside Stocks—They don't take your breath away when the economy is cooking, but you breathe easier when it slows down. They are usually things you can't do without, such as gas and food.

Dividend stock—They don't move much in terms of share price growth, but they pay a healthy dividend. Utilities are the prime example. Dow Jones has a "utility average" that includes companies such as ConEd, Duke Energy, and the Southern Co. Their yield (dividend as a percentage of the share price) at one point in 2000 was about 9 percent, 4 percent, and 5 percent respectively, which beats most savings accounts.

Dot-Coms—A relatively recent addition to the Wall Street mix that befuddles some who watch the market and intrigues others. The jury won't be back anytime soon on this sector despite the "news" in mid-2000 that the bubble had burst.

Financial—Banks, brokerages, and other companies that make their money by handling other people's money.

Growth Stock—Until it edged into blue-chip land (sans dividend), Microsoft was your classic growth stock. It poured everything it earned into its own growth. Good idea. This includes many high-tech stocks that keep churning out profits and grabbing market share.

Value Stocks—Everything seems strong about these stocks but their stock price. They may be operating in the shadow of their industry peers or simply in an industry that isn't in favor at the moment. (Restaurant stocks are notorious for running hot or cold.)

International Stocks—A sophisticated buy even for the pro, but there are mutual funds that buy these under the guise of portfolio diversification.

Initial Public Offerings—Stocks just coming available on the market. They have been the source of great fortunes and even greater busts in the last five years. Many dot-coms that have folded were financed through IPOs.

PROFITS MATTER

So you know how to read a stock table, and have a general idea of the kinds of stocks that are out there. You might have also noticed that the stock market is a chaotic mess that people try to explain in rational terms, occasionally succeeding, and very often missing the mark.

One way to better understand publicly traded companies, the term used for companies that sell stock to the public, is to examine earnings. Earnings are the profit, also called net income. It's why companies exist, or viewed from another angle: They can't exist without them.

If you kept track of a company's profit increases over a period of five years or more, you'd probably find that its stock price kept pace with its growth in earnings. It's a pretty simple idea: The more profits a company earns, the more it's valued in the market. One

CHAPTER 4: STOCKS

study shows that since World War II, the stock market's gains closely match the similar increase in corporate profit growth.

As mentioned above, one way to use earnings as a measure is to calculate the earnings per share, also known as EPS. (Look, if tennis player Anna Kournikova can do it in a TV commercial, so can you.) You simply divide the amount of the earnings by the number of shares currently outstanding. As we showed above, it is a pretty simple equation. There's one little wrinkle: These are trailing earnings per share. It's called trailing because it's from the last four quarters, not the previous calendar year.

However, earnings per share by itself, doesn't tell you that much. You know the company has made a profit (you hope). It is the relationship between the price of the stock and its earnings that will give you some insight on how to evaluate this company. This is called the price/earnings ratio.

IS THE P/E STILL USEFUL?

Many investors used to look at the P/E ratio and not much else when they evaluated a stock. If a company's P/E ratio was low, it was either a bargain or in an industry that didn't grow very rapidly. The ratio, also called a "multiple," showed what investors thought about the stock and its earnings future. Sometimes you'd run across a company that hadn't made a lot of profit but had discovered a new drug or made a technological breakthrough and it might sell at a high multiple, say 30. But historically over the last century, this multiple has been 14. In other words, on average in the last 100 years, stocks have traded at 14 times earnings (and additionally had a dividend yield of 4%.)

Almost anytime in 2000, you would find the average multiple of about 30 times earnings (and with a dividend yield of 1.1 percent).

Experts say the high P/E reflects the fast-moving, high-tech economy, and the anticipated efficiency that companies hope to gain. It's in a way asking investors to accept the idea that the economy is moving faster than in years past, so get used to a higher multiple. Some of this belief is based on real data: People are a lot more

> **Here are a few P/Es from 2000, from a variety of economic sectors.**
>
> Microsoft—43 times earnings
> Wal-Mart—46 times earnings
> Donna Karan—12 times earnings
> Delta Airlines—6 times earnings
> Philip Morris—7 times earnings

productive than they used to be, meaning you need fewer workers to get something done; computers play a big part in this. (Of course, this does not apply to the government, which needs more workers to get less done!)

A finance professor at the Wharton School at the University of Pennsylvania says he believes that a P/E range of 25 is probably where the market should have been in 2000—so the 30 P/E number is a little high.

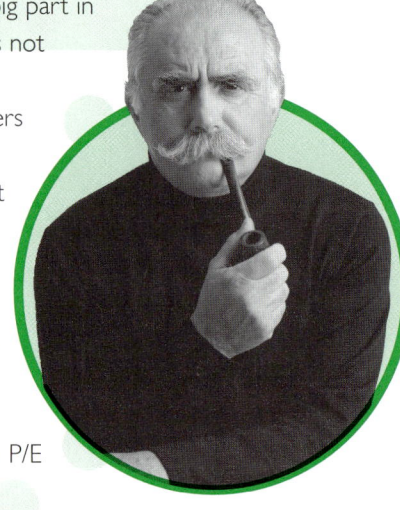

Keep in mind the outside factors that can influence stock prices. High oil prices hurt transportation companies; a lawsuit that threatens a company's existence can wreck the stock price; internal management turmoil can send investors scurrying. And some of the factors driving up stock prices come from outside the stock market or individual industries. For example:

Interest rates

Interest rate changes can play a role in the way the stock market behaves. In recent years, as interest rates have remained low, the market hasn't been affected in any significant way. But when interest rates go up enough, fixed income investments, like bonds, become more attractive. There is less money chasing stocks and that brings stock prices down. On the other hand, when interest rates stay down, then investors tend to shift money into stocks.

Rule Changes

A lot of factors have worked to make the market of the 1990s and beyond a unique success. Changes in tax laws are one. The creation of 401(k)s and IRAs with their tax deferred and tax exempt aspects have helped the stock market. The flow of money into stock mutual funds—where most 401(k) assets reside—gave the market an extra boost.

ARE THERE OTHER RATIOS?

You betcha. Lots. You can use devices called "stock screens" to take virtually any kind of measure of a company you want. (We discuss stock screens more in "How Do You Build a Portfolio?" later in this chapter.) Remember that these are simply formulas that mathematically measure a company. If you are delving this deep, also remember there are professors and portfolio managers who spend their professional lives studying these things, meaning that a little knowledge might be very dangerous. But if you read a report or hear an observation that mentions one of these, then at least it might ring a bell. Also make note that a measure that can apply to one company might not work well for another.

Types of Stocks (Technically Speaking):

Common Stock—Stock is ownership of a corporation represented by shares, and most shares of stock are called common stock, but there can be different classes with different rights. To the average investor, however, the everyday "common" share is the one he or she is holding, and that's the share price quoted on television or in the newspaper. Shareholders of stock are entitled to vote on company matters (usually once a year). This agenda is set by the company's board of directors. Common stock can pay a dividend or not, depending on the judgment of the company's board of directors. Remember why companies sell stock: It's to raise money from investors for expansions or to fund ongoing operations. Also, when a new company sells stock in what is called an IPO (Initial Public Offering), it not only raises money for the company, but it also allows the owners to sell some of their stake to the public and in turn establish a value for the shares they hold.

Preferred stock—Shares issued by a company that usually have certain limits on voting but pay a fixed dividend. In some ways, preferred stock is like a bond, which pays interest. Preferred shares trade on exchanges just like common stock. They often are listed underneath the common share price with a little pf beside the name of the company.

Other—There are also ways to own the "right" to buy stocks, often at a set price. One way is through warrants. These "rights" can be bought and sold just like shares of stock.

CHAPTER 4: STOCKS

Here are three ratios you might run across:

1. Most people react to the term cash flow the way Woody Allen did in the movies when he said of his financial woes: "Something's not flowing." Cash flow is probably the most frequent way of valuing companies used by the pros. Cash flow is literally the cash that flows through a company during the course of a quarter or the year after taking out all fixed expenses. Cash flow is normally defined as earnings before interest, taxes, depreciation, and amortization. (Don't worry about these terms at the moment. The "Research" section at the end of the book offers multiple sources for definitions.)

Why look at earnings before interest, taxes, depreciation, and amortization? Interest income and expense, as well as taxes, are all tossed aside because cash flow is designed to focus on the operating business and not secondary costs or profits. You divide that remainder by the number of shares and you have cash flow per share.

Cash Flow ($25 million) divided by Number of Shares (5 million) = Cash Flow Per Share of 5.

This is especially useful when you research a company that has paid out money to build its franchise. It could be raking in cash but still recognizing on its books the expense of building its business.

2. While profits are important, revenues (sales) are where it all starts. And sometimes companies might not be doing that well in terms of profits but their sales are still strong. Naturally, someone developed a measurement to take this into account. It's called the price/sales ratio.

Companies that may be temporarily losing money—have earnings depressed due to short-term circumstances (like product development or higher taxes), or are relatively new in a high-growth industry—are often valued by their revenues and not their earnings. Revenue-based valuations are made using the price/sales ratio, often simply abbreviated PSR.

The price/sales ratio takes the current market capitalization of a company and divides it by the last 12 months of revenues.

The next step in calculating the PSR is to add up the revenues from the last four quarters and divide this number into the market capitalization. Say XYZ Corp. had $200 million in sales over the last four quarters and currently has no long-term debt. The PSR would be:

$$PSR = \frac{(10{,}000{,}000 \text{ shares} \times \$10/\text{share})}{\$200{,}000{,}000 \text{ revenues}} = 0.5$$

What's it mean? While the company might not be burning up the track in profits, its revenues and the way it's valued in the market still make it a healthy company and possibly a bargain.

3. Another measure is the P/E growth ratio, sometimes called the PEG and popularized by the Motley Fool financial service. It's a "guesstimate" on how a company might do in the future and whether the current stock price accurately reflects a company's potential. Most of the time it does, but there are glitches.

It simply takes the projected growth rate from analysts' projections and compares them with the P/E ratio. If a company is expected to grow at that same 10% a year over the next two years and has a P/E of 10, it will have a PEG of 1.0.

$$\frac{\text{P/E of 10}}{10\% \text{ EPS growth}} = 1.0 \text{ PEG}$$

A PEG of 1.0 shows that a company is fairly valued. Lower and it may be undervalued in terms of stock price; higher and it may be overvalued.

These numbers are just a taste of what the pros deal with all day. The real work is done when you dig into research, a task that is definitely easier than it has ever been in the past.

CHAPTER 4: STOCKS

LEARNING THE ROPES WITHOUT BEING HUNG

The rise of new brokerage firms must have some direct relationship to the amount of free information available to an investor. There is simply a wealth of data about companies, whether from the brokerages themselves, business research companies, consumer groups, or the government.

Now that you know how to look at the price of the stock and understand in general terms what those little crimped-looking numbers are trying to tell you, you might be ready to dive in a little deeper.

There are hundreds of services that provide fairly cold-blooded reports about public companies. Remember that there are only three kinds of research: a report compiled by the company itself; a report compiled by a third party; a report issued by the government.

Unless you're just guessing or acting on a tip (we deal with that later in this chapter), here are some basics you need to know:

CHAPTER 4: STOCKS

ANNUAL REPORTS

Some companies like to show off with their annual reports, giving them the slick look of a stylish magazine. However, the basic job of the report is to deliver financial information to the shareholders, who receive the report for free.

Much of the company's fundamental financial information is published in the report, but as you might expect, bad news isn't highlighted. There are parts of the annual report that you might want to investigate. Reading these reports and then digging for further information are what professional investment managers do for a living. They want to understand the basics of the company as thoroughly as possible, ferreting out information both pro and con about the company's performance.

If you are bent on learning about companies and investing in them, this is the first place to look. These reports can be ordered from the company itself, plus there are Web sites that offer the service.

Here is the basic format most annual reports follow:

Independent Auditor's Report:
They come in several forms: two paragraphs, three paragraphs, even four paragraphs. They usually all say the same thing. They are the verification that the accounting company has checked the books and the report meets with accounting and government regulations.

Financial Highlights:
Usually the company will run a condensed form of its income statement at the very front of the report. It will give a snapshot of revenues and profits and other pertinent information, like earnings per shares or dividends the company might pay.

Message from the Chief Executive Officer or President:
This is an assessment of where the company stands financially, what kind of year it had, and what it expects in very general terms to do in the future.

If there is a really significant issue—a hostile takeover attempt or a big-time lawsuit—sometimes the CEO will allude to it. But usually these are more like the welcoming addresses at a conference.

CHAPTER 4: STOCKS

Report on Operations:

If a company has different divisions, it will break out each one and report how it performed during the previous year. It's a good way to learn about the different businesses of a company. Sometimes you might wonder if all the parts tend to fit together. For example (this is real), does a homebuilding company need to own a chain of jewelry stores, coal mines, and a savings and loan?

Consolidated Financial Statement:

Contains the balance sheet (so called because the assets are equal to the liabilities and shareholders' equity). This is where you find the company's nitty-gritty financials. This will be followed by other types of analysis: consolidated cash flow, consolidated statements of shareholders' equity, and more. It will have comparisons with previous years.

Some analysts go first to the section at the back of the report that contains footnotes to the financial statements. There usually is some interesting information buried back there. They often have detailed explanations of potential problems the company might have with environmental violations, pending lawsuits, as well as the details of an acquisition or the sale of some assets.

At the very back you'll find a list of the board of directors, the company's legal counsel, and the address for the corporate headquarters.

GOVERNMENT REPORTS

Public companies have to file reports with the Securities and Exchange Commission on a quarterly basis. This report is called a 10-Q. The annual filing is called a 10-K, and it is simply a response to a standard set of financial questions that the SEC believes should be answered publicly for investors to know about the performance of a company. Much of what is in the annual reports is in the quarterly and annual filings with the SEC, but the 10-Ks and Qs are more in-depth.

Also, there is a record of shareholders proxies, a document sent to shareholders before a company holds an annual meeting. It's a good place to find who owns what percentage of stock in the company, what sort of salaries the executives are earning, and other financial tidbits. There is a whole cult built around watch-dogging excess executive salaries, which occurs in some tightly held companies.

Anyone (even you) can obtain these financial reports from the SEC's handy EDGAR database (www.sec.gov/edgarhp.htm). And it's free! So, with this

CHAPTER 4: STOCKS — 74

awesome resource at your hands, you can check to see whether a company is even registered with the SEC and, if so, to read its more detailed financial reports before you actually invest.

Naturally, in a perfect world, all companies would have to register their financial reports with the SEC and make them available to the EDGAR database. However, some companies raising smaller amounts of money to go public have different regulations governing them than the big companies. If you can't find a company on EDGAR, use the SEC Web site to contact SEC regulators or call them at (202) 942-8090 to determine if the company in question has filed an "offering circular." If so, request a copy.

THIRD PARTY

It seems everyone has an opinion about the stock market and that opinion is published in reports you can get for free on the Web or subscribe to as a service to build your "wealth of knowledge" about companies. What follows is just a small sampling of what is available for research. Clearly, some sources are better than others, but how can you tell? Here's one old reliable:

Value Line (No Relation to Value Jet)

Value Line is one of the oldest and steadiest sources of information available about companies and their stocks. Anyone seriously investing in the market has used this reference. It comes with a fat blue binder that holds the reports, which are only one sheet. There is nothing visually inviting about the reports, which cover more than 1000 different companies. They are crowded with charts, graphs, and numbers—graceless capsules of information sitting on the page like bricks.

But this is a nifty way to learn about stocks, and you can take a look for free at most libraries. It is also available online. The subscription price is about $570 a year (you can try an introductory offer for $100). After you review it you might actually decide it is worth it, because Value Line does a lot of the thinking for you.

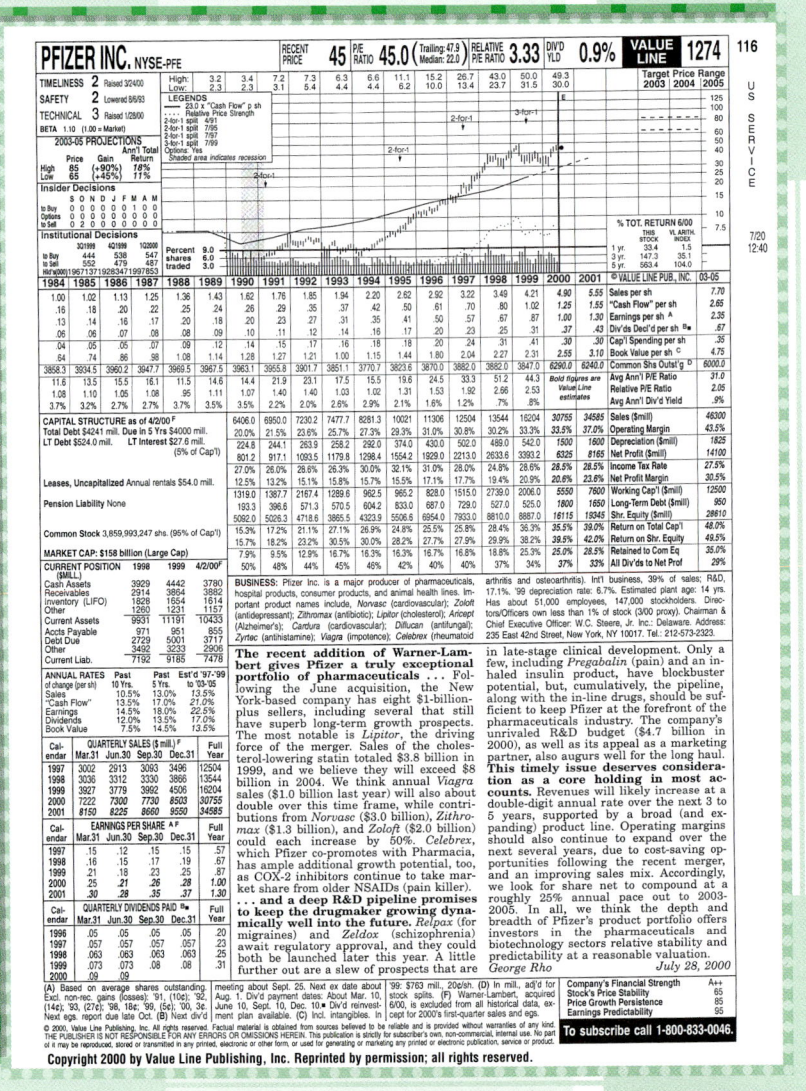

The key to the page is the upper left hand corner. There are three numbers there: One rates the timeliness of purchasing the stock, essentially predicting whether the stock will perform well and whether this is

CHAPTER 4: STOCKS

a good time to buy in relationship to price. One is the best rating; five is the worst.

Another box rates the safety: Is this company going to be around tomorrow? Does it owe too much money or have some skeleton in the closet that could cause problems. This category is also rated one through five. One is the safest, five is the riskiest.

There are also some technical formulas that are used, but few people really understand these, much less a beginning investor. So forget about it.

Value Line is expensive for the novice, but you can order individual company reports for $30 a piece. Try to find someone else who also is interested in Value Line companies and split the cost. You have to subscribe to the print or software to have any in-depth access.

SITES THAT CAN HELP

There's an ocean of stock research data available on the Web, and it is considerably more convenient to cruise at home or in the office than having to zip down to the local library or wait for the mail. The downside is that it is almost too convenient; sorting through the electronic data can be extremely time consuming. Thankfully, a few sites stand out for their expert analysis and information.

Standardandpoors.com

Standard & Poor's, the self-described leading provider of comprehensive, unbiased investment information and guidance, is a tough start for beginners, but it's a complete shop. The main site is a jumpstation to S&P's network of Web sites. Through the main site, investors can access everything from data and analysis of emerging markets and commodities to retirement guides and stock/fund advisors. This is the site you're going to want to become familiar with—if your goal is to become a real investor.

The research options are full-service and basically do it all. You can get your stock and fund comparisons, or research industry trends. There's a section devoted to investment ideas that will encourage out-of-the-box thinking for the marketplace. And if you're just plain tired of bugging your advisor for his professional opinion, go buy it yourself: Get the four full pages of information on each of 6,900 U.S. corporations that analysts rely on for their research.

You will have to pay a monthly fee to become a

CHAPTER 4: STOCKS

member and access the hidden parts of the site (and there are a lot of them). As far as the free stuff goes, there are profiles and data for each of the companies listed with S&P and a Java-based, desktop, real-time financial information program that is fully customizable. There's also a tutorial for beginning investors buried within the personal wealth site. It's a good, sequential guide that appears in a separate pop-up browser window, ensuring that you don't get lost within the many branches of this complex but useful site.

123jump.com

Some news sites are scatterbrained collages of stories, tied together through senseless webs of hyperlinked headings and subheadings, and they ensure that new users will come away from the site thoroughly confused. Hey, nobody's perfect. 123jump.com is *not* one of those sites. News articles aren't buried inside columns where the content rotates based on the whim of the author. This isn't a magazine. It's a well-organized archive of financial news stories, and it's easy to surf. Stories are organized by category: Internet Stocks, Tech Stocks, IPO Corner, Earnings, Global Review, and CEO Interviews. Each section allows you to browse a few stories by content (reading the first paragraph), or see the entire list of articles by headline. The two stock sections reference specific stocks by industry sector and ticker symbol in columns on the side of the page; a convenient way to get familiar with the companies on your field. And everything is free here, from portfolio monitoring to real-time quotes. 123jump.com wants to provide the "right" analysis of news and events in the financial world and they claim to be able to do this with a global team of reporters who report the news up close and "as they see it." At the least, they've managed to put together a friendly and easy-to-use Web site.

Stockpoint.com

At first glance, Stockpoint seems to be just another research portal. There are a lot of them out there, and each has its strengths and weaknesses. From a novice's perspective, Stockpoint's strengths will probably outweigh its weaknesses. In terms of ease of use, it's right up at the top. You're not confronted with a bunch of random articles and menus when you hit the main page. Instead, there's a straightforward portrait of several U.S. markets and a simplified menu. The portfolio manager allows you to choose your stocks from any of eight world markets plus all the U.S. markets (an unusual breadth, but providing global financial info is a chief part of its mission), and you can stack your various stocks and funds up next to each other on the same page for comparison.

One benefit the site provides is free real-time quotes, which are slowly becoming more common on the Internet. However, the Stockpoint service only permits you to retrieve them one-at-a-time. Another great service you can get through Stockpoint is a daily e-mail market report, mailed at midday or at the end of the trading day. Also on the site are top twenty-five stock and fund searches by sector, and a stock/fund finder you can set by personalized criteria.

CHAPTER 4: STOCKS

An attractive feature for some is the world markets section, which is geared toward those who speculate overseas. Through it, you can get easy-to-read data for markets from Paris to Amsterdam to Milan. Stockpoint offers a comprehensive package of basic tools that isn't full of baffling distractions, and that makes it one of the easier sites for beginners.

Stocksniffer.com

This may be the most useful news source available for super-fast alerts on important market information and company announcements. If your trading style depends on knowing exactly what's going on exactly as it's happening, Stocksniffer may become, with practice, an invaluable tool.

Stocksniffer can be used to customize news article search engines that deliver relevant news stories based on user-set definitions right into a separate browser window on your home computer desktop, all in real time.

The news it grabs comes to you hot off the Businesswire and PRNewswire, unfiltered and timely. You can work with other programs and run the sniffer in the background, out of the way. Because it updates automatically every sixty seconds and notifies you with audio and visual signals whenever it finds a match, you're less likely to miss any important tidbits. Registration is painless and simple (not to mention free). Editing your criteria is also a breeze. Suppose you want all news articles dealing with Initial Public Offerings. Just create a new search tab devoted to IPOs and define your keywords as "IPO" and "Initial Public Offering." You can set the sniffer to monitor news stories on specific stocks you're tracking or to look for mergers and acquisitions news.

You can also easily get quotes through the service from any of five different sources such as Yahoo!, Quote.com, or Freerealtime.com. With Stocksniffer you'll be set to make your move—before the market moves along without you.

WhisperNumber.com

The "whispernumber" is an emerging cousin and extension of the "consensus number," which is the term used to describe the pooled projections of financial analysts to forecast a stock's future movement. Some Web sites use consensus numbers for just this purpose. The difference is that the whispernumber comes from regular, everyday investors. It's a number that represents investor sentiment toward a stock as it performs in comparison to the analysts' projections.

These numbers are, technically, positive or negative expectations regarding a company's earnings report, IPOs, and other indicators. The Web site uses polls, flesh-and-blood human data miners, and software that scans over 100,000 messages daily, from message boards such as Yahoo!, Silicon Investor, Motley Fool, Raging Bull, and America Online, in order to build an idea of the public feeling for various stocks.

The whispernumber is gaining credibility on Wall Street and is starting to have an impact on the direction of a stock's price after earnings have been announced, but investors should be aware that bulletin and message boards are not always foolproof indicators of sentiment, as they're sometimes used to hype stocks, spread rumors, and other evils. Approach at your own risk.

CHAPTER 4: STOCKS 78

Internet Stock News

Have you ever wanted to ride the wave of the Internet all the way to the bank? Perhaps you've seen people making mad money off of Internet stocks and thought "that's my ticket," only to be confounded with choices. Which rockets are going to get you to your destination, Rich City?

If that little voice sounds like the one in your head, then Internet Stock News is a start. It's a specialized financial portal dealing only with Internet Stocks. Very thorough and extremely easy to find your way through, the ISN Web site isn't burdened with anything you're not looking for. And most of it is free. Just register and you get access to free real-time stock quotes and a full range of research tools from portfolio managers to news and charts, company profiles, IPO info, a huge glossary, and a bookstore dedicated to Internet stock investing.

The Internet companies the site deals with can be researched by inputting a symbol or the company name, or if you want, you can browse by category. They're indexed and ranked by sector, which is a great way to get a feel for who are the frontrunners and what the competition is like. Enter the "e-tailers" section and compare Amazon to CDNow. Which one will go broke first? Or head into the IPO section? Anybody buying that junk? Spend some time here and read the articles, research the companies, and soon you'll be on your way to making good Internet stock picks. If there are any left.

Okay, here's one for fun:

Ask Nancy Reagan?
http://www.moneyminded.com/investor/stars/78star11.htm

Here's a site dedicated to "Financial Astrology." Hey, it might be better than your broker. The Web master claims that "astrology is increasingly recognized as 'the third force' in the marketplace." He believes financial success derives from a combination of good analysis, good luck, and good timing. This last factor is what the site is designed to help you achieve. If astrology was good enough for Ronald and Nancy Reagan, it's good enough for you. Discover your personal money style, check the sector forecasts, and take a cosmos quiz. Click on "inside indicators" to get market clues and investing ideas from the sky. Astrology can be fun, and to be fair, sometimes it appears to work. So, what's your sign?

CHAPTER 4: STOCKS

HOW DO YOU BUILD YOUR
PORTFOLIO?

Every new investor asks this question, and the answer is always the same. Stocks can be risky investments (especially if you buy and sell on a short-term basis). But as you are staking out your financial future, it probably should include some risk, according to many financial planners.

The question is whether you want this to be a do-it-yourself job when there are pros out there in mutual funds to do it for you. But if you are this far along, you might want to give it a whirl.

In buying individual stocks, you'll need to develop some strategy. What do you want to own? Are you influenced by the product? Is the company by far the best in its field? Does it look cheap?

You can get a well-balanced portfolio with about two dozen stocks, according to many professional managers. As mentioned earlier there are numerous categories of stocks—blue chip, cyclical, growth stocks. And there are a variety of ways to measure them.

Most advisers agree that these picks need to be spread out over various sectors of the market. In other words, a portfolio of twenty technology stocks isn't a diversified selection. Neither is a portfolio of twenty banks.

In case you think that applying these criteria will be difficult, think again. There are services on the Web that offer virtually every kind of selection criterion imaginable and then alphabetizes the stock choices. These are called stock screens.

Screening devices chase after stock candidates based on the criteria you feed it. They can be stocks that pay high dividends, or stocks with high earnings' growth rates or stocks that seem to be under priced. The variables, depending on the screener, can number around twenty and some screens sort through more than 7,000 companies. Many are free.

As you look at the various companies that pop up on the screens, you also might begin to see the value of diversification. It's very unlikely that a diverse portfolio will have all its stocks advance or decline at the

CHAPTER 4: STOCKS

same time, ensuring you won't lose your investments (and your mind) in one horrible downturn. For example, oil stocks will tend to do well when energy prices are high; airline stocks tend to be hurt by rising oil prices.

There isn't a magic formula for diffusing the risk. But keep in mind that if you have purchased stock in one category be extra cautious about the second purchase. Says one professional manager, "Once I have one stock that has exposure to one set of risk factors or one industry, I require a substantially higher hurdle for a second stock that will provide exposure to the same set of risk factors."

And every company and industry comes along with their own special risks.

For example, the cable TV industry can be a solid investment, but it has its potential pitfalls. For instance, the industry's technology could become obsolete or the government could step in and ruin the industry's profitability.

If you are looking for guidelines for your portfolio, you might look to a broad stock index. An index is simply a compilation of stocks that gives a measure of how the market is performing. One is the S&P 500, which is a selected group of 500 stocks. There's also the Wilshire 5000. The vast Wilshire index comes the closest to representing the entire market, and the pros who compiled it have about 30 percent in technology, 12 percent in health care, and 6 percent in financials. Those aren't hard and fast rules, but they can serve as guidelines for the beginner.

BABY STEPS

If you want to experiment with buying your own stocks, you can just take a small amount of expendable cash—maybe 10% of your total portfolio—to start learning rather than putting everything on the line at once. In researching and following the stocks you buy, you'll get an inexpensive education in how the markets and companies work. Says one stock player, "It's fun to buy a stock, watch it go up, sell it, and think you're a genius."

STOCK SCREENERS ON THE WEB

There are a variety of sites available for free. To delve into the companies that you want to know more about, however, the service usually charges a subscription price for you to do more in-depth research.

Hoover's StockScreen (stockscreener.com)— Has 20 ways for you to classify the type of stock you want, and then lists the choices alphabetically with the stock symbol. Easy to use and free for the screening process.

CHAPTER 4: STOCKS

MarketGuide's Net Screen
IQ Net Basic Stock Scan (iqnet.com)—Fewer variables but up-to-the-minute in terms of stock price. Monthly rate is $24.95, with a free two-week trial.

MSN Investor (msn.com)—Has individual stock screens like the other services and scans more than 8,000 companies.

DAY TRIPPER

Some people have done well by day trading in stocks, meaning you buy and sell the stock the same day. However, some people have lost a bundle and that downside can be pretty awful.

Disgruntled day trader Mark Barton went on a shooting spree killing nine people at two Atlanta stock trading firms in the late 1990s. He'd lost $153,000 in a three-day period of day trading, and had accumulated losses of more than $500,000.

Other people have been left destitute by day trading, including a 28-year-old California bank employee who lost $40,000 he raised from credit cards in two months of day trading. And there was a Chicago waiter with no experience who lost his $200,000 inheritance. All this was presented in testimony given during hearings before the U.S. Senate.

The come-on to lure day traders by people trying to sell books or "inside advice" can be ludicrous. Here's one spiel: "Day trading is a rapidly growing field with the potential for high profits. With day trading, you can achieve financial independence by being your own boss. You can handle your own retirement fund and maximize your gain. The day trading handbook is your key to day trading. In just 60 minutes it gives you step-by-step, clear instructions on how to get into and prosper in this lucrative and exciting business."

Even if you don't precipitate a personal tragedy by becoming a day trader, there are other drawbacks.
—You pay a commission when you buy in or sell out. While online trades with discount brokers are fairly cheap, it still eats into your profit.
—Taxes are now part of your life. You have to keep up with every gain or loss because you have to include these on your income tax report. Do you really want to have 300 stock transactions sent to the IRS?

THEN THERE'S GINA

She is a lawyer by training who plays the market to earn her living. She grew up in Los Angeles, practiced law, and now lives in New York City. When she's eating dinner at Elaine's in New York City, she says "hi" to a model she met in the south of France. "She's a good friend," says Gina, who never seems to actually smile. "We're going to Cannes this spring!"

Gina is tall, almost 6 feet, blonde, and in great shape. She has no dependents and values her freedom above everything else. She invests in the stock market as if it were a job. Then she

CHAPTER 4: STOCKS — 82

goes out and spends the money. "I've had a great run," she says.

Like most people in this game, she looks for an edge. She spends a good portion of her time e-mailing or talking to people who also aspire to making their living this way. She's always looking for sources to tap into so that she can get a jump on the market.

"People hear things," she says. "You pick up something here and there and you add it up."

A workday in her life: She turns on the computer at 9 a.m. and goes to a chat room where she knows the players. A good source clues her to what he's doing, but it's a cryptic message.

Prophetakin says, "MSFT—even if the department of injustice breaks it up—is a winner for shareholders—look at what happened to AT&T shareholders—most became millionaires or close to it from the break up."

blondeattorney29 says, "Buy, Buy."

Gina, who is aka "blondeattorney29" logs out and buys 1,000 shares of MSFT, the stock symbol for Microsoft, from her online broker where she has an account. It is an $80,000 plus investment. As the day passes she constantly checks the stock quote ticker from one of the services she subscribes to; she heads to the kitchen for a tuna sandwich, but she is never far from the computer. She lets her regular telephone ring until the answering machine picks up, but she keeps her cell phone handy. It rings.

"Yeah," she answers, then listens. "Someone heard something about Microsoft," she says. The prophet of profit tipped me in the chat room. Are you checking the price."

MSFT starts to go up in share price: $81.50. $82. As 2 p.m. approaches, it's at $85. Gina taps her fingers nervously by her computer keyboard. $86. $86.50. She makes her move. She was in at $81 and out at $86.50. Gross profit for the day: $5,500.

"So where do you want to go for dinner?" she says to no one in particular. "I'll buy."

CHAPTER 4: STOCKS

OTHER WAYS

Traditional analysis has its limits, and requires a lot of hard work. So naturally people look for the easy way out. This grab-bag approach to making good stock picks has its weaknesses but some people swear by it.

KNOW THE PRODUCT

There are so many theories on stock picks, they are bound to be contradictory. Some people suggest buying stock in products you like. If you are an Apple computer advocate, owning shares of Apple could be for you. In 1998, it would have been a scary choice, but if you had held it until 2000, you would have seen the share price increase by 80 percent. And every time you bought Apple products, you would be helping your stock pick.

Another way to judge a company is to ask the people who work there. One stock analyst in Florida used to go to the bar across from the main factory where a company manufactured tile and listen to the workers. He started doing this with other companies, and it seemed to work—until he developed an alcohol problem.

KEEP YOUR EARS OPEN

Everyone hears tips. It is the way of the human race that people talk, and there's nothing (other than sex, maybe) that generates talk more than money. A comment could be overheard in a restaurant or an airplane or an elevator—all places where people somehow think they can say anything and no one will hear them.

The trouble with overhearing tips is that they can be notoriously unreliable. Also, there is a kind of gossiping about companies and stocks that is actually illegal. It's called insider information. Sometimes a person is privy to a company's strategy and passes it on to his brother-in-law or friend, and the SEC, which tracks stock purchases pretty closely, can detect whether a stock that has been dormant for months starts to blossom with people buying thousands of shares. If, in a few days, a takeover or some other news becomes public that drives up the price, the SEC will take a look. If you get caught, you can be prosecuted. People actually go to jail for these types of violations. Nevertheless, meet G.C.

Name: G. C.
Age: 32
Occupation: Bodyguard
Income: $42,000
Marital Status: Married
City: Brookfield, Illinois
Goal: Continue listening closely and investing soundly for his family's future.

CHAPTER 4: STOCKS

While G. C.'s job may sound exciting, in reality he spends a lot of time chauffeuring around rich CEOs in the Heartland. But G. C. doesn't mind. "I'm getting a little too old for all of that macho stuff anyway," says the burly 32-year old. "Plus, my wife sort of frowns on it as well."

Surprisingly, G. C. has found himself in a unique position to pick up helpful tidbits on investing. "You'd be surprised what rich people tell their drivers," he explains. "Directly or—indirectly." G. C. says he's taken those "insider" tips and used them to start investing, however modestly, for his family's future.

"With our first child on the way," G. C. reflects, "I thought it was about time I started investing. Just glancing at a college catalog the other day gave me the cold sweats. Imagine how much it will cost when he, or she, grows up!"

G. C. admits that it's not always a hot stock tip that sends him running to his broker. "I tend to invest in people, not just stocks," says the stocky stock philosopher. "For instance, after guarding the owner of John Deere for a couple of months, I grew to like and respect him. After that assignment was over, I bought a few hundred shares of his stock because I trusted him. I guess you could call it an 'inexact science.'"

G. C. also realizes that he might have to shift to a second career one day. "It's not as if I want to spend the rest of my life in a gym," he explains. "One day I'd like a desk job."

WALLSTREET

"Greed, for lack of a better word, is good."
—Gordon Gekko
(Michael Douglas), *Wall Street*

It is quite doubtful that the mastermind behind the '80s blockbuster *Wall Street*, Oliver Stone, named his slimy protagonist Gordon Gekko (Michael Douglas) by accident. (Replace one "k" with a "c" and you've got the "gecko" lizard of the same name.) After all, the reptilian Gekko certainly lives up to the connotation, delving daily in such questionable practices as insider trading and leveraged buyouts, this Wall Street power broker trades millions of dollars a day and literally lives by the motto, "Time is money."

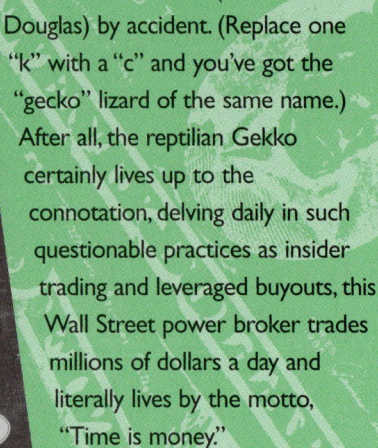

Along for the ride is eager beaver Bud Fox (Charlie Sheen), who soon finds himself a job as Gekko's latest protégé and sucker player, feeding Gordon the latest insider info on Bud's father's airline company before finally seeing the light at the end of the tunnel. (Or, in this case, prison cell.)

Combining his own brand of "insider information" and a grand dash of Hollywood dramatics, Oliver Stone weaves a tale of greed gone wrong and power gone mad. And could there be a more appropriate backdrop for the fast-paced world of stocks?

While few individual investors ever attain the level of play witnessed in this movie, there is no doubt that, in fact, greed is a motivating factor for many of us playing the stock market game. We invest a little, watch that ticker, and hope our stock goes up.

And up, and up, and UP! While few of us are willing to sell out our loved ones in quite the same way as Bud and Gordon do, fewer still would refuse the amount of return on investment shared by both of the above.

So, is greed "good," as Gordon tells Bud Fox, not to mention a packed to the rafters shareholder's meeting? Or is greed just—greed?

So, checked on your stocks lately?

CHAPTER 4: STOCKS

FUN, FUN, FUN: LISTENING TO THE EXPERTS

One Saturday, a TV show on Fox called *TheStreet.com* did its review of the week in the market. This, of course, used to be the domain of PBS stations and that odd-looking guy named Rukeyser, who still does what he's done for 30 years, except now some other people are doing it. Sort of.

While it's not illegal to listen to these people, it probably ought to be. There were a lot of trumped up arguments about what stocks were going up or down or bouncing back or U-turning south. There were charts and graphs and predictions.

But there was almost no mention of what the companies did. One had the word "micro" in its name, which means it might be hard to see its profits; the other's business was not discernible by its name. All said, they were the subject of a heated debate, meant to persuade viewers that these experts had very strong feelings on the subject, which looked about as persuasive as professional wrestling. In fact, it was a *lot* like professional wrestling.

From chat rooms to TV to the guy next to you on the train, everybody knows something.

CHAPTER 4: STOCKS

THE DOT COMS

In mid-2000 *The Wall Street Journal* published a series of stories titled "Life After the Dot-Com Crash." It dealt with the high fliers that were now grounded, some permanently. Dot-com-ville is an area of investment that the hipster generation has an affinity for. You're their customers. Is this boom over? Hardly. The shakeout will have its effect, but it didn't take long after the "crash" for companies like Yahoo! to report great financials and for similar companies to go from looking sickly one day to healthy the next.

It's impossible to predict what new innovations or breakthroughs or downfalls could be in the offing. But if you are looking at the dot-coms and other companies with a technological bent, you might keep the following in mind.

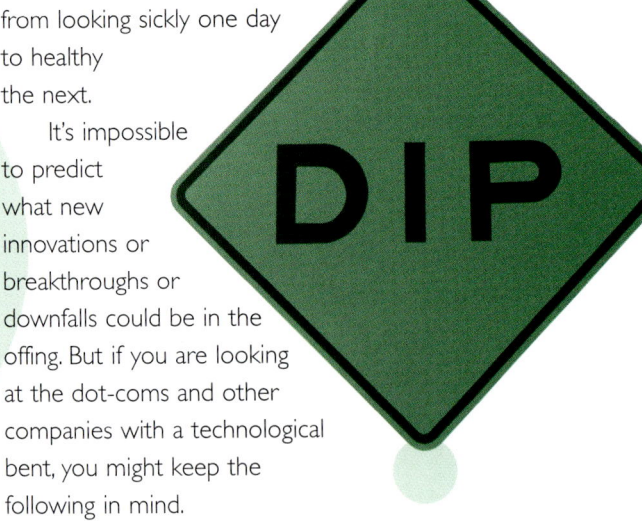

NO NET

The newspaper *USA Today* compiles a list called the Internet 100. In early 2000, they ran a list of some stocks and how they had fared, comparing the current price with the high for the last year. The striking aspect of the list is that it was changing awfully fast.

From Value America (down 94%) to Emusic (down 77%) to TheStreet.com (down 78%), these stocks lost huge amounts of their market value in a year and were venturing into penny stock land, and that's not good.

There were some early caution lights that didn't attract much attention.

One came from a report by The Responsibility Research Center, which studied 39 Internet companies, and found about one-half (47%) of the board members at these firms are company insiders.

87 CHAPTER 4: STOCKS

Generally, a company has a board with about 60% of its directors from the outside. But the rules that typically govern companies—i.e. that somebody other than a bunch of colleague-buddy types are keeping an eye on things—seem to not apply to some Web companies.

SELF-FULFILLING PROPHETS

Also consider a study conducted by NFO Interactive and the Spectrem Group, showing that 45% of all 7.1 million online investors own the stock of an Internet company.

"Interestingly, online investors tend to have more than twice the appetite for Internet stocks as do the general investing population," says Lee Smith, vice president of NFO Interactive. Clearly, online investors appear to be infatuated with the Internet stocks. Nearly three-quarters of all online investors who have ever purchased an Internet stock continue to own one or more Internet stocks, representing 23% of their entire investment portfolio measured in dollars, or an average of $38,000.

Net Stocks Held by Online Investors

America Online	38%
Yahoo!	17%
Amazon	15%
eBay	11%
EGroup	8%
Cisco	5%
Excite	4%
Lycos	4%
CMGI	3%
Microsoft	3%
Barnes & Noble	3%

The general investing population and online investors tend to prefer the same Internet stocks. "Those investing in Internet stocks tend to classify themselves as 'aggressive investors.' This appears to be a common denominator," said Smith.

Today's Hottest Stock Tips

Here is another survey, this one a Web poll of investors who buy on the Internet:

Which Stocks Interest You Most?

Bargain Stocks	9%
Good Value Stocks	13%
Growth Stocks	27%
Aggressive Growth Stocks	20%
Technology/Internet Stocks	29%

How Do You Select Stocks?

Fundamental Analysis	33%
Technical Analysis	21%
Newsletter/Advisor Recommendations	25%
Dart Board	11%
Indexing	9%

CHAPTER 4: STOCKS

MODEL INVESTOR: IN FOR THE LONG TERM

Name: Jody Poenisch
Age: 32
Occupation: Model
Income: $55,000–$70,000
Marital Status: Single
City: Miami, Florida
Goal: Retire early and live off investments . . . for a while

As a successful model who is rapidly approaching the "retirement age" for her particular profession, Jody realizes she must act fast if she wants to continue to live in the style to which she has grown accustomed. The blond, green-eyed, 5' 10" model does not see herself entering the land of cubicle careers any time soon. She quite realistically considers herself too "spoiled" for that.

However, she does look forward to finding another career for the second half of her life. She just wants to be "set up" in case it takes longer than she expects to find that all-important "rebound job." Jody thinks she might like to be a talent agent, scouting out future models and booking them for steady work. But she realizes that it will take time to build a client, not to mention a talent, base.

Therefore, she has decided to scale down her lifestyle (for now) and be less "selective" in her photo shoots. "When I was younger," she admits, "I turned down lots of print ad campaigns just because I didn't like the brand name or store it was for. But now I'll gladly do catalog work for a place like Sears or Ace hardware and turn around and invest the money."

Having been "burned" in the past on bad stock tips and an admittedly "excessive" nature, Jody admits that she's toned down her investing act lately. While she still plays the market, she's not the "super freak" she says she was in the past.

"I know now that finding the right stock, investing in it while it's hot, riding it to the top and then selling it off for a quick profit is just as hard as winning the lottery," she admits. Instead, Jody listens to trusted friends, follows suit, and joins them in their respectably tidy long-term profit sharing.

"Sure," she says. "I watch the news when I can and take note when they say the market's had a 'good' day or a 'bad' one. But it's the same way I look at the weather report. Unless a hurricane's coming, I don't really get too excited."

"Besides," Jody admits, "I still can't remember which one's good and which one's bad: The bull or the bear!"

Until then, Jody continues to work hard, spend less, and go long term.

CHAPTER 4: STOCKS

BOILER ROOM

"The trick is to stop thinking of it as 'your' money."
—IRS Auditor

Billed as the "*Wall Street* for the new millennium," *Boiler Room* is a gritty tale of urban greed and cagey con men all hoping to make fast money in the even faster-paced world of trading stocks. Working for a renegade brokerage, Seth (Giovanni Ribisi) finds himself using any and all means necessary to sell his naive customers the latest hi-tech or pharmaceutical stock being pushed by the shady superiors at his brokerage. (Most shares of which will be worthless when the storefront companies close up shop and go broke.)

Perfectly timed for a modern audience hearing nightly about dot-com millionaires and Microsoft secretaries living high on the hog off of their stock options (this fact is even alluded to, jealously, in a voice-over by Ribisi's character), *Boiler Room* taps into today's greed-driven, day trading psyche.

Despite the moralistic ending (the worst guys go to jail, supposedly) much of the film's attraction is the love/hate relationship the audience feels for the main characters, even as they do unspeakable things to entice innocent people to invest their life savings into stocks that will soon be worth less than the paper they're printed on.

Boasting a talented cast full of Hollywood's hottest young stars (Ribisi, Vin Diesel, Nia Long, Nicky Katt, and an unforgettable performance by none other than Ben Affleck), *Boiler Room*'s real star is greed. It drives the brokers' actions, drives the customers' willingness to believe them, and drives the audience to dream of itself trading or buying up shares of stocks that are days away from "going through the roof."

After all, in the words of *Wall Street*'s own Gordon Gekko (Michael Douglas): "Greed, for lack of a better word, is good."

Isn't it?

NERVOUS WRECK

Name: J. R.
Age: 31
Occupation: Property Manager, Small Business Owner
Income: $43,000
Marital Status: Single
City: Cape Hatteras, North Carolina
Goal: Plan for retirement; start investing

As an integral part of J. R.'s early retirement plan, he has recently begun playing the stock market. And, now that he has, he can't remember a time when he hasn't!

"It's like when I got my first cellular phone," he explains. "After a week, I couldn't remember a time when I didn't have one. I don't know what I'd do without it."

As such, J. R. has become an Internet junky of late. "I still use a traditional broker," he claims. "I mean, it's worth the extra money to me to actually talk to a real live person." But J. R. has bookmarked Yahoo! Financial, too, and checks it regularly.

"Too regularly," he admits.

He checks it whenever he has free time, and he has already had quite a roller coaster ride. "Even though I invested in 'stable' stocks," he explains, "it just so happened that I did so before the Fed raised the interest level twice in four months. It seems like every time they do that, the stock dips a little. Sometimes— not so little. It's really scary the first couple of times you watch your stock lose money. *Your* money. But then you walk away for a couple of days, keep yourself busy, and check again to find that it's gone back up. Then you can breathe again . . . ."

CHAPTER 4: STOCKS

5

Mutual Funds:
"FUN"-ds FOR EVERYONE

Mutual fund managers pool your money with other people's money and invest it in securities—stocks and bonds—as well as some other accounts that pay interest. So when you invest in a mutual fund, instead of buying some shares in corporation X, and some other shares in corporation Y, and then some bonds issued by the government of Freedonia, you let the mutual fund manager pick the investment for you.

The manager of the mutual fund will choose which corporate stocks and bonds to buy, and what government bond issues to include, and how many of each. Or, to put it another way, when you buy shares in a mutual fund, you are buying partial ownership of a pre-established and carefully crafted investment portfolio. That is, if you buy from a good mutual fund. There are more than 10,000 of them available to investors.

You make money through a mutual fund investment pretty much the same way you would make money through a direct investment in a selection of securities: When your shares in the fund are sold (at a profit, you hope), through dividends, and when the fund itself sells shares, you receive what are called capital gains.

ARE Mutual Funds A GOOD IDEA?

Generally speaking, mutual funds are an excellent way to invest, especially for an individual who has other things to do with his or her time besides investigating market trends and corporate earnings statements and watching daily stock fluctuations for thousands and thousands of potential investment opportunities. No civilian should ever have to watch those cable television business reports for more than a minute a day.

When you invest in a mutual fund, you give your investment choices over to a team of managers and researchers who really do have nothing better to do than investigate and oversee whether your investment is, and remains, a sound one. Such is their job, and there is no reason why you should not take advantage of their expertise, just as you take advantage of your doctor's years of medical training rather than trying that "appendectomy at home" kit. Of course, as in every profession, some practitioners are more skilled than others.

Mutual funds offer other advantages as well. The best of them combine low-cost with low-risk, which is especially good if you are the type who gets financially seasick from the sometimes violent ups-and-downs of the stock market. And in terms of risk, mutual funds offer safe harbor if you simply cannot afford to lose a significant amount of your hard-earned savings. (Who can?)

They are low-risk because they provide you with a single purchase, a valuable trait of a healthy investment portfolio—diversification. With a mutual fund, you have some of your eggs here, some over there, here an egg, there an egg—actually it's not eggs, it's money and it's a good idea to spread the risk around.

Mutual funds can provide this type of diversification not only because they have the time and the expertise to do so, but also because they have so much more money to invest than you are likely to come up with, billions and billions of dollars. So though you are a small investor, perhaps even a tiny investor, since many mutual funds will allow you to start with as little as $50, you get the benefits of being a very big investor with some experienced pros doing the work for you; and you know where you stand by checking the fund's Web site or making an occasional phone call.

CHAPTER 5: MUTUAL FUNDS: "FUN"-ds FOR EVERYONE — 92

ALL MUTUAL FUNDS ARE NOT ALIKE

With the thousands of mutual funds around today, and more coming, they generally can be distinguished in three major ways: What they invest in, the overall goals behind their investment strategy, and whether they perform well (or poorly). Mutual funds are like cars, some are better for driving around town, some are for long trips, some are for rough terrain, some run into trouble more often than others, and some are big and showy but guzzle gas. Fortunately, mutual funds can be divided into certain broad and easy to understand categories, as follows:

BOND FUNDS

invest mostly, if not exclusively, in bonds. A bond is a kind of loan you make to a corporation or government, which issues the bond, pays interest on the bond, and redeems the bond at full value after a set amount of time has passed, anywhere from two years to two decades, at what's called the "maturity date."

Generally, bonds are a conservative investment, without the potential for growth and high returns of stocks, but with much less risk, and may be a good place to put a substantial amount of your money, if receiving regular checks from dividends fits in with your lifestyle.

With a bond fund, as opposed to a direct investment in bonds, your investment will be continually reinvested in new bonds by the fund managers in accordance with the overall goals of the fund.

EQUITY FUNDS

invest mainly in stocks ("equity," in this context, is a fancy word for stocks). Within the general grouping "equity funds," there are a number of varieties. Some are riskier than others, some invest more for dividends, and some invest more for potential growth. Some stick to smaller companies, as measured by market capitalization, some concentrate on larger companies, and some look for bargain basement buys, while others concentrate on sure-thing, long-term, high-priced investments. Equity funds are generally riskier than bond funds, but have greater potential returns.

INDEX FUNDS

are equity funds that spread their assets over a given stock index, like the Dow Jones or Standard & Poor's (or one of a great many other indexes), and rise or fall in value exactly as the index itself rises or falls in value. The strategy behind index funds is so simple and formulaic that they are almost entirely overseen by computers, and are therefore cheaper to manage than other funds, and have cut-rate fees. Index funds will never beat the index, as some investments will, if you're lucky, but will never do worse than the index either.

CHAPTER 5: MUTUAL FUNDS: "FUN"-ds FOR EVERYONE

HYBRID FUNDS

HYBRID FUNDS, also known as balanced funds, try to get the best of both worlds, the safety of bonds with potential returns of stocks, by investing a significant percentage of the fund in both. Some hybrid funds, like some equity funds, are more careful, and tend toward longer term purchases and a set ratio between bonds and stocks. Others vary the ratio between bonds and stocks according to how they see the market reacting, retreating to bonds during stock market downturns, and returning to stocks when they appear to be on a rise.

MONEY MARKET FUNDS

MONEY MARKET FUNDS are minimum risk funds with a high yield in interest payments. A money market fund invests in what are called "money market securities," which are sold by financial companies in a variety of denominations and by the United States Government in the form of Treasury bills and notes, as a way of borrowing money for a short period of time. A good money market fund will act like a savings account with, usually, higher interest than a bank savings account and with the added benefit of unlimited free check writing. Mutual fund money market accounts, however, unlike bank accounts, are not insured.

INDUSTRY FUNDS

INDUSTRY FUNDS invest in specific service categories and industries, like banking, HMOs, high tech, energy, etc., carry generally higher fees because they require more research and are more difficult to manage, and usually ask for a larger initial investment than other types of funds.

FUNDS OF FUNDS

FUNDS OF FUNDS are mutual funds that invest your money in a series of other mutual funds as a way of maximizing diversity for your investment. It is a sort of exponential cross breeding.

SOCIALLY RESPONSIBLE

SOCIALLY RESPONSIBLE mutual funds will choose investments according to how a given corporation meets or fails to meet certain ethical criteria. Some socially responsible funds, for example, will not invest in tobacco manufacturers, others will not invest in firms that make pesticides or nuclear power. Some refuse to purchase government bonds to protest defense spending. Some socially responsible funds are going to be more restrictive than others, and the best way to find out is to check the fund's investment portfolio and then call them and ask how, precisely, they limit their investment choices.

Note!

It is important to note that these broad categories are not all inclusive. There are also mutual funds, for example, that invest in real estate mortgages, where you, in effect, loan money to people who want to buy themselves a home, and, as with a bond, make returns on the interest they pay. Utility funds that specialize in power company stocks have recently become fashionable as well.

And most mutual funds, while concentrating on one type of investment, don't do so exclusively, so that many bond funds will have stock and money market holdings as well, just as many stock or money market funds will also have holdings in bonds. Many times you'll find that you can invest in one of these three types of funds with a company that has all three under its roof, and can even switch your money back and forth between bonds, stocks, and money market accounts, as you desire. Some will charge fees, however, either hefty or nominal, for doing so. Fees in general are something you must pay very close attention to when choosing a mutual fund, and will be dealt with in more detail later in this chapter.

CHAPTER 5: MUTUAL FUNDS: "FUN"-ds FOR EVERYONE

WHERE MUTUAL FUNDS INVEST

If you've already been perusing mutual fund literature, you have probably noticed that some describe themselves as Worldwide, Global, or International. Some funds are pretty much exclusively tied to U.S. markets and invest in businesses and institutions based in the United States. Funds that describe themselves as International, generally do not invest in U.S.-based businesses, but limit themselves to one or more international markets, such as Asia, the European Union, or Latin America. A fund that describes itself as Global or Worldwide might invest just about anywhere.

What Difference Does It Make?

It can make a significant difference on several counts. First off, you may be one of those people who, along with perennial presidential candidate Pat Buchanan, thinks that America is where your loyalty lies, and therefore your money belongs. If this is the case, however, you should keep in mind that U.S. firms these days are as likely as not to have international holdings and manufacture their products in Southeast Asia or in partnership with a company based in Germany, though they sell their stocks on a U.S.-based exchange and pay their taxes, or most of their taxes, to the U.S. government. On the other side, an internationally focused mutual fund might have foreign firms that pour significant business and salaries into the U.S.

It also makes a difference regarding the quality of your investment portfolio. International markets, like Japan's Nikkei stock index, may be heavily influenced by the muscular U.S. economy, but that does not mean they will follow U.S. markets with any precision. A foreign market may be going up, while the U.S. market goes down, and vice versa. If you have both domestic and foreign holdings in your portfolio, you may be able to take advantage of whatever market is rising faster at a given time, and cut your losses during domestic or foreign market downturns.

You should be aware, however, that a mutual fund, especially one that describes itself as global, may be spreading itself too thin. Remember, what you are using a

CHAPTER 5: MUTUAL FUNDS: "FUN"-ds FOR EVERYONE

mutual fund for is the expertise of the fund's management. Mastering the vagaries and complications of the U.S. market alone is a nearly impossible feat. So, as you might imagine, it would be very difficult indeed for any one fund's management group to have enough expertise regarding the economies of the entire globe to be especially effective in choosing the best places to invest your money. With international mutual funds, the same thing holds true. You'll want to know if they are limiting themselves to those markets with which they are familiar and aren't blindly tossing your money off to London and Bangkok and everywhere in between.

HOW MUTUAL FUNDS EARN MONEY

As mentioned above, mutual fund investments, like direct investments in stocks or bonds, earn you money in three ways.

Share appreciation is the first way. As with shares of any company's stock, shares of a mutual fund will increase in value over time if the mutual fund is successful. To realize this profit, however, if you want to use it for a down payment on a macaroni farm, for example, or to help pay your rent, you must sell shares in the fund. Remember that some funds will penalize you for selling too early, and that you will have to pay capital gains taxes on any profits you realize.

Capital gains distributions are number two. As when you yourself sell shares of a mutual fund at a higher price than when you bought them, so the manager of the fund may sell shares of stock, with the resulting profit (you hope), or capital gains, then being distributed to you and all the fund's other shareholders as either good old fashioned money or as more shares in the fund. Either way, such distributions are taxed.

CHAPTER 5: MUTUAL FUNDS: "FUN"-ds FOR EVERYONE — 96

Dividends are number three. Some investments pay out a percentage of the total investment in the form of dividends, which, in the case of a mutual fund, will, like capital gains distributions, be either given out as money or automatically used to buy you more shares in the fund. And dividends too will be taxed.

How to Choose a Mutual Fund

The main thing to keep in mind when looking at mutual funds, behind all the various investment practices and strategies, is whether a given mutual fund fits your needs. Just as some stocks are good for dividends and other stocks pay little in the way of dividends but may double or triple their current worth, so in mutual funds there are two basic possible goals: value and growth.

Value funds are good, low-risk places to keep your money and have it work for you, if slowly. Value funds, like bond funds or balanced hybrid funds, are managed for stability. A value fund manager buying stocks will look for solid deals rather than for rapid appreciation. Value funds should be able to at least keep up with, and hopefully keep ahead of, the rate of inflation. If they don't at least keep up with inflation, your investment is decreasing in actual value, though it may increase in specific dollar amount.

Growth funds, on the other hand, seek to do more than merely outmatch the rate of inflation. They seek to keep up with the rate of increase in the stock market itself, which has averaged, over its history, some 8 percent per year. Many funds attempt to do yet more. They claim to beat the stock market average and show returns of up to 15-20 percent per year. Of course, they are taking on higher risk when doing so, and one should keep in mind that there is no shame whatsoever in merely keeping up with the stock market, which, over the long haul, can prove to be the smartest and even the most lucrative investment strategy. And mutual funds that promise more than this often charge higher fees for their market savvy.

CHAPTER 5: MUTUAL FUNDS: "FUN"-ds FOR EVERYONE

FEES? WHAT FEES?

Glad you asked. Inflation, it turns out, isn't your only enemy when trying to get a healthy return on money invested in mutual funds. The mutual funds themselves can charge you an excess of unnecessary and sometimes hidden fees.

Loads are commissions charged by brokers for selling you shares of a mutual fund. If the load on a fund is, say, 5 percent of your total investment, then for every $1,000 you spend, you actually only buy $950 dollars worth of shares, while the broker gets $50 as part of his income. There's nothing shady about this; stock brokers get paid commissions. But there are questions to be asked about such "loads."

Loads seem especially problematic when you realize that viable alternatives do exist, namely brokerage houses that pay their brokers salaries rather than commissions, and mutual funds, known as "no-load funds," that do not come loaded with commission fees. Loads seem yet more problematic because studies have shown that no-load funds do just as well on the market as load funds. And your investment must appreciate the amount of the commission, which can go as high as 8 percent or more, to so much as break even on loaded funds.

You must also beware of hidden loads, like back-end loads that charge you for selling your shares, and redemption fees charged to discourage frequent trading. While they may disappear if you stay with your investment long enough, decreasing often at a rate of 1 percent per year, both of these hidden loads can tie up your principal unnecessarily. Funds with hidden loads may be called "no-load" funds but are not.

The answer is to invest your money in a true no-load fund. You can do this, by the way, directly from the mutual fund itself, simply by calling its 800 number.

Surprise!!!

Surprise!!!

Surprise!!!

CHAPTER 5: MUTUAL FUNDS: "FUN"-ds FOR EVERYONE

Operating expenses are attached to all mutual funds, and are deducted from your returns, as a percentage of your total investment. So if you are paying 1.1 percent in operating expenses, and your investment appreciates at a healthy 11 percent over the course of the year, a full 10 percent of these earnings will revert to the mutual fund to pay salaries and other expenses.

You can find the operating expenses listed on the fund's prospectus. It will be substantially higher for stock funds than for bond or money market funds because stock funds are generally more difficult to manage, and because they have a higher profile and tend to attract better known managers who can charge exorbitant salaries for their services. Such salaries are passed on to you in fees. The question is whether such expensive expertise is worth it, and the answer is a definite, "probably not."

Fate is even more fickle in the world of finance than in the entertainment industry, and the stock market even more difficult to predict consistently than it is to come out with a theater hit every year. Last night's Oscar nominee is this morning's waiter. The truly good mutual fund managers often are not the ones most well-known, but those who invest wisely and help insure you a good return by not taking so much off the top for themselves. Remember that for every big name your fund puts on the payroll, and for every lavishly produced 60-second advertisement your fund puts on nationwide TV, your investment's return decreases. Because of this, some of the best-known funds are some of the weakest investments.

The answer is to go for a solid fund that charges low operating fees.

Taxes are not fees in the sense that you pay them to a mutual fund, but they are fees in the sense that they can be higher as a result of a given fund's investment strategy. Some fund managers are set and stay set with purchased investments for as long as seems reasonable. Other fund managers choose to chase the market around, trying to predict which stocks are overpriced and selling before they come down, and which stocks are bargains, and buying before they rise. While the latter strategy is certainly more fun and exciting, and can also be more lucrative, it also means that the fund must be distributing losses and capital gains more often to investors like yourself.

Every fund will distribute capital gains at least once a year, and you will either get actual money or automatically be given more of the fund's shares as a result, but you will have to pay the capital gains tax on your earnings either

99 — CHAPTER 5: MUTUAL FUNDS: "FUN"-ds FOR EVERYONE

way. The more capital gains a fund generates, the more taxes you pay, and the more taxes you pay, the less you get as a return on your investment. So a fund that trades a lot, and generates a lot of capital gains, and can brag about rates of return, may not be making as much money as a fund that trades less, and brags less. So while a fund may advertise a wonderful profit on investments over the past three or five or ten years, you, the potential investor, on whose back such profits are made, need to take into account how much of that profit you'll lose in taxes.

Note!

Note that chasing the market may seem like the natural behavior of your basic investor, mutual fund manager, or other predator. It may also suggest expertise and a charmingly aggressive personality, and that your fund manager is one of those real go-getter types with those leadership qualities people are so quick to applaud. But chasing the market may not actually be the wisest thing to do. It is rarer than you may suppose for experts, however savvy and aggressive, to beat the market for any length of time. And when they do so, they are taking on a lot of risk, risk which may lose them money too, over the long haul. Stocks, and especially mutual funds, are not get-rich-quick opportunities, and should not, for the most part, be treated like a roulette wheel. We say for the most part because there are people who gamble and who do come away with extraordinary returns, and more power to them. But most people can get a healthy profit over a number of years and the financial security they derive from this is prize enough and well worth the effort.

HISTORICAL PERFORMANCE

Another thing you need to examine is the historical performance of the fund. If a mutual fund has been in business five or ten or twenty or more years, how has it fared over this period of time? Remember that managing a mutual fund is a matter of making sound investments, and investing is like being a batter in baseball. Just about anyone might have a really good game, get three or four hits or a home run, but you wouldn't want to hire a player on the evidence of one game alone. You'd want to know if he will be a consistently good hitter, game after game after game, over the course of an entire season, before you decided to hire him and make him part of the team. And you would not assume a given player's headed to the Hall of Fame just because of a good season or two. For that, you'd need to see at least a decade's worth of the player's stats. So too with mutual funds. You want to know not only how the fund has performed over the past few years, but how it has

CHAPTER 5: MUTUAL FUNDS: "FUN"-ds FOR EVERYONE — 100

performed over the life of the fund, which will hopefully be long enough to give you some idea of how consistently the fund performs well.

The problem with baseball and mutual funds is that even the best hitters slump on occasion, for a month or even a year or two, before making a dramatic comeback or finding that their career is over. With even the best mutual funds, no matter how stellar the historical performance of a given fund, there is always the chance that it may fall to earth not long after you decide to buy into it.

Another thing to consider, then, is the fund's parent company and what other funds that parent company has under its umbrella. If the parent company is old, established, and trustworthy, this may make it more likely that the mutual fund is a solid one. If the parent company's other funds are relatively solid with good records over the years, this may bode well for the fund you're interested in, just as you may be more comfortable buying a new and untested Honda if you have a good overall sense of Honda Motor Co.

Of course such information is relative, and you can't judge a fund's record or its fees without doing a careful comparison between it and a host of other, similar funds, just as you can't judge a given batter's performance without knowing how other batters might perform under similar circumstances.

Note!

Note that historical performance is most relevant for funds with a major percentage of their portfolio in stocks. Bond funds can be better judged by their "current yield," that is, what they pay in dividends.

Money market funds are best judged simply by how much interest they pay (compared to savings accounts and to other money market accounts) and whether they give unlimited check writing privileges. Both bond funds and money market funds should carry very low operating fees.

101 — CHAPTER 5: MUTUAL FUNDS: "FUN"-ds FOR EVERYONE

FINANCE DIARIES

Unbeknownst to Marie, Bill had been doing a little work on the side (of interviewing for a real job, that is) to help their frustrating financial situation out a little bit. After all, it was a little embarrassing to be a grown man (well, sort of) and have his girlfriend still supporting him. So he decided to start up a mutual fund in the best sense of the word: He'd add a little money to the pot so that their funds were, quite literally, "mutual." (Get it?) He started by mowing a few lawns with his old pal Scully, who, despite his claim of being an Internet entrepreneur extraordinaire, actually ran a successful lawn business as his main source of income and, in fact, worked (hard) at it six days a week. (Bill had no idea how hard. Yet.)

Unfortunately, Bill was not the go-getter that Scully was. (At least, not physically, anyway.) Three days of weed whacking, lawn mowing, Gatorade chugging, and, most of all, sweating half to death, left him ready to write Scully off of his Christmas card list permanently.

However, the three hundred bucks he made, and that Marie didn't know about, left him quite refreshed. (Once he was finally rehydrated, that is.) Despite the fact that he could barely walk, he somehow managed to make it to the local bank branch one morning and start up a savings account in his own name, with his own passbook and even his very own clever folder full of financial information and literature. (Which he never read.)

He knew that having his money in a savings account wasn't exactly the wisest investment move he could have made, but for three hundred bucks he didn't think he could swing much more. He was quite sure that the more profitable investment opportunities, like IRAs, money market accounts, CDs, annuities, and mutual funds, all dealt in thousands (and lots of them), not just hundreds of dollars. Still, there had to be some better way to invest than what was available to all those high rollers.

Strolling through the library on the way home from the bank, he checked out a book called *Investing for Cheapskates*. It was a thin volume, Bill was guessing not many cheapskates were interested in investing in the first place, but it held a lot of practical information between its hundred or so lofty pages.

For instance, in the chapter entitled, "Every Day Investing," Bill learned tips on how to spend less money. After all, one way to save more money was to have more money to save from the get-go. Fired up, Bill left a message on Scully's LawnsCrafters answering

CHAPTER 5: MUTUAL FUNDS: "FUN"-ds FOR EVERYONE

machine asking for a few more days worth of work, and then decided to give up his precious Yoo Hoos. Cold turkey.

At a dollar or so a pop, and at six or seven a day, he could have quite a nice deposit slip going after just one week on the wagon!

After reading yet another chapter, called simply, "Spend Less Now," Bill picked up valuable tips on how to shave dollars and cents off the money you did have to spend. For instance, Bill could hardly survive his long weeks of interning, interviewing, and "Internetting" without his weekly movie (or two.) Most often, this celluloid luxury took up most of his week's allowance, not just in the price of a ticket (or two, if he felt like a double feature) but also in necessary handfuls of popcorn, soda, and candy. However, thanks to his budget busting book, Bill brought his backpack with him starting immediately and stopped into the local convenience store on the way to the theater. Grabbing a bag of generic potato chips, a can of soda, and a candy bar, he paid with a five instead of a ten and spent a third of what he would have once inside the theater. Naturally, he felt like white trash with his crinkling potato chip bag and that tell-tale "crack-hiss" of the soda can, but with his new monetary mentality, he hardly cared.

And so, in between mowing lawns and missing Yoo Hoos, Bill somehow managed to pad his building bankroll as the weeks slowly added up. His trips to the bank became more common, and he even renewed his finance book at the library. And then something strange and magical happened.

Curiously, the more money Bill actually made, the more careful he got about it. He interned less (working for free was definitely a "no- no" in his finance book, and worked for Scully more. The days of Yoo Hoos and movies were long behind him. He quit buying CDs and paperbacks, started clipping coupons for his weekly trip to the grocery store, and even (gasp!) gave up his beloved AOL and switched to one of those free Internet providers!

Eventually, Marie could hardly help but noticing her boyfriend's new spendthrift attitude. Not to mention, suntan from working outdoors three or four days a week.

"Have you been laying out by the pool?" she asked him as nonjudgmentally as possible one day after work.

105 — CHAPTER 5: MUTUAL FUNDS: "FUN"-ds FOR EVERYONE

"And, if I'm not mistaken, isn't that a glass of water in your hand? Where's your hourly Yoo Hoo?"

Bill stammered and stumbled his way though a clearly illogical explanation, but Marie was so busy scarfing down her dinner she hardly heard him.

"This hamburger tastes funny," she said around a mouthful.

"That's because it's not hamburger," he said proudly. "It's tuna."

"Bill," she said, "I'm too young to start eating tuna casserole. That's what they serve in nursing homes. Hamburger Helper is one thing, at least there's meat inside and, if none of our friends know about it, I don't mind. But tuna and casserole are two words I don't want to hear in this house anymore."

"But, honey," Bill whined. "Tuna's so much cheaper than hamburger. And it goes twice as far."

"That's because no one can stand to eat a whole plate full," explained Marie. Eventually, Marie finished her plate and apologized. Not every woman had her very own Mr. Mom (minus the kids) doing the grocery shopping and cooking the meals back home. She could hardly complain. Still, she drew the line at tuna fish. Yech!

She had to admit, however, that she was impressed with Bill lately. Not only was he looking tan, quite a contrast to his normal pasty Internet white, but he looked, dare she say, muscular, as well. His stomach was lean and, was it possible, he'd lost his premature Yoo Hoo belly? Come to think of it, she hadn't seen a single Yoo Hoo bottle around the house in, could it be, weeks! Not to mention, he hadn't had to ask for an extension on his "allowance" in over a month. A first.

"Bill," she said that night after the dishes were done and he had logged off for the night. "Are you having an affair?"

"What?" he asked, nearly spitting out his mouthful of water. Water? When had he started drinking water? "Are you kidding? Who do I see sitting around the house all day? I'm going to have an affair with the UPS man?"

"I don't know what it is, then," she continued. "But something is definitely going on with you. You're tan, you're strong, your tennis shoes have grass stains, and you've lost that bittersweet Yoo Hoo breath I'd almost just gotten used to. You tell me. What am I supposed to think?"

Bill knew the masquerade could go on no longer.

TOP-5 WORST PART-TIME JOBS

5 Assistant crack head.

4 Mafioso manager trainee.

3 Kinko's head paper shredder.

2 Chief coin wrapper at the laundromat.

1 The guy who holds the top up while your buddies dumpster dive.

CHAPTER 5: MUTUAL FUNDS: "FUN"-ds FOR EVERYONE

Marie was an intelligent woman, and, once she'd finally confronted him, he found himself surprised that she'd been clueless for this long.

And so, bringing out his cherished passbook, not to mention his dog-eared copy of *Investing for Cheapskates*, Bill ran the whole thing down for her. The weed-whacking, the Yoo Hoo celibacy, the sneaking food into the movie theaters, the coupons, and, finally, the savings account.

When he handed over the passbook, he saw Marie's eyes bulge at the numbers inside. She couldn't believe he'd done all of this behind her back, and to such a great extent. Her mind whirled with ideas and her mouth didn't stop making plans for most of an hour. She ran down the long list of technology stocks she was interested in, the 401(k) plan she could add to at work, the IRA account her Dad had started, and on and on and on.

Like a mother giving her newborn child up for adoption, Bill watched Marie slide the passbook over to her pile of paperwork where she kept the checkbook, and knew that his stint as a financial hero had come to an end. He found his mouth watering over-hot, buttered popcorn instead of stale, gas station potato chips. He yearned to escape the blinding sun and stinging sweat of his days as a lawn boy. But more than anything else, he found himself drawn to the refrigerator.

There, hidden in the back, in case of emergency only, was his very last Yoo Hoo. Reaching for it with trembling hands, he popped it open and sucked at the bountiful, chocolate-y, sweet-tasting cocoa concoction. Ah, sweet relief!

"Bill," Marie was saying, "I just wanted you to know how proud I am of you. Here I was imagining you in some illicit affair, and all the while you were hard at work preparing for our financial future. How sweet."

"Sweet," murmured Bill, deep inside a Yoo Hoo high and feeling cozy and relaxed. "Listen, Marie, could I have an advance on next week's allowance? I seem to have deposited all of my extra money in our savings account...."

PASS BOOK

"It is better to have a permanent income than to be fascinating."
— Oscar Wilde

CHAPTER 5: MUTUAL FUNDS: "FUN"-ds FOR EVERYONE

WHERE TO FIND OUT ABOUT MUTUAL FUNDS

It might be best to start off with an idea of where not to look. Avoid dispensers of so-called wisdom who take in investor disciples like fanatic cult leaders with promises that they will make money forever if only they give themselves over to their guidance absolutely. The cult-style financial advisor's main goal is to sell his book or newsletter or motivational videos or what-have-you, which is where he makes his money, and he will say whatever he thinks will get you on board.

Season all advice with a dash of skepticism, in any case. Look for the information you need to make a decision that makes you comfortable and provides you with the services you want. Read the fine print and resist the hard sell.

Sources

That said, there are a host of publications, available through subscription (though subscriptions in the specialized financial press tend to be rather expensive) that describe and rate thousands of available mutual funds.

Value Line and *Morningstar* are two such publications, both of which should be available at a well-stocked public library. They both give each mutual fund listed its own page, complete with relevant historical data and current yield information, information on the company and on its manager, and a rating of the fund from 1 to 5, which is based on both returns and the amount of risk the fund took to generate those returns. Risk is ignored by many other such ratings systems, and is important if you are to understand and are concerned about the level of volatility you will be subject to in your investment. They do not, however, include fees and loads in their ratings.

CHAPTER 5: MUTUAL FUNDS: "FUN"-ds FOR EVERYONE — 106

Popular financial magazines like *Barron's*, *Money*, and *Kiplinger's Personal Finance Magazine* also provide rated lists of top mutual funds. Such lists are often based solely on rate of return, which is, of course, for better or worse, how much investing in securities is determined in the current market. Where older generations would try to pay close attention to the health of the business, today's brokers have limited themselves to the issue of profitability, often looking only at the stock's value and recent history, with the idea that once a stock starts going down you sell and buy another. This is fine, perhaps, if you want to spend all your time watching the market, but defeats the purpose of investing in mutual funds, really, and you should certainly consider as many relevant factors as you can when choosing which fund to invest in.

There are also a wealth of Internet sites you can view dedicated to mutual fund investing, such as the Mutual Fund Education Alliance's Mutual Fund's Investor's Center at **www.MFEA.com**, where you can get tips and advice on investing in no-load funds, not to mention a create-your-own-portfolio service. Free reports on mutual funds and a Frequently-Asked-Questions list (with answers) are available at **www.mutualfundcenter.com**.

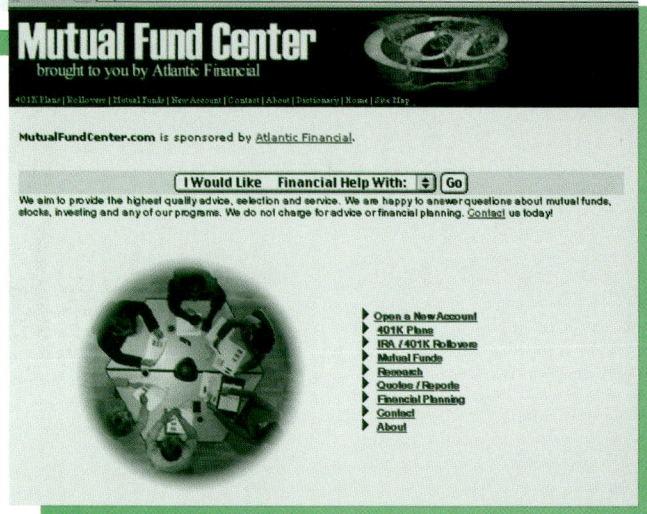

Meanwhile **www.labpuppy.com/funds/html** will happily provide you with links to mutual fund screening tools and to a selection of mutual funds' own Web sites.

Many of these sites will provide you with step-by-step guidelines on how to invest online, for those who feel more comfortable buying with a modem rather than with a telephone.

If that's not enough, it's more than likely your daily paper will carry a weekly column offering advice on mutual funds, as will many non-finance magazines, due to the rapidly increasing popularity of mutual funds.

CHAPTER 5: MUTUAL FUNDS: "FUN"-ds FOR EVERYONE

that if there weren't adults around he would have said something mean like, "Hurry up, little girl."

Or worse. So she willed her feet to move, the sound of her sandals slapping in her ears, and held out her hands to receive what he was to give her. He reached to the ground, straining against the pinstriped polyester of his suit, and stood up bearing a huge money bag with a big dollar sign on it like they always had in those Scrooge McDuck cartoons.

When Marie's principal tried to hand it to her, she woke up. Screaming!

"What was up with you last night?" asked Bill over corn flakes and Yoo Hoo the next morning. "You must have been having one of those *Nightmare on Elm Street* dreams, huh?"

Marie barely heard her boyfriend from beside the filing cabinet in the other room. She was on a mission, chasing the tail-end of her dream/nightmare before the last remaining wisps of it disappeared from her short-term memory. Not an entirely organized couple, Marie and Bill had inherited the rusty cabinet from an old college roommate who had spilled many a beer inside and out. Mostly they used it as a convenient spot for storing their income taxes and passports, and it made a handy nightstand in the guest room to boot.

Now Marie sorted through old pictures and report cards from her elementary school days, chasing down a dream in more ways than one. She found it in between a homemade Mother's Day card and her faded Presidential Fitness Award: A Series-E savings bond for $25! It looked vaguely official in her trembling hands, with its pictures of eagles and national monuments on the face and its money green border. Not faded at all, it looked as fresh as the day she'd received it, from her elementary school principal, for having perfect attendance for one entire year in third grade.

Sitting back on her heels, the savings bond brought back a flood of ancient memories, like a replay of her dream the night before: The band had played, her Dad had worn a tie, the kids in the audience had been given watermelon Jolly Ranchers to keep them quiet, and her principal had handed her the savings bond, and not a bag of money.

So what was the dream telling her? It was pretty obvious, wasn't it? This savings bond in her hand was worth, well—a bag full of money by now. Feeling her heart beating against her night-gowned chest, Marie wanted to race out to the bank and cash

119 — CHAPTER 6: BONDS AND MORE, FINDING YOUR BEST BETS

Marie couldn't quite remember when all of this "economy envy" started, but she guessed it was because she was in the software business herself. With all of those stories about dot-com millionaires on the news every night and in *Yahoo! Life* magazine each week, she guessed she felt a little insecure. Why wasn't she a dot-com millionaire yet? Though she made decent money for a (young) woman her age, Marie couldn't help but feel downright poor compared to those cyber geeks laughing all the way to the bank.

And so she worried over their budget, troubled over their checkbook, brought her own lunch, and secretly prayed Bill would get a (good) job. Until then, she slept fitfully and wondered if she and her long-term boyfriend would ever have enough money to actually get married and buy a house of their own, let alone retire!

Then, as she slept (fitfully) one night, she had a dream. A waking dream almost, steeped half in reality, half in sleep. She saw herself in pigtails, little white sandals, and her favorite pink dress. There was a loud band in the background, playing patriotic songs, and the faint taste of watermelon Jolly Ranchers was in her mouth. She saw her parents smiling, and her Dad wearing a tie, so she knew it was serious business. The American flag was waving and the sound of scattered applause sounded like waves hitting the sand.

Her principal was waiting for her. Smiling, but tightly, as if more for the crowd and less for her. He seemed impatient, and she knew

CHAPTER 6: BONDS AND MORE, FINDING YOUR BEST BETS — 118

Corporate bonds pay taxable interest. Most are issued in denominations of $1,000 and the period of maturity is incredibly wide: from weeks to a century. Because their value depends on the financial reliability of the company offering them, corporate bonds carry higher risks and, therefore, higher yields than government guaranteed Treasuries. Top-quality corporates are known as investment-grade bonds.

Corporates with lower credit are called high-yield, or "junk," bonds. Junk bonds typically pay higher yields than other corporate bonds. The rates for some junk bonds have been well over 10 percent. The investment strategy is that if you buy several junk bond issues, even if one defaults, the others pay such a high rate, the investment is still a good one.

FINANCE DIARIES

BONDING

Marie and Bill weren't exactly blazing a brilliant financial future for themselves, but, to their credit, they had taken that all-important first step: They had admitted that they needed to plan for the future in the first place. They just weren't sure how to go about doing that just yet. The whole financial world was just so confusing, so—intimidating.

Sure, the boundless opportunities of modern America were endless, from mutual funds to the stock market, from annuities to CDs, from IRAs to money market funds, the world was your oyster—as long as you had a safety deposit box full of pearls, that is. If they had only been millionaires with plenty of pocket change to spend, investing their money would have been no problem.

As it was, however, Bill was still working part-time doing yard work for Scully, Marie had just gotten another promotion at work, and yet they still found it hard to set aside a little money at the end of each month to invest in their future.

Aside from a little money in their savings account, the IRA they could never quite seem to add to, and Marie's meager 401(k) contribution through her job, they were probably right about where they should have been as young, twenty-something lions, but not quite anywhere near where they wanted to be. And that was the rub.

117 — CHAPTER 6: BONDS AND MORE, FINDING YOUR BEST BETS

a bond for more than it cost you in the first place is taxable; the tax-exemption applies only to your bond's interest. Other bonds free from federal taxes can include:

General obligation bonds are issued by the governments of cities, counties, or states to pay for bridges, roads, and so on. They are repaid with taxes collected by the government.

Revenue bonds are issued by a government enterprise, such as a city-owned utility. The bond's security is only as good as the enterprise.

Industrial revenue bonds are issued by the government of a city or county usually, but the promised pay back is only as good as the company that is using the bond money to build a factory or office or, in one case, even a bowling alley.

Business Bonds On the other side of the bond world is the corporate bond—the promise from a company that it will pay you back, just like the government. These interest payments are taxable and while the rate is higher than the government pays, there is a chance the bond issuer could default.

CHAPTER 6: BONDS AND MORE, FINDING YOUR BEST BETS

Treasury bills, or "T-bills," are short term. They mature in thirteen weeks, twenty-six weeks, and one year.

Treasury notes mature in two to 10 years. Interest is paid semiannually at a fixed rate. Minimum investment: $1,000 or $5,000, depending on maturity.

Treasury bonds are long term. They mature in 10 to 30 years. As with Treasury notes, they pay interest semiannually, and are sold in denominations of $1,000.

Inflation-indexed Treasuries. Maybe a sleeper in years to come. Issued in 10- and 30-year maturities (plus some five-year bonds are still trading on the secondary market), these pay a rate of interest on a principal amount that rises or falls with the consumer price index. You don't collect the inflation adjustment to your principal until the bond matures or you sell it, but you owe federal income tax on that unrealized interest each year—in addition to tax on the interest you actually receive.

Mortgage-backed bonds represent an ownership stake in a package of mortgage loans issued or guaranteed by government agencies such as the Government National Mortgage Association (Ginnie Mae), Federal National Mortgage Association (Fannie Mae), and Federal Home Loan Mortgage Corp. (Freddie Mac). Interest is taxable and is paid monthly, along with a partial repayment of principal. Except for Ginnie Maes, these bonds are not backed by the U.S. government. They generally yield up to 1% more than Treasuries of comparable maturities. Minimum investment: typically $25,000.

OTHER GOVERNMENT BONDS

Municipal bonds are issued by state and local governments and agencies, and mature in one to thirty or forty years. Interest is exempt from federal taxes and, depending on the state, local and state taxes as well. However, the capital gain you may make if you sell

CHAPTER 6: BONDS AND MORE, FINDING YOUR BEST BETS

The Treasury offers the bond with two separate rates, both set by the government: A fixed rate of return, which once it is set won't change, and a variable rate tied to inflation. (The two are added together to give the total rate.) The inflation rate is adjusted every six months so it gives an investor some protection if inflation gets out of hand. The return on these bonds has been in the 7 percent range.

Series HH bonds have a redemption value that remains constant at exactly the amount you invested. Your interest is paid to you every six months. When you cash an HH bond, you receive your original investment back. The return on these bonds has been in the 4 percent range. They can only be exchanged for EE Bonds and in increments of $500.

The bond process becomes more sophisticated when you look to purchase Treasury bonds, bills, or notes. The buying process can be done by mail or through the Internet. You can check your balances, and see your money in all of its glorious safety. The address is www.publicdebt.treas.gov/sec/sectdes.htm.

The auctions for the debt are held almost every week. While there are two kinds of bids, the only one you are interested in is the noncompetitive bid. The interest rate will be determined by those who are in the government securities business. You're just along for the ride. Remember that bonds issued by the U.S. Treasury are the safest bonds of all because the interest and principal payments are guaranteed by the U.S. government. You can buy Treasury bills, notes, and bonds for a minimum of $1,000.

TOP-10
MOVIES TO WATCH BEFORE INVESTING IN A BOND

10. The Bond of Blood
9. Mr. Bond
8. Bond of Fear
7. The Invisible Bond
6. Bond Street
5. The Bond
4. Blood Bond
3. Plead Guilty, Get a Bond
2. The Bond Between
1. Fatal Bond

CHAPTER 6: BONDS AND MORE, FINDING YOUR BEST BETS

TYPES OF BONDS

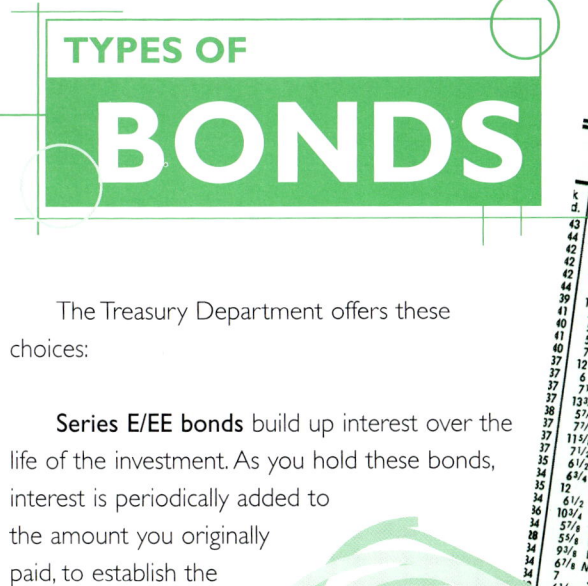

The Treasury Department offers these choices:

Series E/EE bonds build up interest over the life of the investment. As you hold these bonds, interest is periodically added to the amount you originally paid, to establish the current redemption value. As this interest accumulates, the value of your bond increases. When you cash an E/EE bond, you receive this redemption value, which represents the return of your original investment, plus the interest that you have earned while you held the bond. The return on these bonds has been in the 5 percent annual range.

I Bonds are slightly more sophisticated. They offer some chance of protecting the purchasing power of your money against inflation. I Bonds are an accrual-type security—meaning interest is added to the bond monthly and paid when the bond is cashed. I Bonds are sold at face value—you pay $50 for a $50 bond—and they grow in value with inflation-indexed earnings for up to 30 years.

CHAPTER 6: BONDS AND MORE, FINDING YOUR BEST BETS

Name of the bond: This is an abbreviated name of the company that issued the bond. In this case it's Duke Energy.

Interest rate: This number follows the name and is the original interest rate at which the bond was issued.

Another number right after the interest rate: This is the date the bond matures, in this case 2025.

Current yield: This is figured by taking the interest paid (6.75 percent) divided by the current price ($87.875). This equals 7.7 percent.

Volume: Bonds traded that day.

Close: The price of the bond at the close of the day, or 87 7/8 ($87.875).

Net Change: How the bond price changed, or in this case, up $1.875.

As you can see, the volume and volatility of the stock market contrast with the sluggish world of corporate bonds. This predictability has a certain appeal to many people, especially those who look in the mirror one day and see—a squirrel. Yes, your fur is thickening for the upcoming winter months, and you want to make sure your investment is safe. Absolutely safe. None of this market downturn stuff or "whoops, bad choice."

This desire to seek safety can be fulfilled by the United States government. The bonds are guaranteed and there's no brokerage fees.

The U.S. Treasury Department sells different types of savings bonds. Yes, these have been peddled under the slogan "Invest in America," and they are simple, easy ways to invest. They can be purchased (there's a $25 minimum) in a variety of ways. Almost all banks, savings and loans, and credit unions sell these. They take the order and your money. The government sends you the bond through the mail. Some companies have a payroll deduction plan for savings bonds.

Invest in America

CHAPTER 6: BONDS AND MORE, FINDING YOUR BEST BETS — 112

And whether it's Rudy or the federal government, the rules are pretty much the same. The borrower promises to pay you interest, usually every year.

A bond's interest payment is known as its "coupon." A $1,000 bond paying 7 percent a year has a $70 coupon. If you buy the bond for $1,000 and hold it to maturity, the "yield," or actual earnings on your investment, is also 7 percent. That is: Interest paid divided by price = yield.

Maturity refers to the specific future date on which you expect to get your money back. Bond maturities can range from one day up to 30 years. Your choice of maturity will probably depend on when you want or need the principal repaid and the kind of investment return you want.

COUPON
(A Bond's Interest Payment)
INTEREST PAID ÷ PRICE = YIELD

You probably can't find bond listings in your daily newspaper. Specialized financial publications carry them, and the listings, like the stock listings, have their own code.

MATURITY
(THE FUTURE DATE YOU EXPECT TO GET YOUR MONEY BACK)

CHAPTER 6: BONDS AND MORE, FINDING YOUR BEST BETS

WHAT GIVES WITH THE BOND MARKET?

Nothing exciting these days, but some financial observers believe that as the stock market cools a little in years to come, bonds could bounce back. Here are the basics: Most personal financial advisors recommend that investors maintain a diversified investment portfolio consisting of stocks, cash, and bonds in varying percentages, depending upon individual objectives. For example, older investors may typically have a higher proportion of bonds in their portfolio than younger investors.

When you buy a bond, you are loaning your money for a certain period of time to either a company or a government. The ability of the company or government to pay you back plays a big part in whether this is a bond you might want. If your friend Rudy down the street, who has never had a job, decides he is going to issue bonds, you probably would consider that a very risky investment. If the U.S. government issued the bonds, you'd see that as safer. That's really the scope of the bond market: Some bonds are safer than others and that plays a role in the interest rate you would receive. The higher the risk, the higher the rate.

CHAPTER 6: BONDS AND MORE, FINDING YOUR BEST BETS

6
BONDS AND MORE, FINDING YOUR BEST BETS

You've heard about bonds, as in the phrase, "Your bond is $500 for public intoxication." But that's not exactly the bonds we'll deal with. These bonds are debt, promises from governments and companies that they'll pay you back with interest.

At this juncture in financial history, with wild-eyed crazies bent on driving stock markets into high frenzies, the staid, gray investors in the bond market seem more a page from the past. Bonds almost always have been a safe harbor, a steady if unspectacular investment, generally centered around the idea of going to the bank and clipping little coupons to cash in an interest payment.

And because interest rates have remained low in recent years, bonds have not received much notice, except in articles and television programs asking the same question:

CHAPTER 6: BONDS AND MORE, FINDING YOUR BEST BETS

The Prospectus

Be careful, information overload is not what you want, nor do you need advice from every hack with the print space to give it. When you have found a fund that fits your criteria, then go to the fund itself, call its 800 number and request copies of its prospectus and most recent annual report. A mutual fund's 800 number, by the by, is not, or should not be, staffed by clueless minimum wage slaves, and is a good place to get in touch with a knowledgeable representative and to ask a few questions.

A mutual fund's prospectus is what you really want to look at. A prospectus is not an advertisement. It is a legal document that has been reviewed for accuracy and audited by the U.S. Securities and Exchange Commission. And while much of it will be as technical as you might expect, too technical, that is, for most of us, it should open with a clear statement of the fund's investment goals, which you may match to your own, or not. Following this will be a summary of the rest of the report, in clear enough English, so that you can get a handle on fees, loads, and the historical performance of the fund.

After You Invest

One last thing. After you invest you may have caught the bug that makes people immediately think about selling and finding a better fund, or makes them try to "time the market," to wait, that is, until they think they've got as much as they can from this particular fund and then sell to buy another fund at what they hope will be a bargain basement price. You should resist such impulses for two reasons. First off, it probably won't work out. If you bought well in the first place then you should stick it out for a while and see what happens.

Don't run for cover at the first sign of a dip. Second, the point of buying a mutual fund rather than buying stocks in a company yourself is to get other people to do the worrying and research and the buying and the selling for you. Let them do their job, and be glad that you don't have to.

CHAPTER 5: MUTUAL FUNDS: "FUN"-ds FOR EVERYONE 108

in her savings bond immediately. Unfortunately, it was Sunday and the only banks open were those "Easy Cash" check-cashing places on the wrong side of town.

So Marie did what all modern hipsters do when they have to wait a whole day to put their best laid plans into action: She got online. Keying into the U.S. government's savings bond site, she was soon greeted with a plethora of online options. She scrolled and double-clicked until she found a section on her bond. It took a while, only because she was so excited.

Visions of sports cars and early retirement danced in her head. Bill could take his time and find the job of his dreams, whether it took one year or ten. Or not. Who cares? Let him drink Yoo Hoo and eat bon bons all day! They could afford it. She could do a little extra clothes shopping, every single day, and fill her closet with the latest styles and fashions. She could buy all those retro-cool Beatles CDs she'd been secretly eyeing on Cdnow.com during her lunch break. Why, she could even afford to take a well-deserved day off! (Or two.)

Forcing herself to focus, she scrolled and hyperlinked, browsed and double-clicked until, wham, she wound up on a page with a "bond calculator." Keying in her bond series, the year it was issued, and the denomination, she hit the "submit" button and sat back like a king watching the court jester count his riches. She smiled, she blinked, she sighed, she crossed, and uncrossed, her legs, wishing Bill would have splurged on a better lap top.

And then, like a revelation, came her answer: $5,764! Amazing. Fantastic. Great. Could it be true? Was that all? Hey, wait a minute, what was that pesky, little dot doing there between then "7" and the "6"? The dot goes in the Web address, not your financial future! But, wait? Was she still bleary eyed from last night's dream? After all, it was plain to see that her crappy, hokey, government issue savings bond was only worth $57.64, and not even close to six thousand dollars!

Adrenaline receding from her body, exhaustion overtaking her now that the emotional roller coaster ride was over, Marie sagged against the lap top and couldn't help smirking.

"So," she thought, "this was what it was like to be a day trader?"

CHAPTER 6: BONDS AND MORE, FINDING YOUR BEST BETS — 120

TOP 10 SONGS TO LISTEN TO WHILE CONSIDERING BONDS

10 Slick Rick
"Bond"

9 Barry Adamson
"007, a Fantasy Bond Theme"

8 Andrews Sisters
"Any Bonds Today?"

7 Barmy Army
"Billy Bonds"

6 Emperor
"Acclamation of Bonds"

5 Groundhogs
"3744 James Bond"

4 Jam
"A Solid Bond In Your Heart"

3 Byron Lee & Dragonaires
"Bond Is Bliss"

2 Keith Methven
"Big Band Bond"

1 Spy Who Loved Me (Soundtrack)
"Bond 77"

BEYOND THIS POINT, THERE LIE DRAGONS

If you like it fast and loose, then commodities are for you. These markets don't make much sense to the people who play them for a living. Ultimately, it is a product that someone has a use for—such as heating oil. You are betting on perceived shortages or oversupplies. We explained this in more detail in Chapter 2. But in truth, Nostradamus couldn't make a dime in this game. Here are some of the commodity exchanges. Go there at your own risk.

NEW YORK MERCANTILE EXCHANGE

Nymex.com
In 1994, the New York Mercantile Exchange and the New York Commodity Exchange, the city's two largest exchanges, merged to become the world's largest commodity futures exchange. The

CHAPTER 6: BONDS AND MORE, FINDING YOUR BEST BETS

Nymex division trades oil, gas, and metals, while the Comex division moves metals and European stocks.

The Web site (Nymex.com) offers a history of commodities' markets and an explanation of how trading works within them. It also has one of the most detailed, comprehensive, and colorful educational sections for futures trading on the net among the exchanges. You can come away from here with a new understanding and respect for what those men down in the pits have to handle every day. After all, a thousand contracts bought and sold per minute makes the floor a busy, stressful place. It's a simple Web site, with news articles, links to research sites and papers, an extensive financial glossary, commodities traded on the exchange. The "Fastfacts" section shows you how to get real time market information through your telephone.

The New York Mercantile Exchange is the preeminent trading forum for energy and precious metals in North America. Come to it if you seriously want to trade electricity, crude oil, natural gas, gasoline, propane, coal, aluminum, copper, gold, or other metals at the largest exchange of its kind in the world.

CHICAGO
MERCANTILE EXCHANGE

cme.com

The CME is the world's largest financial marketplace in terms of open interest, which is a measure of the number of futures contracts and options outstanding at the close of trading. It is an indicator of what's called liquidity; many open positions

TRADING PLACES

Greed again plays a central role in a movie about finance. This time it's the commodities business in the movie *Trading Places*. Two old rich guys decide to test their theory on heredity over environment by trashing their young colleague, Winthorpe who has had all the advantages in growing up, and replacing him at their commodities trading firm with a street hustler named Billy Ray Valentine. Meanwhile, the greedy Dukes want to corner the frozen concentrated orange juice market (FCOJ) by illegally obtaining a report on the upcoming Florida orange crop.

Winthorpe (Dan Aykroyd) and Billy Ray (Eddie Murphy) find out the Dukes are behind their change of fortune and join up to trick and financially ruin the Dukes. They secretly switch the crop report, and the Dukes go to the commodity trading floor in New York unaware that they've been had.

Trading opens and the Dukes corner the market. While this works in Hollywood, it doesn't happen in a day in the real commodities market. The price of FCOJ can only go up or down so much in a day and then trading is suspended. (The terms are called limit up and limit down.)

The movie version is more fun than real life: The Dukes go broke, Winthorpe and Billy Ray earn a fortune and go to an island and ogle co-star Jamie Lee Curtis.

The business angle of the movie is worth watching; the scenes are really on the exchange trading floor and the frenzy is a good re-creation, but there's one scene not to miss: A down-on-his luck Aykroyd, dressed in a Santa Claus suit on a bus and eating a whole salmon filet he's pilfered at a Duke Christmas party.

CHAPTER 6: BONDS AND MORE, FINDING YOUR BEST BETS — 122

indicate a group of participants who are likely to buy or sell at a good price when anyone wants to make a transaction. Liquidity gives you choices.

There is much to see on this user-friendly site. When you go there, you'll learn that the CME trades a wide variety of futures options and contracts, ranging from currencies you've never heard of (the Brazilian Real?) to pork bellies, emerging markets products, interest rate products, lumber, and boneless beef (known in the field as "the rubber cow"). One of the best parts of the site is "A Day In the Life of a Trader," which is a graphical walkthrough tour of, you guessed it, a trader's day. There's also a one-of-a-kind section called "Trader's Toolbox," in which you can learn how to signal for a buy or sell as if you were down in the trading pits yourself. There's a brief financial glossary and a broad educational section. You can quiz yourself online, take an Internet class with tests and all, or you might want to browse through various trading styles as you formulate your own investment plan. One amazing page will actually show you what to look for within the research you uncover—those graphs and charts will finally speak to you.

The CME has a full range of research tools and links, and an interactive program to help you learn trading (monthly fee required). And if you end up loving trading so much that you just can't stop, you can get a membership and access the GLOBEX system, an around-the-clock after hours trading system.

Overall, the CME Web site is an excellent educational resource, conveniently attached to one of the world's major exchanges.

MIDAMERICA COMMODITY EXCHANGE

Midam.com

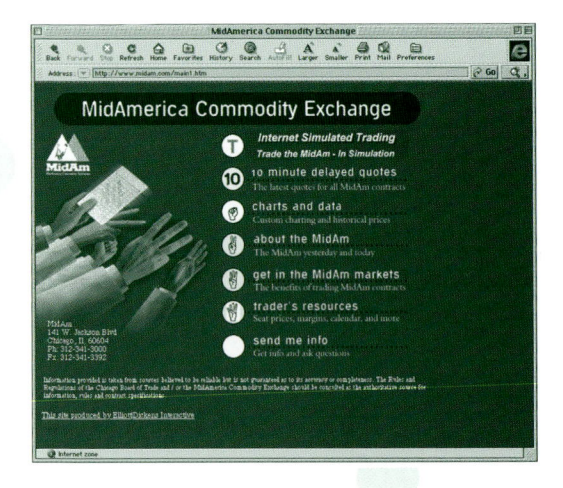

The MidAmerica Commodity Exchange, based in Chicago and affiliated with the Chicago Board of Trade, is the place to go if you're interested in starting to trade futures but don't have the dough to jump into the larger markets. MidAm futures contracts are one-fifth to one-half as large as similar contracts traded elsewhere. This exchange is a good place to learn while minimizing your risk in a very risky world.

Of course, the site has all the market data you need on the exchange's futures, which range from the agricultural (cattle, soybean, corn, hogs, oats, and wheat) to currencies and metals (gold, silver, platinum, Japanese yen, Swiss francs, U.S. treasury bonds and notes, and the Eurodollar). It also has a "ten rules of trading" section with tips ranging from the obvious (buy low, sell high), to the equally as important suggestions for planning a smart investing strategy. One of the most clear and visual explanations of trading mechanics on the net resides within these pages, too.

You can order more information about the exchange and have it delivered by e-mail or, if you prefer, as snail-mail brochures. And there's a version of an interactive program here that lets you simulate trades on the MidAm floor with other players through the Internet, for a $29.95 monthly fee.

125 — CHAPTER 6: BONDS AND MORE, FINDING YOUR BEST BETS

CHICAGO BOARD OF TRADE

Cbot.com

The Web site of the world's oldest, largest, and leading futures and options marketplace is a good place to learn how futures are traded and how they are different from stocks and other types of investments. Easily navigable, the site is set up so that visitors can browse through the information sequentially without getting lost in a maze of links. Some of the commodities traded on the CBOT include Treasury Bonds and Notes, corn, wheat, and other agricultural products, and Tennessee Valley and ConEd Hub Electricity. There are comprehensive overview and FAQ sections that do a lot to clarify the mechanics behind futures trading, plus history, headlines, and news. If you have questions that are not answered on the Web site, you have the option of e-mailing the webmasters, and you can subscribe to a list server to get "week in review" updates by e-mail.

COFFEE, SUGAR AND COCOA EXCHANGE, INC.

www.csce.com

Did you know that cocoa trees take up to ten years to reach maximum yield and that Africa's Ivory Coast is the world's leading supplier? Or that Brazilian droughts in 1994 sent coffee prices soaring? The Web site of the Coffee, Sugar, and Cocoa Exchange, Inc. has dedicated sections for each of its commodities and is a great place to learn about the factors that can determine the performance of your futures options.

The CSCE is the world's leading marketplace for the exchange of coffee, cocoa, sugar, and dairy products. Formed in 1882 in response to a disastrous speculation-fueled oversupply of coffee that ruined several large coffee trading houses, the CSCE was created to serve as a more orderly process for trading coffee. Over time, sugar and dairy futures were added, and the exchange merged with the New York Cocoa Exchange to become what it is today. Make the CSCE your first stop on the web if you're of the opinion that the road to riches is paved in chocolate bricks.

The exchange's Web site lets you download historical data on its futures, create custom tracking charts that use a variety of technical indicators, order informational brochures, and receive by e-mail the latest margin rates and changes. There's an interactive program you can download for free which will help you build a working knowledge of options trading. Click on "history" to get a step by step walkthrough of the trading process and to learn how the CSCE works, or how markets in general work. Then try clicking on "market economics" to get some great insight into each of the commodities on the exchange. You'll never get lost on this site; someone had the foresight to keep the table of contents in a convenient frame that stays put throughout your stay.

CHAPTER 6: BONDS AND MORE, FINDING YOUR BEST BETS

7
INVESTING AT HOME

For many people, owning a house is a step toward, well, something: success, stability, and status; debt, doubt, and depression. A house says you've "made it," along with all the other people in your neighborhood who thought being near the converted landfill "park" would somehow be a plus. (What is that smell?)

Basically, owning a home shows that you qualified for a mortgage and now work to pay off the single biggest expense most people will ever incur. There are as many wrinkles to buying a residence as there are different locations: A Brooklyn brownstone and a split-level ranch house outside Oklahoma City are very different animals. And buying a house comes with its own lingo, such as escrow accounts, mortgage points, and title insurance.

You may feel an anxious trepidation not only at the immense cost of buying a house, but also at the time and effort it necessarily involves if you do it right, and it is something you have to do right to avoid some potentially disastrous pitfalls. And it also has a chance to be the best investment you'll ever make.

FEAR AND DESIRE

IS IT WORTH IT?

You may have not yet come to that stage in your life where you're ready to settle down: Your job is not quite right, or you're changing jobs often, or you're unsure of where you'd like to live (country or city, east or west). The basic rule of thumb is that you need to stay in a home for three years to give it a chance to be a worthwhile investment.

Or perhaps you think it is just not worth the effort, that renting is just fine, easier, and, in fact, cheaper. After all, you don't have to maintain the property, your landlord does, and you don't have to pay taxes on it, or pay interest on a massive mortgage, or worry about declining property values, or mow the lawn, or replace the fridge when it quits, or anything much at all, besides putting your rent check in the mail at the beginning of the month. And you are freer this way, free to move on or to take a job a thousand miles away. Your money's not tied up in property, but can be used for a trip to Europe or an extended stay in Napa Valley or to make you filthy rich in the stock market. And while they say real estate is a good investment, nothing is certain, even valuable property depreciates when an area falls out of fashion, and you may well make little or no money or even, heaven forbid, take a loss, if you do decide to sell in a few years.

And, even with all those reasons, it's still probably much better to own a house.

TO BUY OR NOT TO BUY

While the above argument may be convincing for many, it is not the whole truth. Renting, for example, may seem cheaper on the surface, and may be so in the short term, but when you look closer, a house makes more sense financially. First, your mortgage payments may not be a whole lot more than your monthly rent. For a $100,000 home you may be paying as low as $700 or $800 a month, and unlike rent, which is not tax

CHAPTER 7: INVESTING AT HOME — 126

deductible, you may itemize on your taxes the interest on your mortgage, which is most of the payment, at least for the first few years. This could substantially reduce your income taxes.

The money you spend on rent is gone forever, but when you pay off a mortgage, you are buying something. You will have equity (the difference between the market value and what you owe). If need be, you can usually borrow against this equity to take a loan out to help pay for a college education or to start your own business. Home equity loans carry some of the lowest interest rates available and offer a much better deal than the interest charged by most credit card companies.

The world is rife with people who sit on the fence when it comes to buying a home. A guy named Dave lost years of rent money before he finally took the plunge with his wife and two sons. For him, it was a head thing. He'd finally realized the freedoms conferred by being a renter rather than an owner were mainly psychological, and were not as important to him as long-term financial security.

Also, remember that your house becomes your home not after you pay off your mortgage, but just as soon as you begin paying for it. There's no landlord to decide orange is just the right color carpeting, or the grimy stove will do, or to tisk-tisk at the nail holes where you hang a picture.

A HOUSE IS A HOME IS AN ASSET

It is true also that real estate is not always a good investment, and that even in a strong economy, some houses will decline in value. There's always a chance a given house will prove to be a loser because it is a particular type of house that has since gone out of fashion, or because, to be blunt, it was a shoddy house made of second-rate materials designed solely to make the developer a quick buck. And the real estate market sometimes goes cold for a specific area, or even freezes over for a time, and if this is the time you are forced to sell, for whatever reason, you are doubtless going to feel a

CHAPTER 7: INVESTING AT HOME

financial pinch. A woman, middle-aged and divorced, named Kelly, lost a good sum of money on a beautifully styled four-bedroom house because the market went sour for a year or two.

For the most part, however, if you do your homework and go into a deal on a given house with both eyes wide open, knowing the neighborhood, the quality of the house's construction, how well it will suit your own needs as well as the needs of prospective buyers down the road, buying a house is a wise way to invest your hard-earned dough.

FINANCING YOUR PURCHASE

Actually, financing should be a consideration from the moment you start dreaming of owning your own home, and should remain an issue throughout the entire transaction. You most likely are going to be paying for your house for the next 15 to 30 years, and it helps to keep finances a conscious part of every decision you make. For example, you'll want to get a credit report on yourself, and clear up any blemishes or discrepancies, and pay down debts. (See "What Savings Aren't & Your Credit," Chapter 1.)

HOW MUCH CAN YOU AFFORD?

Part of this question is up to your lender, and your lender will want to know about your personal finances in detail before deciding how much money to lend. The general rule is that your monthly housing expense (mortgage payment + property tax + insurance) should not exceed one-third of your current monthly pre-tax income.

What this means is that the amount you can pay will depend on the terms of your mortgage, particularly the interest rate, and on how much cash you use for a down payment. The optimum down payment is 20 percent of the price of the house, since this will get you the best mortgage, though down payments can go as low as 5 percent and even 0 percent of the price of the house. Another general rule is that you can afford a mortgage up to three times your gross (pre-tax) annual salary.

CHAPTER 7: INVESTING AT HOME

FINANCE DIARIES

Some experts recommend making the financial stretch and getting as much house as you can afford, the idea being that you will make more money as the years pass; today's costly castle will look like tomorrow's reasonable rancher. It remains up to you, not your lender, to apply such conventional wisdom, and to make sure you are not threatening your retirement funds and other major expenses, curtailing your lifestyle in a way that you will regret, or that you won't end up getting your new car repossessed when you sign on the dotted line.

"Only in American banks can you find the pens chained to the counter and the doors wide open."
— Branden Kerr

LENDER FEES

Your lender will require an initial cash outlay, several hundred dollars usually, for a credit report, an appraisal to ascertain the house's current market value, and to process your application. You will not be refunded this money, even if you are rejected or decide not to take the loan.

Despite this, if you are on a tight deadline and are worried about rejection (be as up front as possible about your financial situation to avoid wasting your money), you may want to apply with more than one lender to be sure you get the loan.

You should also consider getting pre-approved for a loan. Pre-approval is not legally binding to either side, but may save you from paying fees to a lender who can't or won't help you.

YET MORE FEES

Before we go on to discuss mortgages, be aware that there are other cash costs involved in buying a home, most particularly title insurance, escrow, and legal fees.

HOUSE (OF BLUES) HUNTING

Bill and Marie think that they're finally, actually, *almost* ready to buy a house. A real house. With four walls. And windows. Possibly an attic. Maybe even a basement. With a yard. And a garage. A nice driveway, too. With no downstairs neighbor to complain when Marie goes through one of her fitness fads and decides to do two hours of Tae-Bo at midnight three nights in a row. And no one upstairs to keep them up as they stomp around in what sounds like cement boots while they listen to dreadful music that, to Marie and Bill's ears anyway, sounds like it consists solely of thumping bass and lavish (not to mention loud) drum rolls.

Naturally, this monumental decision was reached just after they'd signed another year's lease on their current apartment, for which they paid over $800 a month. Which was, after all, more than some of their

CHAPTER 7: INVESTING AT HOME

more mature friends were paying for a mortgage. The place was nice, all right, with gates at the front entrance, several well-maintained pools, a 24-hour gym, and even a volleyball court just downwind of the garbage dumpsters. But an apartment is an apartment is an apartment, after all.

Besides, they were getting a little tired of having to buzz in the delivery guy each time they ordered a pizza. And the pool was always crowded with college kids guzzling beer, listening to God awful music, and belching (those damn kids), and they couldn't even play volleyball because the local pet walkers found it the best place around to make their doggie deposits.

But what really made them turn the bend on their decision to go house hunting was, of all things, *The Matrix*. No, they weren't packing it all up and leaving for L. A. to go camp out on Keanu Reeves' front lawn (or as close as they could get to it, anyway). And, no, they weren't shaving their heads and plugging into their easy chairs to await the return of "The Chosen One." In fact, despite their reputation as bona fide tech heads, they weren't exactly all that thrilled with the movie themselves. (Aside from the ever-cool Laurence Fishburne and some wicked special effects, what did you really have? *Bill & Ted's Excellent Adventure in Cyber Space?*)

No, it was their downstairs neighbor's love of the ultra-cool cyber flick that had them foregoing the Sunday funnies in favor of the hefty real estate page every Sunday for the past three weekends. Apparently, their nocturnal neighbor had not only invested in the latest DVD version of the fist-flying film, but in a hi-tech, surround sound, digital audio stereo system that let him (not to mention everyone in the bordering three states) enjoy the action as if he, too, were a martial arts expert.

Unfortunately, black clothes and black belts weren't the only dark thing about their *Matrix* loving neighbor. The hearing impaired Keanu fan also enjoyed the night life, often returning from late evening/early morning trips to God knows where only to show a two-hour *Matrix* fest for his friends, and always at the loudest level possible, if only to show off his new hi-tech toys.

Complaints had been made, doors had been knocked on, and even a handy broom stick had been employed for knocking on the offending film fan's ceiling, yet all to no avail. In the end, Marie and Bill would shuffle off to the guest room and cuddle up on the too narrow futon until the alarm went off at 6 a.m. the next morning and sent Marie off to work, still hearing every karate kick, bullet hole, and helicopter

CHAPTER 7: INVESTING AT HOME — 130

blade from the night (and early morning) before.

And so, one Sunday morning after actually making it through an entire evening without hearing the neighbor's noisy surround sound film fest, Marie and Bill showered, dressed, hopped in the car, and made it as far as the nearest convenience store, where Bill snatched up all the free real estate guides he could muster, while Marie poured them both 24-ounce frozen coffees with extra long straws.

Tooling around town with a full tank of gas and two bona fide caffeine buzzes, Marie and Bill "oohed" and "aahed" over houses from the west to the east, from the north to the south. They saw two-stories, duplexes, Victorians, and A-frames. There were grassy green lawns, towering basketball hoops, fish shaped mailboxes, manicured bushes, precious flower gardens, monogrammed door knockers, and even a "For Sale" sign or two.

Naturally, Marie and Bill never made it inside any of the gorgeous houses they passed that first Sunday. Eventually, however, house hunting became a true passion of theirs. They would meet in the evenings after Marie got home from work, have a quick bite to eat, and then head off to any address mentioned in one of Bill's real estate guides that was selling a house for about a hundred grand.

They would cruise the neighborhood as the sun slowly set and porch lights turned on, one after the other. As they drove, they looked for unsightly blemishes in the neighborhood that might prevent them from ever wanting to live there, such as Hells Angels headquarters, KKK meeting grounds, nuclear waste dumps, and an overabundance of frantically practicing garage bands.

Sometimes, in especially quiet neighborhoods, they would park the car off to one side of the scenic street and just sit there patiently, enjoying the silence and imagining the day when they, too, wouldn't have to cringe each time they walked inside their front door, waiting for the beginning strains of gunfire, karate chops, and chopper rotors to welcome them "home."

As Bill sipped his Yoo Hoo, Marie would close her eyes and imagine their own front yard, their own basketball hoop, heck, even their own fish-shaped mailbox. Eventually, Bill would reach over and gently hold her hand, squeezing it tight, as if to say, "One day, Marie, one day we'll have a place to call our own."

After all, their lease was up in a mere 354 short days. How many times could the practically deaf kid who lived downstairs watch *The Matrix* in that amount of time?

CHAPTER 7: INVESTING AT HOME

TITLE INSURANCE

The title to a house is the deed of ownership, like a title to a car. Title insurance, which is usually mandatory with the purchase of a house, insures that you and the lender aren't the losers, should any problems arise with the legitimacy of a title. If someone, for example, an ex-wife or ex-husband of the seller, has since moved away, and after you've bought the house, returns to claim partial ownership, you will not be liable for potential financial losses. Other problems that may occur with a title include those resulting from recording errors, forged signatures, unpaid property taxes, and mistakes in deed indexing.

Title insurance is not cheap, and could run you over a thousand dollars; the insurer will investigate the title to make sure it is clear and reduce his own risk. So why not just hire someone to investigate the title? Because there's always an outside chance that the investigator will miss or simply not know where to find a crucial, damning detail, and the potential loss could be very high. You don't want to spend $250,000 on a house to find out you don't really own it at all.

ESCROW FEES

Escrow fees are paid to a third party who makes certain the purchase and sale of the property in question is handled properly. For example, if you put a deposit down on a house, that is the seller's money, and the seller is free to gamble it away in Reno. But in most real estate deals, such money will be held in an escrow account by either the agent or a lawyer until the sale is completed or not. If, for example, agreed upon repairs have not been made, and you therefore decide not to buy the house, you should be eligible for a refund, which would be difficult to recover from a spendthrift seller, but easy to get out of escrow.

CHAPTER 7: INVESTING AT HOME

LEGAL FEES

Things can always get muddled in situations where large sums of money are at stake, either intentionally or accidentally. It is not a bad idea to keep a lawyer handy, working for you, to consult with and make certain you are not in for any nasty surprises regarding hidden costs or unkept promises. Consulting a lawyer is an especially good idea if the agent includes an arbitration clause in the home purchasing contract that may prevent you from suing the agent or seller after the sale is complete.

MORTGAGES

There are more varieties of mortgages available these days than anyone can possibly keep track of, and it is important to shop around and read the fine print. Don't be afraid to ask your lender, no matter how many stupid questions it takes for you to know precisely what type of financial obligation you are in for.

Mortgages do fall into two main categories, however, fixed-rate and adjustable-rate, and usually are available in either a 15- or 30-year repayment plan.

Adjustable-Rate Mortgages

Adjustable-rate mortgages, or ARMs, are designed to take advantage of the fluctuation of interest rates. They are offered by the lender with the idea that interest rates may rise over the course of the loan and increase the lender's profit margin. They are attractive to the borrower because interest rates may fall over the course of the loan, reducing payments. This is no small consideration. The interest you pay on a mortgage will alone be much higher than the cost of the house.

The interest rate on an ARM is determined by a formula, the sum of an index rate (usually the six-month U.S. Treasury bill rate) plus what's called a "margin." If the Treasury bill rate is 6 percent and your loan carries a margin of 3 percent, than your interest on the loan will be 9 percent, going down to 8 percent if, say, the Treasury bill rate goes down to 5 percent. This interest rate may be recalculated anywhere from every month to once a year. An annual recalculation is probably in

CHAPTER 7: INVESTING AT HOME

your best interest, as it will cut down on surprises.

Many lenders will offer low start-rates on ARMs, also known as teaser rates, so your first few payments will be comfortably small. But the payments will jump up within months to the normal, higher rate, and since you'll be paying your mortgage for years, the starter rate, which is really just a sales gimmick, is insignificant, and you'd be better off with a lower margin than with a low start-rate.

An ARM should come with caps on both the annual rate increase and the cumulative rate increase. Find out what these are and how high your monthly payment might be under the terms of the loan, and decide if you'd be comfortable paying this.

Fixed-Rate Mortgages

Fixed-rate mortgages have a set rate of interest and therefore a set monthly payment amount for the life of the loan. This is good for those who are uncomfortable with the idea that their monthly payments are dependent on the economy and the maneuvers of oracles at the Federal Reserve (which influences interest rates in the United States), and for those who simply don't want to spend the next 15 or 30 years checking and worrying about interest rates.

But a fixed-rate mortgage can cost you money if, over the course of your payments, the interest rates average less than the interest rate of the mortgage.

Points

All fixed-rate mortgages come with points, with one point equal to one percent of the loan. Two points on a $60,000 loan equals $1,200. This is the up front fee charged by your lender for making the loan. Different lenders will give different points on different loans, and the number of points may make a given loan more or less attractive. But remember that lower points are not always a good thing, and a low-interest loan with substantial points may be better for you in the long run than a high-interest loan with few or even no points.

Length of the Mortgage

Responsibly choosing between a 15-year and 30-year repayment period on a mortgage may seem like a no-brainer, and that you should take the 15-year period if you can afford to do so, and the 30-year period as necessity dictates. But you should also take into account how you might be shortchanging other investments, like retirement plans and stock portfolios. You should consider, that is, the larger financial picture, and your decision should not be determined by the simple idea that you should fully own your house as soon as you are able. And remember that you can, if you like, pay off a 30-year mortgage at the rate of a 15-year mortgage, but not vice versa.

CHAPTER 7: INVESTING AT HOME 134

SOME THINGS TO LOOK OUT FOR

Negative amortization on a mortgage is the same as being allowed to pay off less than the interest charge on a credit card balance, so the amount you owe actually increases (if slightly) with each payment. This is obviously the road to future problems. Make sure your payments are not set for negative amortization.

Prepayment penalties penalize you for paying your loan back early, if, for example, you decide to refinance your mortgage to take advantage of a drop in interest rates, or simply if your income rises and you decide to invest some extra money in home equity. Make certain your mortgage does not carry prepayment penalties.

Balloon loans carry an often low, fixed-interest rate for several years, seven and ten are usual. Then the entire balance comes due at once. Certain circumstances may make a balloon loan practical. If, for example, you know that you will only be keeping the house for a set number of years, and plan to sell well before the end of the loan, it might make sense. Otherwise, if you take on a balloon loan, you will be forced to refinance, and you're taking a chance since you may not be able to refinance due to short-term financial difficulties, in which case you may lose your house. Or you may have to refinance when interest rates are substantially higher than when you took out the initial loan.

SHOP AROUND

Both fixed-rate and adjustable-rate mortgages are potentially loaded with fees for the lender. Make sure to request an itemized list of such fees from any potential lenders and, again, shop around, remembering that lenders include both banks and mortgage brokers.

Mortgage brokers buy loans wholesale and retail them to you at, for the most part, the same terms as the original lender would have given. A good mortgage broker is like one-stop shopping, and could save you a

CHAPTER 7: INVESTING AT HOME

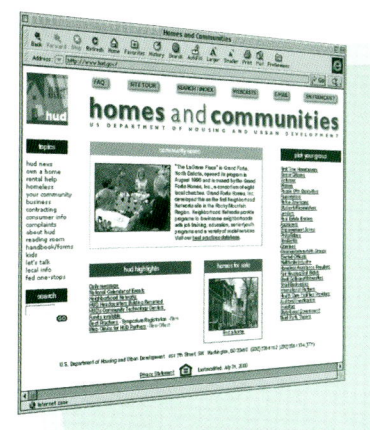

lot of running around from bank to bank to check terms and conditions.

There are also alternative sources of financing available, including loan packages available from the Federal Housing Authority (FHA) and through the Veteran's Administration, and there's help available for poor families, single mothers, minorities, and people with disabilities. A good place to research such opportunities, as well as to gather general, useful information about buying a house, is the Housing and Urban Development Web site at www.hud.gov, which includes links to other valuable Web sites.

MAKING AN OFFER

In Mexico, buying a pair of shoes from a street vendor can involve hours of haggling, the trading of insults, and all kinds of exaggeration concerning the poverty of the seller and the desperation of the buyer.

In the United States, one gets used to the idea that prices are fixed, and that rather than haggle with a clueless and powerless retail clerk, one must just try another store and compare prices. An exception used to be the Times Square area of New York City, where moaning and complaining were as much a part of the purchase as the similar dramatics in a nearby Broadway theater. But many people have not had the experience of negotiating prices.

In real estate, this is a mistake that can cost you thousands of dollars. You need to be willing to negotiate, and the first step in negotiating is making an offer that is lower than the seller's price—not so much lower that the offer won't be taken seriously, but low enough to find what the seller's situation might be. The seller may not be desperate at all. Perhaps the market is hot and all the seller needs to do is sit back and wait until his or her price is met. Or perhaps the seller is merely testing the market, and is not ready to give up the house, or does not need to sell the house any time soon.

What you offer will also, of course, depend on how much you want the house. You may be unwilling to risk extended negotiations, afraid another buyer will jump in, but remember, you'll like even a seemingly perfect house much better if you haven't paid too much for it. Offer some 10 percent (and even up to 20 percent) lower than the asking price, depending on the situation, the price, and how much the house seems worth compared to other houses in the area. Say you offer $200,000 on a $240,000 asking price, and the seller makes a counteroffer of $235,000. You've already saved $5,000 dollars. Now offer $220,000, and see if the seller is willing to come down even more.

CHAPTER 7: INVESTING AT HOME 136

To Negotiate Is to Profit, Usually

Know that the price of a house is not the only thing open to negotiation. Your offer can be made with a series of terms. Say the seller is stuck on the idea of getting a particular price for the house. You might accept this price on condition that the carpets are replaced and certain, specific work is done on the kitchen. Never fall in love with a house, in any case. If the seller and/or the agent you are dealing with is unwilling to make concessions of any kind, it's probably best to just walk away.

An Offer Is a Legal Agreement

Offers on houses are nothing to play around with, of course. Your offer will be in writing and will be legally binding if the offer is accepted. You will set a time limit on your offer from a day or so up to a week. You can set as short, or as lengthy, a time limit as you like, actually, but you should not put yourself in suspense any longer than one week, though the agent and seller may ask for a longer period, especially if they expect to be fielding other offers. You can cancel your offer, or refuse an acceptance, at any point after the offer expires.

DEPOSIT

The next thing to worry about is the amount of your deposit on the property. This is cash money given to be held in an escrow account either by the agent (who should have such an account available for this very purpose) or an agreed upon third party (usually a lawyer). The deposit is earnest money, to make certain you won't easily walk away from an offer that's been accepted and will therefore tie up the property until the closing. They may ask for from 1 percent to 5 percent of the price of the house, but usually less. Even a thousand dollars, for example, should satisfy them as to the seriousness of your interest.

PRORATED PAYMENTS

You will be expected to pay prorated house insurance and property taxes. If the seller has paid taxes on the property or housing insurance premiums that cover time you will be living there, you will be asked to refund these expenses to the seller.

PERSONAL PROPERTY AND PROPERTY FOR SALE

Know that a distinction will be made between property that comes with the house (which is physically attached to the house), and property that is personal, and which the seller will remove after the sale is made. If, for example, you are expecting gorgeous drapes to remain in place, or plush carpeting that is not attached to the floor to be there when you move in, you should make certain what the seller does not consider his or her own personal property.

CHAPTER 7: INVESTING AT HOME

WHAT TO LOOK FOR IN A HOUSE

When you are looking for a house to buy and to invest in, you always need to consider two things: What's right for you, and what will be right for the market a few years hence. You may, for example, be one of those hardened souls who doesn't get easily ruffled by vagrants or having a halfway house in the immediate vicinity of your home, but when you go to sell the house in five or ten years, if these situations remain, they may well cause you serious inconvenience of another sort by scaring off potential buyers. And even if you do not have or plan to have children, the quality of the area's schools may seriously impact the value of your investment.

LOCATION, BABY

You probably already know this, but where the house is located is pretty important. What type of neighborhood are you looking in and what type of neighborhoods surround it? An oasis in the center of economically depressed neighborhoods is likely threatened to go the same way. How are the schools? What are the services like—the fire department, the police, the library, public transportation? Is it a high crime area? Has crime risen or decreased substantially in the last few years? Make some phone calls, talk to people in the area. Local business owners are a good bet. Is the guy behind the counter at the independent video store down the street ready to bolt for fear of robbery and because his customer base is too transient?

Talk to the police. They can tell you a lot about the quality of life in a given area, as can a member of the local school board. Are there restaurants in the area? How busy are they during the day, at night, on weekends?

CHAPTER 7: INVESTING AT HOME — 138

Do people keep their lawns maintained? And how convenient is a good grocery store or will you be driving a half hour in one direction to get food and a half hour in another direction for dry cleaning and forty minutes in yet a third direction to see a good doctor? These might seem like inconveniences you'll be able to "put up with" to get a house that's "charmed" you, but over the long haul may make your home seem like a ball and chain.

What about you? How far is the house from where you work and how are you planning to get there and back? Is this a neighborhood you'll feel comfortable in, whether you like lots of privacy and quiet or vitality and bustle? Is it a place you can take a walk in on a Sunday afternoon or is everything car-oriented, without sidewalks?

Check the area out at night, during the day, and on weekends. What type of cars do your potential neighbors drive, clunkers or BMWs? Family vans or sporty coupes? Ask a resident if the basements flood and then ask this resident how long he or she has been there and how long they plan on staying.

Location is important enough that, as a general rule, it is a better investment to buy a modest house in a good area than a mansion in a bad one.

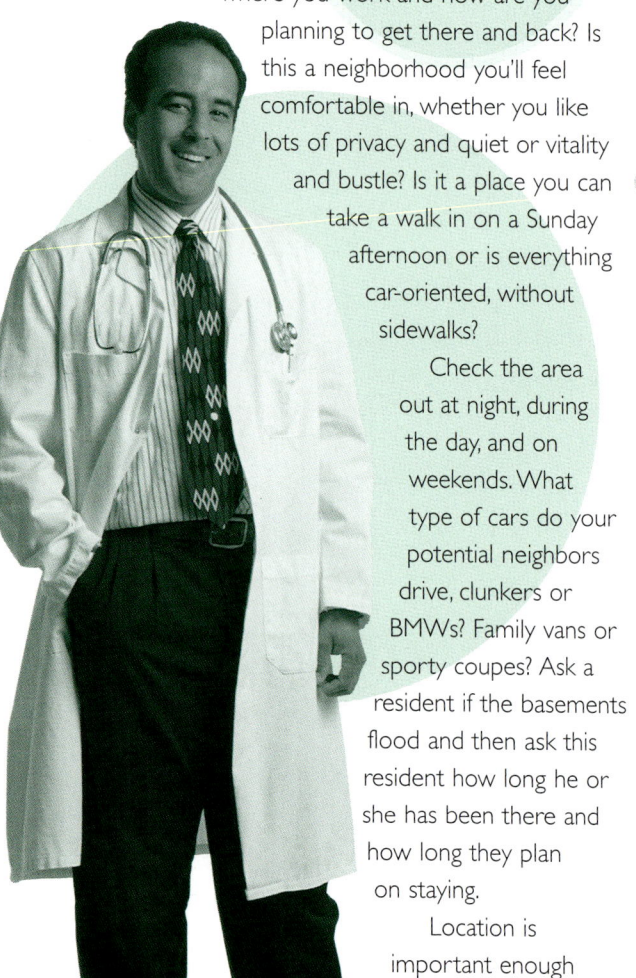

SIZE

You should start looking at houses with a general idea of how big a house you will be looking for, two or three bedrooms, one or two or three bathrooms. A house with only one bathroom would be tough to resell, and you probably want at least three potential bedrooms for the same reason.

You have to ask yourself how much room you'll need and how many rooms, whether you entertain a lot and therefore would like an ample living room, and whether you like to work at home and will therefore need a convenient and comfortable office space.

Size will of course be related to the price of the house, as will location, and everything else you are looking for, so in deciding this you will also be deciding how much you can afford to pay for a house. But there's nothing wrong with fantasizing a bit at first, asking yourself what your ideal house would be even as you enter into the more practical question of what type of house you can actually have.

LAYOUT

Houses are designed by architects, and architects, like members of any profession, have their good days and their bad ones. A house that's poorly laid out can cause headaches that will never end.

What you need to do when looking at a house is imagine how it would be to actually have to live there, not just as an idealized daydream, but with chores such as taking out the garbage included. Ask friends what they do and do not like about their houses, what they regret, and what turned into a pleasant surprise. Think of houses you've felt perfectly at ease in and houses you've felt oddly uncomfortable in and ask yourself why. It may have merely been poorly executed decor, but it may have been intrinsic to the house's layout.

CHAPTER 7: INVESTING AT HOME

APPLIANCES AND UTILITES

The type of stove a house has installed, the washer, dryer, and dishwasher (assuming these things come with the house), the heat and air-conditioning, whether it has storm windows, are all important because they may, if found unsatisfactory, not only cost you a lot of money to replace and modernize, but will affect the overall value of the house in years to come. If it is an old house, appliances and utilities may be rundown or simply outdated, and while you may think you don't need to think about such things right off the bat, you should make sure the price you're paying for the house allows for the needed repairs and updates. If it is a new house, beware the use of substandard equipment. Someone, a developer, a builder, a subcontractor, may have been cutting corners and it will be you who will have to pay for their savings in the long run.

BUILDING MATERIALS

All building materials, from window panes to paint to the shingles on the roof to plywood, come in a variety of grades, from basic to high quality, and what grade of material has been used in a new house or to rehabilitate an older house with a solid foundation and sound structure will determine whether you will be buying a money-pit or a house that will need little maintenance. You don't want to start repainting a house within a year of moving in. If several (two or three) layers of high quality paint have been applied over a layer of primer throughout the inside of a house, this will save you money and time and effort in the future. If the house has recently been repainted on the outside, has it been done for show to get the house sold, or has it been done right?

CHAPTER 7: INVESTING AT HOME — 140

You can investigate the building company as well. Find out what type of reputation it has, what other work it has done, and when you have your house inspected (see below), make sure to get someone with construction experience to take a look at it.

SOME THINGS TO WORRY ABOUT

With older houses, in particular, there are certain dangers, now well-known, but not always addressed. The main ones are lead used in old paint and plumbing, and asbestos in the walls. When you have a house inspector look over a place you are considering, these are things you'll want to know about. If the house inspector is not qualified to look for these things, find someone who is. Also, if the seller insists that such problems have been taken care of, make sure to get documentation to that effect.

Another potential danger is radon, the invisible and odorless radioactive gas that can cause lung cancer and exists in a significant percentage of old and new homes—estimates are 1 in 15. Find out if the house has been tested for radon, and, if not, insist on a test being made, paid for by either the seller or yourself. A radon test will cost two or three hundred dollars.

GIANT

Set smack dab in the middle of the big, old world of Texas, the Oscar award-winning film *Giant* poses the investment question: What's more valuable than land? Answer: How about land with oil on it?

Lucky Jett Rink (played by James Dean in his last film) begins the movie as a penniless cowpoke on a huge ranch, with his hat pulled so low you'd think he was country music star Dwight Yoakam. But when he inherits a tiny corner of the 500,000-acre ranch, Jett decides that land is a pretty good thing to own. When ranch owner and cattleman Bick Benedict (Rock Hudson) tries to buy him out, Jett says he'll be holding said property for the long term, thanks anyway, Bick.

Then Jett discovers that his land just happens to be resting over an ocean of oil. ("Texas tea" in the venerable words of those other savvy investors, The *Beverly Hillbillies*.) He becomes the classic nouveau riche Texan (there's another kind?) and manages to fall over drunk in public with a grace everyone seems to admire, including Liz Taylor, who plays Rock Hudson's wife in a screen marriage combo that leaves the imagination reeling.

Unfortunately, few investors can ever hope to own parcels of land, let alone ones that sit atop a prime oil gusher. But if Liz and Rock can get together, even on the screen, well, anything's possible.

CHAPTER 7: INVESTING AT HOME

HOW TO FIND A HOUSE

Checking the classifieds in the Sunday papers and the Internet are the easiest ways to get started. The Web allows consumers to use the medium to its full advantage. The space on the Web enables sellers to show everything about the house in detail. The better sites have virtual tours of the home, where you can get a closer look at amenities like patios and pools.

Still, the best way to get a good idea about a house is to go over and look at it, with a camera and a pad and pen handy, to take pictures and make notes and sketches to consider later so your memory doesn't play tricks on you, which it will if you look at enough houses over a short period of time.

You might also simply ask around, let friends and colleagues know you are in the market, put word out on the grapevine, and see if anything comes back to you. Who knows, you might strike gold quickly, or at least hear some things that might help you better define your goals and needs. Either way, don't get too impatient. Buying a house is one occasion where you don't want to be rash. Take your time, and be picky.

EVERYWHERE A SIGN

FSBO stands for For Sale By Owner and you've no doubt noted this phrase on For Sale signs hung on cars and houses. It means that if you buy a house directly from the house's owner rather than through a real estate agent you are cutting out the middle-man and saving the price of the agent's commission. If the seller is an honest person you can talk to, you may be cutting out a lot of unnecessary wheeling and dealing as well.

But owners of property, especially houses, tend to have a certain psychological connection to that property, which may lead them to be even more stubborn and to overvalue what they own. Like a man going to trial and refusing the advice of a lawyer who could get the sentence reduced if only the man would agree, an owner may be avoiding real estate agents because they recommended a lower, more realistic asking price.

AGENTS

Other For Sale signs will have the name of a real estate agency and/or the name of a real estate agent with a phone number. Like agents for writers and movie stars, real estate agents work on commission, which is a percentage of the selling price, and make money when the deal is done. Theoretically, they are experts in real estate, and are another good place to start. Agents will have access to a large number of listings in the area, and, if they are a good agent, and know their territory, will be valuable guides and sources of information even if you do ultimately go the For Sale By Owner route.

CHAPTER 7: INVESTING AT HOME — 142

WHAT TO KNOW ABOUT AGENTS

First, agents tend to specialize in a given territory, and will be most valuable if you already have a pretty definite idea about where you want to live. If they start showing you houses outside their territory, you may want to consult another agent as well.

Second, agents don't work for you, the buyer. They may seem to be working for you, serving your interests, and acting very friendly, but legally and ethically they are responsible to the sellers they represent. So, for example, if you tell them how high you're willing to go on a given property, but make an offer initially lower than this, they will tell the seller to hold out for your high price, but not vice versa, that is, the agent will not and can not tell you how low the seller is willing to go.

In recent times a person called a buyer's broker has come into being, supposedly to alleviate this discrepancy. But even if a so-called buyer's broker signs a contract saying your interests are paramount, they still only get paid by commission, and are therefore still primarily motivated to close a deal at the highest bid they can get. Representing the seller remains the more natural relationship for an agent.

Third, there are good agents and bad agents. This is not necessarily related to how much selling they do. Closing a lot of deals may simply mean they know how to sell.

There are certain things you can look for to help you judge a given agent. First, is the agent part-time or full-time? Many people take up real estate as a hopefully lucrative sideline, and really don't know all that much about real estate, houses, or their territory. You probably want a full-time agent. Next, are they a member of the National Association of Realtors? These should be the top realtors, the most ethical, best educated, and the ones who take pride in doing their job well. Judging an agent is also a matter of judging character. Are they giving you the hard sell? Do they change their story when they find out you are or are not interested in a given property? Are they patient with you and willing to answer your questions? Are they ignoring what you say you want? You are allowed to try out several different agents, and find one you feel comfortable with.

WHAT AGENTS ARE GOOD FOR

First, they have access to the Multiple Listing Service (MLS), a database listing properties for sale. Second, they want to close a deal and so will lead you through the maze of paperwork and explain all the legal requirements involved in buying a house, like mortgage types, title insurance, appraisals, and house inspections. They can recommend lenders and lawyers and inspectors. While you should shop around on your own as well, these recommendations may prove helpful when you are at a loss, or just want to get the sale done without a lot of hassle or uncertainty.

Note that most agents do not know anything about construction values, like what the best type of insulation is or how warm a house will remain through the winter. This is not their job, though they may try to make themselves seem like all-around experts. For technical information, you need to go to the inspector or a construction expert.

What is a subagent? Since the MLS gives listings from various real estate agents, the agent you're working with may show you properties listed under the name of a different agent, and is acting as a subagent in doing so. The important thing to remember is the subagent is still responsible to the seller, not the buyer, even though the original agent will also be representing the seller.

WHAT TO DO ONCE YOU'VE FOUND A HOUSE YOU WANT

The first thing to do is make certain the house is what it appears to be, and that you do in fact want this house, and the first thing you need to do on this account is have the house inspected. There are people who are listed in the phone book under "housing inspectors," waiting for your call, and your agent will no doubt give you a name or two as well.

There are hard inspectors and easy inspectors. An easy inspector is in the best interest of the agent and seller, a hard inspector is in the best interest of the buyer. An easy inspector may slide over problems, a hard inspector will not, and this is good because, first, you do want to know if there are any problems before you buy a house, and second, because substantive problems may force the seller to lower the price or to promise, in writing, to fix the problems before the sale. And just as you never want to buy a used car without having a mechanic take a long hard squint at its engine, so you won't want to buy a house without an expert or two (get references) double-checking the plumbing and heating and electric systems, or, if the house is new, without investigating the builder and finding out who put in what and how well they are respected for their work.

Things to know about: plumbing, foundation, roof, pest control (termites especially), and overall condition. Also: potential for flood, hurricane, or earthquake damage in areas where such natural disasters are realistic threats.

On the day before the closing, do your own investigation, walk through the house and make sure it's in the condition promised, the walls have been repainted, a new furnace installed, and that the carpeting hasn't been taken up.

AFTER YOU'VE BOUGHT YOUR HOUSE

Every house will require a certain amount of redecoration and maintenance, both to keep it up and to improve its value over time. Don't go the cheap route, buying the least expensive furnace you can find, or using low-grade house paint. You spent lots of time and energy making sure to get a good house for your money, now you must treat your investment with the respect and care it deserves, because it is where you live, because you'll save money that way in the long term, and because you might want, or need, to sell your house in the future.

TOP 5 SIGNS YOU'RE NOT READY FOR A HOUSE JUST YET

5 "What do you mean 'cable's not included'?"

4 You still have three boxes of checks that say Apartment #8-C.

3 "But the rental office has those hard-to-find green starlight mints!"

2 You keep forgetting the "up or down" rule on that little red flag on your mailbox.

1 "What do you mean I have to plunge my own toilet?"

CHAPTER 7: INVESTING AT HOME — 144

REFINANCING

Refinancing is the best way to improve the terms of your mortgage, especially if interest rates have dropped substantially since you bought your house, or your credit has improved and you can get better terms on a mortgage.

Scams abound in the refinancing business, and you can, if you are not careful about checking what you sign, end up paying more per month than you did before. Be especially suspicious of unsolicited refinancing offers that include a big, too-good-to-be-true loan with which, the sales rep will tell you, you can buy new furniture or get the house in better shape or "even take a vacation." Also: Make sure to do the math yourself, rather than trusting the numbers of an overly insistent lender.

Refinancing will cost you several thousand dollars in any case. While refinancing your mortgage is often a very smart and cost-effective measure to take, remember it is not free and should be done as carefully as choosing a mortgage in the first place.

OTHER KINDS OF REAL ESTATE INVESTMENTS

There are plenty of people who have made money by investing in real estate other than their own home. They have built hotels, erected office buildings, and supplied America's renters with apartment space. Unfortunately, you probably are not one of those people. Real estate is a rough and tumble business that can generate huge profits, but it is not for the weak of heart. The sucking force of a bad real estate deal can bury you and your lender forever. Bad real estate loans fueled the savings and loan crisis of the late 1980s.

If you are just edging into investing, you probably don't want to take the plunge into real estate outside of your own home.

For those who do, here is the landscape:

GLENGARRY, GLEN ROSS

It is probably no accident that a full-size map of the state of Florida is placed prominently in numerous scenes in one of the greatest grifter flicks of all time, *Glengarry, Glen Ross*. After all, the huckstering investment salesmen in this gritty classic are the direct descendants of the slime balls from the state that virtually invented land swindles. Everybody needs some swampland, right? And who has more than the Sunshine State?

The all-star cast of Al Pacino, Jack Lemmon, Ed Harris, and Alan Arkin hammer home the one universal truth of the movie: Property is the ultimate investment lure.

Stocks? Bonds? Who needs 'em. And the Internet? Forget about it. You won't find any of those computer gadgets cluttering up these guys' desks. All they need is a phone, some shoe leather, and a few great leads. That, and some shady property deal to sucker in a few unsuspecting families.

Clad in sharkskin suits and atrocious ties, these slick salesmen from the old school make cold calls from bad leads and show up late at night for in-home visits. They sell such "prime investment opportunities" as Rio Rancho Estates in Arizona, and of course the more sought-after Glengarry Highlands in, where else, Florida. They're not just selling property, they tell their unsuspecting clients, they're selling "the dream."

What dream is that? Property. Land. Real estate. Buy it up. Parcel it out. Lay it on thick, and you, too, can own your own eight units of Rio Rancho Estates in sunny Arizona.

Hey, don't forget about those "highlands" in Florida.

CHAPTER 7: INVESTING AT HOME

RENTALS

This is sometimes referred to as a "learn as you go" business and that should tell you something. It can take as much time as a full-time job and definitely as much as a part-time job. If that's not enough to scare you off, do you know what an estoppel certificate is?

Still some people love to own rental properties and if you have the knack for it, there's money to be earned. Rental properties in good areas usually are in demand, and the rates rarely go down. So over time you can profit, both on an income basis and as a way to reap an even bigger gain if the property is sold.

LAND

There is an old saying: "You can't get hurt in dirt." Yes you can, especially if you own it. It requires property tax payments, and probably some upkeep, no matter what. Unless you are renting it to a farmer (in which case there may be pesticide residue), this is something you want to avoid.

SECOND HOMES

It's true you can itemize interest payments of a second home, though to a lesser extent than your primary residence. But unless this is a rental property that you might use from time to time, it is almost a certain money loser.

BORROWING

The good and bad news about commercial real estate is that banks and other institutions will lend on it with an almost blind faith, until the market turns, and then they won't lend anything at all. Period. So you can't sell it. Timing is everything and that is especially true in real estate.

It does allow some diversification and in periods of high inflation, when investments in "brick and mortar" tend to rise, it's not bad.

CHAPTER 7: INVESTING AT HOME

8
FRAUDS & SCAMS
HOW TO SPOT (AND AVOID) INVESTMENT SCHEMES
With the Internet you can lose your money faster than ever. Here's how!

Consumers lose hundreds of millions of dollars every year to investment fraud. Like malevolent viruses, the schemes that perpetrators dream up seem to transform in seconds, ready to lure people who eventually become victims of their own greed.

Scams, of course, have literally been around for centuries. Pyramid schemes, like the one named for the 1920s Boston scam artist Charles Ponzi, promise big profits from a small investment. Word of mouth, then as now, draws in investors by the thousands.

And, usually, there is a small element of truth or credibility in the larceny these people peddle. A scammer in Florida convinced investors he had developed a "new" oil refining process. Oil prices were high, and the guy selling the plan had a choirboy look and reputation. Some initial investors received whopping returns. And in the small town, word spread fast. People fought to get in; after all, they didn't want to fall behind their neighbors. Outcome: The technology was a hoax; the scammer went to the pokey; the money—millions of dollars—was lost.

Almost anything with a "new" technology aura seems to have fraud appeal. A company sold "specialized mobile radio licenses" for $7,000. Anyone could have applied to the federal government and purchased one for $200. Then, in a truly creative twist, a sister company under another name stepped in and promised to help the defrauded investors recover their money—for an upfront fee, thus plucking their pigeon twice on the same swindle.

And who said American ingenuity was dead?

CHAPTER 8: FRAUDS & SCAMS

THE INTERNET: FASTER, BETTER SWINDLES

If word can spread fast in a small town, just think what a scheme on the Internet can do. One example: An enterprising teenager goes on the Internet and gives the investing public the chance to buy into a $500,000 bond issue for Golden Waters Production. He makes up endorsements, including this gem: "the best bond investment of the century!" The "business" the bonds would finance? Eel farming. People actually responded before the SEC shut him down; the kid said he just needed some cash.

The Wall Street Journal reported that a California man was sentenced to 10 years in prison for conducting a fake stock offering over the Internet. It's among the harshest jail penalties for Internet securities fraud in history. Matthew Peter Bowin offered to sell stock in a technology company, called Interactive Products & Services, over the Internet in the late 1990s. He characterized his company as the "next Microsoft," and about 150 people fell for it. They sent him checks for nearly $200,000, which he proceeded to spend on clothes, stereos, and rent for a luxurious beachfront cottage on the Pacific.

THE "PUMP AND DUMP" SCAM

These con artists use *your* emotions to *their* advantage. Specifically, they seek out the chat rooms, message boards, and usenet groups to post online messages urging readers to buy a particular stock (one they have a vested interest in, of course) because it's ready to "explode."

Another variant of this cyber scam is to urge readers to sell a particular stock before the price "plummets." The hustlers then rush in and pick it up on the cheap. Language, naturally, is a key ingredient.

These people use their handy "scam thesauruses" to add just the right dramatic touch: explode, mushroom, skyrocket, orbit, takeoff, as well as plummet, jettison, black hole, crash and/or burn, disastrous, cataclysmic, and dead cat.

Most of the time, of course, the authors of these bulletins profess to have "inside" information concerning an upcoming development in the company in question and, out of the goodness of their heart, they are "leaking" such information to you, their good readers.

Either way, if you fall for this scam, the only one profiting will be the writer of the message. (And his backers, of course.)

TOP-5 SIGNS YOU'VE JUST BEEN "TAKEN" ON THE INTERNET

5 You just bought 2,000 shares of "Microshaft" for 5 cents a share!

4 Your new online investment password is "you-R-screwed."

3 You receive a thank you e-mail from Don Corleone.

2 The $60 you paid for a virtual pet rock?

1 Your brand new membership on Ameri-Fraud.

CHAPTER 8: FRAUDS & SCAMS — 148

The ease of this type of scamming on the Internet has even attracted that notoriously lazy group—the mob.

In June 2000, about 600 agents of the Federal Bureau of Investigation (FBI) arrested 120 suspects as part of a crackdown on stock fraud. The mobsters had taken over a company called DMN Capital. It had recruited brokers to tout stocks, which DMN had purchased when the stocks were still inexpensive. Some companies were supposedly involved in Internet-type businesses, such as "an alternative online trading system." Another was called "E-Pawn." It was ready to sell anything, from European castles to racetrack timeshares. The mob bribed and intimidated the brokers to mislead customers; and if the brokers started having second thoughts, they would have the opportunity to meet Mr. Corleone. The FBI reported there were threats and even a contract taken out on a squeamish participant.

The fraud netted about $50-million for the criminals. As FBI official Barry Mawn phrased it, "From the fish market to the stock market, the methods (the Mafia) uses are always the same: violence or the threat of violence."

BETTER ASK THE SEC

To aid you in your search for truth, justice, and a way not to get conned, the federal securities laws require the vast majority of public companies to register with the SEC (www.sec.gov). Naturally, an organization like the SEC wouldn't exist if all companies offering investment opportunities were on the up and up. Therefore, it's in your best interest to deal only with companies that actually register with the SEC. Otherwise, you're "investing blind," without the aid of financial reports or even much other information at all. Instead of relying on the so-called experts behind a flurry of spam e-mails, financial bulletin boards, or Internet newsletters, spend your time doing research based in fact.

CHAPTER 8: FRAUDS & SCAMS

A Taste of "Spam"

Gigabyte grifters use spam, much like they use e-newsletters and message boards, to spread false information about one scheme or another. After all, the beauty of spam is that it allows cyber cons to launch massive e-mail attacks to net their victims. By purchasing a simple and easy-to-use bulk e-mailing program, spammers are able to send personalized e-mails to hundreds of thousands of victims at the same time, a feat that would cost much more money if going the traditional mass-snail-mailing or cold-calling route. And money is what this is all about.

And, while most of us are able to spot a spam a mile away, the law of averages dictates that just enough people are sitting around with just enough time on their hands to actually read a spam or two a day and actually act on it. Which is money in the bank to the spammer.

A woman named Darla wrote into a service called Scambusters.com about a supposed "credit" offer from a company called CMA. She received an e-mail, "actually it was 'spam', and something I usually delete right away," she wrote.

However, with the "enticement" of a guaranteed two or three credit cards, with no security deposit required, and needing a laptop for her Web design business and still being at the mercy of her ex-husband's bad credit, she was sucked in.

In the e-mail ad it very clearly stated "risk free," and invited her to "apply now." So, thinking she had nothing to risk, she "applied," to see what would happen. It seems that just by filling out the application she had legally bound herself to pay the company $35. She received an e-mail saying to make a payment on the account now or risk late fees. Totally befuddled and confused, she e-mailed back and said, "What payment?"

The company stated that not only was she obligated to pay the $35, but that she was now going to be charged a $75 late payment fee, threatening that the officials had her "credit report" in their possession. Even more ludicrous was that it had not been 30 days, but only 23 days, so their supposed bill wasn't late, yet they continued their threats. CMA boasted of being listed with "Dunn (sic) and Bradstreet." As the victim noted, the company didn't even spell the name of the credit agencies correctly. It's Dun.

DON'T BANK ON IT

There are a small number of banks that are misrepresenting themselves on the Internet. The government has created a site where you can check to determine if an institution has a legitimate charter and is a member of the FDIC. Visit http://www.fdic.gov/bank/individual/online/index.html

CHAPTER 8: FRAUDS & SCAMS

FEDERAL TRADE COMMISSION'S
TOP TWELVE SPAM SCAMS

12. Vacation Prize Promotions—These e-mail "Prize Promotions" tell consumers they've been selected to receive a "luxury" vacation at a bargain-basement price. But the accommodations aren't deluxe and upgrades are expensive.

11. Credit Repair Scams—These scams target consumers with poor credit records. For an up-front fee, they offer to clear up a bad credit record or give you a completely clean credit slate by showing you how to get an Employer Identification Number. "No one can erase a bad credit record if it's accurate and using an Employer Identification Number to set up a new credit identity is against the law," the FTC reports.

10. Guaranteed Loans or Credit, On Easy Terms—Some offer home-equity loans, even if you don't have any equity in your home. Others offer guaranteed, unsecured credit cards, regardless of your credit history. The "loans" turn out to be lists of lending institutions and the credit cards never arrive.

9. Cable Descrambler Kits—For a small initial investment you can buy a cable descrambler kit so you can receive cable without paying the subscription fees. "There are two small problems with these schemes," according to the FTC. "The kits usually don't work and stealing cable service is illegal."

8. Investment Opportunities—These scams may tout outrageously high rates of return with no risk. Glib, resourceful promoters suggest they have high-level financial connections; that they're privy to inside information; or that they guarantee the investment. To close the deal, they may serve up phony statistics, misrepresent the significance of a current event, or stress the unique quality of their offering. But they are not unique. They're just like the other scams.

7. Get Something Free—The lure of valuable, free items—like computers or long-distance phone cards—gets consumers to pay membership fees to sign up with these scams. After they pay the fee, consumers learn that they don't qualify for the "free" gift until they recruit other "members." "These scams are just low down, high tech pyramid schemes," according to the FTC.

6. Health And Diet Scams—These offer "scientific breakthroughs," "miraculous cures," "exclusive products," "secret formulas," and "ancient ingredients." Some come with testimonials from "cured" consumers or endorsements from "famous medical experts" no one's ever heard of. As Americans continue their quest for a 20" waist, these scams will undoubtedly flourish.

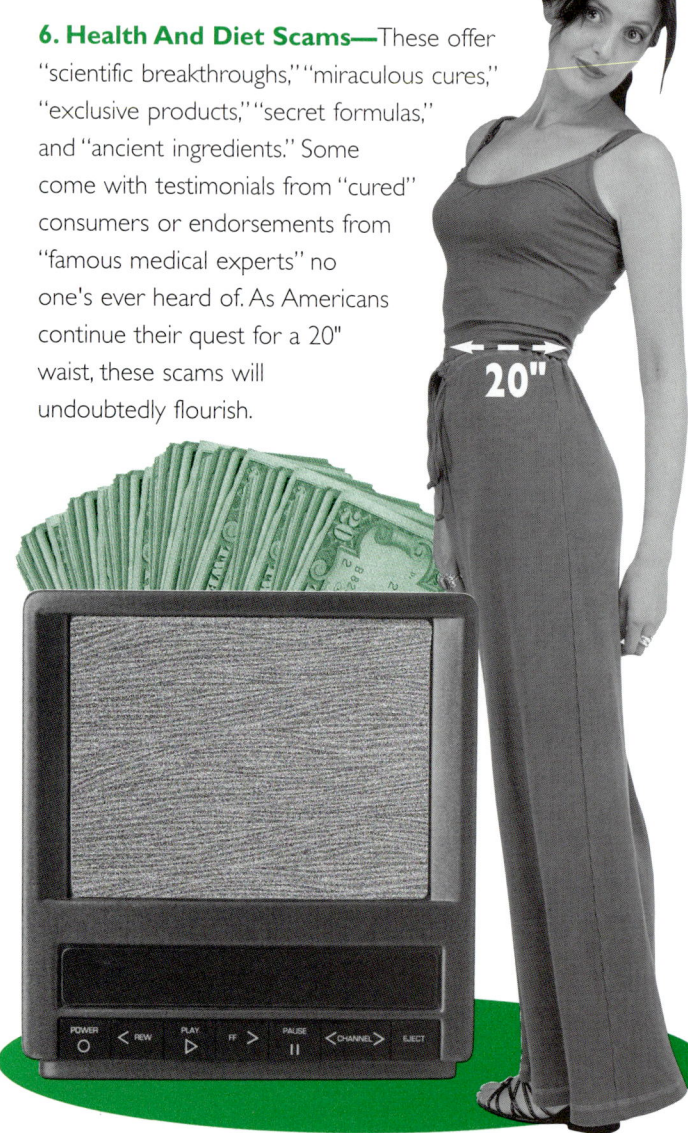

CHAPTER 8: FRAUDS & SCAMS

5. Easy Money—Offers such as "Learn how to make $4,000 in one day," or "Make unlimited profits exchanging money on world currency markets," appeal to the desire to "Get-Rich-Quick." "If making money was that easy, we'd all be millionaires," says an FTC official.

4. Work-At-Home Schemes—E-mail messages offer the chance to earn money in the comfort of your own home. Two popular versions pitch envelope stuffing and craft assembly. But nobody will really pay you for stuffing envelopes and craft assembly promoters usually refuse to buy the crafts claiming the work does not meet their "quality standards."

3. Chain Letters—These electronic versions of the old fashioned chain letters usually arrive with claims like, "You are about to make $50,000 in less than 90 days!" "But you don't," reports the FTC, "and these electronic chain letters are every bit as illegal as the old fashioned paper versions."

2. Making Money By Sending Bulk E-Mailings—These schemes claim that you can make money sending your own solicitations via bulk e-mail. They offer to sell you lists of e-mail addresses or software to allow you to make the mailings. What they don't mention is that the lists are of poor quality; sending bulk e-mail violates the terms of service of most Internet service providers; virtually no legitimate businesses engage in bulk e-mailings; and several states have laws regulating the sending of bulk e-mail.

1. Business Opportunity Scams—Most of these scams promise a lot of income for a small investment of time and money. Some are actually old fashioned pyramid schemes camouflaged to look like something else. "Consumers should be careful of money-making schemes that sound too good to be true," the FTC reports. "They usually are."

OFF-SHORE FRAUDS

One benefit of the Internet is that it has broken down barriers between countries. E-mails can zip from here to there, regardless of language, time zones, or currency rates. Naturally, cyber scammers have realized this fact and, of course, turned it to their advantage. With no international barriers, it's easier to defraud unsuspecting U. S. residents. Sometimes it is just another multi-cultural millionaire offering one and all the benefit of their wisdom by helping you invest your money "their" way. Sometimes it is just a credit card bilk. Not only is it difficult for U. S. law enforcement agencies to investigate the source behind foreign frauds, but it's twice as difficult to prosecute them as well. Even a porno scam:

A guy named David bought into an adult site with a one week trial for $5, after which he could cancel at any time. He received a cancellation notice, but the scammers kept right on charging his Visa. The company's Webmaster e-mail bounced when he tried to cancel, and the phone number in Monrovia was always busy. He disputed the Visa charges, but the company hit him with three more bogus charges.

CHAPTER 8: FRAUDS & SCAMS

PYRAMID POWER

Working from home, of course, is an American (pipe) dream shared by millions of hard-working people across the country. Visions of sipping endless cups of coffee and padding around in your fuzzy, blue slippers all day make us all smile as we stare at our cubicle walls waiting for our precious lunch hour. Naturally, offers to "make thousands from your home computer," lure unsuspecting suckers each and every day. What the cyber scammers making such outrageous offers don't tell you, however, is that it takes a hefty "start-up" fee to set up your "home office suite." And, once you pay your start-up fee, your only job requirement is to recruit other unsuspecting "victims" to join your con-man's company. At which time, of course, you get a small percentage of *their* start-up fee, and so on and so on. Of course, this is the techno version of the age-old "pyramid scheme." It never worked without a computer, what makes you think it'll work with one?

The FTC reports that The Providence Foundation Fund, based in St. George, Utah, set up shop online, selling travel packages (a bundle of discount coupons that cost $500, plus a $40 administration fee.) The easy money would roll in, the online ads promised, when you recruited other people to sell the travel packages. You would earn a portion of those people's commissions.

Investigators say this type of business is also known as multi-level marketing or a "downline club," which refers to the people you recruit as your "downline." Here's some of what the ads promised: "Is It Possible to Make a Fortune Buying and/or Selling Vacation Packages? YOU BET IT IS !!!!! By Showing Others Your Success, You Will Introduce Them and Earn an Additional $20,000 per Person. Turn $500 into your Dream Income!" At first, the Providence Foundation Fund did pay out some good-sized commissions. But then the money stopped flowing, according to a state investigator.

Consumer complaints came pouring in, says Ron Barton, a criminal investigator in the Utah Attorney General's office. The Utah Division of Consumer Protection produced a cease and desist order alleging that Providence was acting as an illegal pyramid scheme, Barton says. The Attorney General's Office seized the company's records and computers, which are being examined as part of an ongoing civil investigation by the Attorney General. The company has not yet been charged with anything.

"There are a whole bunch of pyramid schemes on the 'Net," Barton says. "The people are going from one scheme to another, one location to another." The companies advertise heavily on the Web; in newsgroups such as alt.business, alt.business multi-level, alt.business general; in help-wanted and work-at-home online areas; and in online classified ads.

CHAPTER 8: FRAUDS & SCAMS

THE BUZZ ON FINANCE

October 13, 1999

CYBERSCAM!

Teen Used 'Treks' of the Trade

A Long Island teen cyberscammer who stole $50,000 from online auction bidders was inspired by the ruthless principles of alien businessmen on a *Star Trek* TV series.

When cops in Huntington Station raided a 17-year-old's room, they found hundreds of wadded bills lying on the floor, and posters on the walls detailing the duplicitous "Ferengi Rules of Acquisition."

The Ferengi, space aliens on the *Star Trek* series *Deep Space Nine*, hold business as their religion.

Their take-no-prisoners rules include: "Laws are made to be broken, especially by businessmen"; "Never ask, when you can take"; "When in doubt, LIE"; "More is good, ALL is better"; and "Businessmen are predators, customers are prey."

Investigators said the teen followed the bizarre Ferengi code in carrying out his cyberscheme.

A detective said the parents of the teen "didn't fully understand what was going on."

"The parents just didn't go [into their son's room]. They felt something was amiss but it just didn't click," said the detective. "I basically feel they weren't paying attention.

"There were posted signs all around, about how [their] son feels, morally, about doing business. The signs were there."

"There was a lot of money, a lot of crumpled money lying everywhere."

Police said the teen had even posted a "projected" earnings chart that showed he was way ahead of scheduled profits—raking in more than $50,000 in just two months.

Police said the teen began his scheme on the eBay Web site, e-mailing losing bidders on software auctions to offer them the same products at much lower prices.

Hundreds of people—some as far away as Japan—responded by sending checks and money orders to a Huntington Station post-office box. But the teen never sent them the software, police said.

The teen was arrested and hit with a felony charge of scheming to defraud, which carries a penalty of up to four years in prison.

"It's one of those things kids do to mess up their parents," said a neighbor.

"The computer was a good idea at first, but nobody knew where it was going to go. Just like the atom bomb."

CHAPTER 8: FRAUDS & SCAMS — 134

FINANCE DIARIES

SCAM$

Bill's birthday was coming up, and Marie wanted to surprise him. The only trouble was, she had absolutely no time. In fact, she had less than no time. Further, she was well into the negative hours, as far as time management was concerned. Promotions, dismissals, hirings, firings, and numerous leaves of absence had turned her once orderly company into a quagmire of empty cubicles and pressing commitments. She'd been working overtime on her double-time, and there was just no room in her compact schedule to fit a quick trip to the mall for a new CD from Bill's favorite alternative band or a new hardcover tome from his favorite alternative author.

And so, with no time to spare and even less patience to spare, Marie did what every hot-blooded, modern American female would do when faced with the same exact situation: She got on the Internet. Searching high and low for something, anything, anything at all, that would excite, surprise, or please her down-on-his-luck boyfriend, she sped through search engines, leapt around fire walls without a sound, and deflected spams and bulk e-mails without flinching.

She looked for Dilbert T-shirts and supermodel calendars, considered those kooky beer bong baseball caps and even a lifetime membership to the Hooters of the Month Club. But those were things any old girlfriend would get any old boyfriend. She wanted to get her guy something special, something unique, something that would signify her undying love and passion for—

Wait! There it was, right there in that bright blue and underlined hyperlink on the fourteenth page of her fifteenth keyword search: Yoo Hoo for Yahoos. The fan club for chocolate drink drinkers around the globe. Hats, T-shirts, posters, stickers, and even special Yoo Hoo coolers for individual bottles or six packs, were all hers for the taking.

Marie couldn't believe her good fortune, but thought that the regular yellow and blue Yoo Hoo label she was so used to seeing day in and day out on Bill's favorite drink of choice looked kind of funny on the fuzzy laptop monitor. Or perhaps it was just the bad lighting in their den. Maybe he should get his colors fixed or something. Why, those shades looked downright orange and green, the way she was seeing them.

Oh, well, no matter. She whipped out her trusty credit card, keyed in her information, and clicked on the box marked "special delivery." Now all she had to do was sit back and wait for that 2-4 day express delivery to bring a boat load full of Yoo Hoo for Yahoos products right to her door. Hopefully it would come while Bill was slaving away over yet another revision of his ever-evolving resume. What a surprise that would be!

She felt good that night as she brushed her teeth before bed. She didn't know what all the hubbub about Internet e-commerce was about. The scams and rip-offs, the tricksters and grifters lurking along the information superhighway for hapless hackers to cross their paths and get taken. She had found that Internet shopping was quite the opposite: It was so convenient, so easy. What could go wrong?

Several days later, rushing up the stairs with an arm full of mail and eager to see what Bill had whipped up for dinner (how spoiled she had become), she was surprised to see Bill sitting in the

CHAPTER 8: FRAUDS & SCAMS

middle of the floor guffawing over a box full of orange and green colored, well, crap. Yes, for lack of a better word, it was crap.

"What's that junk?" asked Marie as she sniffed pointedly for a nice, warm dinner that was nowhere to be seen. Or eaten, for that matter. "And what's for dinner?"

"Oh, sorry hon," sighed Bill, trying to piece together a green and orange cooler that looked like it was made out of badly formed Legos. "I've been trying to figure out who would be so inconsiderate as to send me such a wasteful gag gift, I guess I just never got around to whipping up dinner after my latest interview. Sorry."

Grumbling her way into the kitchen, Marie also was wondering who would send such a thoughtless gift. Especially just in time for dinner! Looking closely at Bill and his gag gift scattered hither and yon across their beige living room carpet, Marie tried to figure out the barely indecipherable words on a blearily printed poster: Yaga? Yogo? Yoko Ono? Yahoo?

Yoo Hoo?

Oh no. It couldn't be. It just couldn't. But it was. It *was* her. It was *her*. She was the one who had sent the gag gift, only, for $49.99 (plus shipping and handling) the Yoo Hoo label should have been a lot more readable and Bill should have been a lot more happy! Munching on a cup of yogurt to stave off her impending low blood sugar attack, Marie slowly wound her way around the kitchen counter to peer more closely at what Bill was tinkering with.

The Yoo Hoo pennant she had so looked forward to Bill hanging in his very first office (or cubicle, whatever) was at least one-fifteenth the size they had shown on the Web site, and looked about as flimsy as a wet roll of toilet paper. The special-edition Yoo Hoo jeans were small, too, and the letters were barely legible, looking small and insignificant, but downright classy compared to the hideous shade of sherbet orange and neon green of the socks that were included. All of the other products were similarly shoddy, and Marie felt a sinking feeling in her stomach: She'd been had.

Those Internet scams and rip-offs she'd scoffed at so heartily, those hard-drive horror stories she'd pooh-pooh'd, had finally come to her front doorstep. And she'd paid an extra ten bucks to get them there all the sooner!

"What an awful birthday present, Bill," said Marie as she helped him shove the yucky Yoo Hoo rip-off merchandise into an extra-large size garbage bag and place it outside their front door for an early morning pick-up. "Now, before I go out and get you something else you don't want, too, like that clueless cretin did, why don't you tell me exactly what you want this year."

"Sure, babe," gushed Bill, rushing to find pad and paper. "Let me just make a list—"

Marie groaned. Internet be damned, now she had to go to a gosh darn store after all. She only hoped there was enough left on her credit card to buy Bill a second present. In person, this time.

CHAPTER 8: FRAUDS & SCAMS

9
STARTING YOUR OWN BUSINESS,
OR INVESTING IN YOURSELF

There are an estimated eight thousand small businesses starting up every day in the United States alone. Some people are lured by the prospect of freeing themselves from corporate hierarchies and stifling office bureaucracies. ("You can have a new pencil when you turn the old one in!") Or they may have found themselves at a crossroads due to downsizing, layoffs, cosmic boredom, or disability. More people than ever are choosing to strike out on their own and take responsibility for their own financial future. Sometimes they are called entrepreneurs.

This word can be divided into two parts: *entre*, meaning enter; and *preneur*, meaning from the depths of Hades. (Actually it comes form a French word meaning "to undertake.")

Though not readily apparent, there's also an investment angle to starting your own business. Many people who go into business for themselves develop a unique financial focus. They waste little of their time considering other investments. They tend to believe that the best place to put their financial future is not in the hands of a financial planner, or the stock market, or in a mutual fund. It's in their hands. They pour their profits back into the business, believing that's where they'll receive the best return. Hey, it worked for Bill Gates.

CHAPTER 9: STARTING YOUR OWN BUSINESS

WEB EFFECT

Entrepreneurs today have decided advantages over their counterparts from the past. They're aided by a host of new technologies, from computers to cell phones to the Internet, allowing small firms to compete in some arenas against larger, better-financed businesses.

When you read the headlines of success in the Internet economy, it's hard not to have the Web bug bite just a little. Do you have an idea you'd like to put in play as a business? The goods and services available on the Web run from sublime to silly. There's the high-tech kick scooter produced in Massachusetts and sold worldwide on the Web. The company expects to generate $10 million in revenues in 2000, its third year in business. And then there's the cheese swizzle stick. Revenues on this stroke of genius were not available.

High-tech startups in particular lure the adventurous. A group of entrepreneurs in New York City is definitely hooked. They are in the throes of developing a technology that is used with mobile communications devices. It helps users to select information, such as weather reports or sports scores. There is an abundance of competition in the field and for one partner that makes the challenge more exciting, "It's not just enough for us to play well," the partner says. "We have to put points on the board and win the game."

That attitude is necessary when it comes to business competition. It's estimated that some 90 percent of all new businesses will fail within the first few years of operation. The pitfalls they encounter are plentiful. Some will fold from a lack of capital, others will fall prey to the countless vagaries of a volatile market.

But many of those that fail will do so because of simple, old-fashioned bad planning. And while there is probably nothing anyone can do to manage all the risks involved in starting up a business, you can certainly reduce those by doing your homework and knowing by heart everything from potential competitors to the price of long distance service.

HOT STARTUP BUSINESSES

Here are some new business categories that have attracted entrepreneurs in recent months:

1. Online film distribution
2. Niche label clothing
3. Tot tech (high tech toys for kids)
4. Online file storage
5. Match making service
6. Corporate concierge
7. High tech public relations
8. Juice bars
9. Online education
10. Massage service

CHAPTER 9: STARTING YOUR OWN BUSINESS

ARE YOU THE ENTREPRENEURIAL TYPE?

"No" is likely the most frequent word a budding entrepreneur hears. Consider these episodes from business history:

"The concept is interesting and well formed, but in order to earn better than a C, the idea must be feasible."

A professor's assessment of Fred Smith's report proposing an overnight delivery service. He would take the idea and found FedEx.

"We don't tell you how to coach, so don't tell us how to make shoes."

A shoe manufacturer's response to former coach Bill Bowerman, inventor of the waffle-soled sports shoe and co-founder of NIKE.

"This . . . has too many shortcomings to be seriously considered as a means of communication."

Memo about a new invention by Alexander Graham Bell called the telephone.

Because business startups can be disheartening, they're not the route for everyone. This is a fact to face early on. In truth many people are better off with the security provided by a job with an established company, where they do their work, receive a regular paycheck every week, and are granted the health and retirement benefits that give them peace of mind. If you tend toward introspection rather than action, are soft-spoken, value privacy highly, and like things settled, ordered, and precise, your talents and contributions to mankind probably lie outside the startup realm.

But if you're ambitious, aggressive, tenacious, disciplined, strong-willed, hard-working, have a high tolerance for stress and are, in general, nuts, you may be ready to make a serious commitment of time and resources to a long-term project where the rewards may not be immediately apparent or ever materialize. Yes, you may be the right person to start your own business.

Yet another valuable quality in the budding entrepreneur is an energetically innovative and original imagination. Say you were really, really good at making up excuses in school. This is now called imaginative problem solving and/or convincing the customer to buy the thing you're trying to sell, even if it's delivered late.

Since your new enterprise will no doubt face competition in the real world of the unforgiving free market, you must be willing to seek out "imaginative" new ways of getting your product or service out there and made attractive to the public.

Many businesses have been swinging successes because the people who ran them discovered something new in the way they distributed or marketed their goods.

Someone was the first to place men's cologne in men's clothing stores or to sell magazines in the grocery store checkout lane. Maybe they one-upped the competition with "Three Minute Abs." Improvisation can be a key to success. A man who ran a struggling radio station had an advertiser pay him off in electric can openers. Not knowing what to do, he

CHAPTER 9: STARTING YOUR OWN BUSINESS

decided to sell them on the air. To his complete surprise, they were all gone in a matter of minutes. The result: He took the idea and co-founded The Home Shopping Network.

WHAT'S YOUR BUSINESS GONNA BE, EXACTLY?

You may already know exactly the type of business you want to start before you even begin. But it's not that unusual to *not* know. Many people realize first that they want to be their own boss; they thrill at the idea of embarking on a business adventure. Sometimes it takes a few tries. A reporter for a newspaper, who wrote about a variety of businesses, almost couldn't help himself when it came to trying out new business ideas. He learned to play golf and soon was trying to raise money to build a chain of driving ranges. After a few more false starts, he started a TV production company to produce programs about the mistakes people make in business, an area that had inadvertently become his specialty.

On the other hand, a lot of fumbling around for an idea might mean starting your own business isn't for you. A few years ago a lot of people who found themselves jobless would say they wanted to get involved in "desktop publishing." This usually meant they had no idea what they wanted to do.

Often a business will reflect an interest or hobby that you might wish to make more than that. A fanatical amateur chess player may wish to start a chess magazine or an online chess store. Do you find romance fascinating enough to dedicate yourself to creating a successful dating service, one of the hottest online startups? Are you already involved in designing a better bicycle?

Meshing personal interests, talents, and your business may prove a winning combination. A chess fanatic will not tire easily of writing about chess or cataloguing chess products. It will also keep you involved in something you truly care about, and will enable you to relate to your customers.

Such considerations may seem like asides, but in fact may be the key to your small business becoming an enduring success. You'll believe in your product or service and will therefore be better able to get other people to believe in it with you.

CHAPTER 9: STARTING YOUR OWN BUSINESS — 160

But your ideal business may not be the right one for competitive reasons. A person inquired in a business advice chatroom about wanting to start an Internet advertising company that would specialize in coupons for rebates or other perks to customers.

The hard facts were that some large companies had already weighed into the market and lined up thousands of national and regional retailers. And other large direct-marketing companies seemed poised to enter the competition. "Every single direct-mail company, direct-response firm, and couponing firm is out there trying to figure out what to do online," said one expert.

But that didn't mean the field was totally closed. Another site was enjoying success with coupons, but it had started out as a place where college kids could go to play games and find spring break vacation packages. The site owner got so many hits he attracted coupons on his site from companies like American Airlines. "He was making about $30,000 a month in ad income before he knew it," the expert said.

THE BUSINESS PLAN

Though you may be eager to start your business, you will be much better off if you think through your business idea from A to Z and back again and again and again. Write down your thoughts in a detailed and organized fashion, for it could provide entertainment years later when you see how far off the mark you were.

Writing does force you to clarify your thought, and enables you to review it objectively. Your business must make sense to the outside world, though it may begin in your dreams. Make sure also that your plan is detailed and as specific as possible. Far from restricting you to choices that may later appear incorrect, such discipline will allow you to make adjustments while your business moves from theory to reality.

And remember that some plans start out to be one thing and then morph unexpectedly.

A company called AllApartments in San Francisco had started in the late 1990s as a simple online listing of apartment rentals available in the United States. A couple of years later, the business changed its name to SpringStreet. It reflected a dramatic turn of fortune for the Web site company. It still lists apartments and sells ads on its site, but it has developed new sources of revenue.

CHAPTER 9: STARTING YOUR OWN BUSINESS

The company quotes prices on furniture, insurance, and moving-truck rentals—all for free to its customers and often at very low rates. The added revenue comes from collecting transaction and commission fees from about 35 partners, including Visa and Ryder Moving Services. Every time a consumer requests a car insurance quote or applies for a credit card, SpringStreet gets a fee that starts at $4. "We want to provide people with free services and save them money," says Sophia Kabler, SpringStreet's vice-president of marketing. "The good part is, we make money off of all that." SpringStreet expects the new fees to account for nearly 50 percent of revenues in 2000.

In other words, the company's original business plan didn't anticipate the new revenue it tapped into, but the success of the foundation it laid really did pay off.

"You try to think of everything, but you don't," says one businessman who ran through a dozen failed businesses before hitting on one that worked. "You find you test your ideas as you plan. But with a solid plan you can solve a lot of your problems before you ever open your doors. Then when something unexpected happens, good or bad, you're ready to seize the day."

The first thing to consider is the basic idea or your "business concept." Be very, very specific. Remember, you can change it later as your resources and investigations into your prospective market suggest. And note how these details enable you to develop your plan further: What you are selling may differ substantially if you figure your customers will be hipsters with tattoos or househusbands getting used to a non-traditional domestic routine.

Also, remember that if you are using the Web as a way to deliver information or sell your product, some specialized rules can apply.

Almost everyone agrees that the Internet is a revolutionary business tool. Yet few have been able to make money from it. As one Harvard professor phrased it, "The online world (is) a virtual theme park where most rides are free."

That means that for most content sites, revenues come from advertising, partnerships, and the sale of goods and services that are related—sometimes only peripherally—to the primary focus of the site. For most young companies, those sources aren't sufficient to cover costs—especially given the expensive marketing they must do to rise above the masses of similar sites.

And charging a fee for information is probably not going to work, unless your information is so controlled and proprietary that your site visitors absolutely cannot get it anywhere else. Even so, "you'll be putting people off by charging them at the front gate," says an

CHAPTER 9: STARTING YOUR OWN BUSINESS — 162

Internet expert in Los Angeles. "It's much better business to give some information out freely, so that people will come back to your site and perhaps upgrade and choose to pay for additional content if they need it further."

As people struggle to build the dominant Internet business model, they may face the deflating realization that (Internet company stock values aside) e-commerce is just another kind of business. Says the Harvard professor, "As with businesses that have come before it, there are countless 'right' answers. There will be no magic bullet."

Other things that should go into your business plan include:

Equipment: What equipment will you need to keep track of your business as a business (spreadsheet programs, file cabinets, and folders, etc.), and what equipment will you need for the particular type of business you are starting (special tires for your "superbike"?).

Personnel: Will you be able to do all the work yourself or will you need help? What type of help? Part-time or full-time employees? Or will you contract out parts of your business and which parts will you do yourself?

Marketing: How will you market your product and to whom? Will you want to place advertisements in local papers and how much do these cost? How will you get your Web page noticed on the Internet? How will you characterize your product? Should you hire an advertising agency or a public relations consultant? Would you feel better using the services of a professional salesman, or can you do sales yourself? What other services might you require? Will you need to consult an attorney? An accountant?

CHAPTER 9: STARTING YOUR OWN BUSINESS

Finances: How much will each aspect of your business plan cost? How much do you need to get started? Do a little research, make some phone calls, and write down a list of figures. What do you expect to make in profits? What do you need to make in profits to stay afloat? (Remember that you will have to pay taxes and make payments on a loan if you've borrowed money.) What do you hope to make in profits a year down the line? Two years? Five? Are these expectations realistic?

Obviously, you may not be able to answer all these questions, but by using such questions to pin down what you are doing and why, you will get a clear and practically useful picture of what you do need to know and what to do next. Discouraged yet?

BUSINESS AT HOME

A vast number of today's small businesses are started at home. Houses and apartments across the country are doubling as office space for a generation of savvy entrepreneurs for whom location is not as important as saving money by not renting office space. The advantages of running your business out of your home are many and easy to understand. There's no beating the five second, gas-free commute from bedroom to boardroom, and you may not be able to afford the luxury of a separate work place at first, or really have much use for it. The downside is that you

TOP 10
HOME BASED STARTUPS

10 MARKETING SERVICES

9 TRUCKING

8 CRAFTS

7 PAINTING

6 REAL ESTATE

5 CLEANING SERVICES

4 BUSINESS CONSULTING

3 COMPUTER SERVICES

2 CONSTRUCTION

1 GENERAL CONTRACTING

(Source: County Data Corp./The Lead Sheet.)

(Conspicuously absent from the home-business rankings are the number one and number six most frequently started businesses in the country: miscellaneous retail stores and restaurants, neither of which function well in one's living room.)

CHAPTER 9: STARTING YOUR OWN BUSINESS — 164

also are only a step away from the kitchen and can add 30 extra pounds before you know it.

In truth, location is less important today in the wake of the Internet revolution. And it will be much easier to schedule the very long hours you'll need, at least initially, to put into your business, without making undue sacrifices in other important activities in your life. It will be easier as well to pace yourself, and to take breaks when you need a little fresh air or time to think through your next move, especially in the earliest stages.

Almost everybody has a trick they rely on. A man in Tucson, Arizona, would always make sure he had an hour for lunch and would purposely spend it alone. He used the time for what he called "free thinking," and he routinely came up with his best ideas. For others, nothing clears the head better than a quick walk around the block. Do whatever works for you, because dealing with the amorphous problems a small business encounters takes a good deal of head clearing.

There are drawbacks to consider with using the home for your business. You may be uncomfortable blurring the line so completely between your personal, day-to-day life and the part of you that is dedicated to making money, and between your business and your social activities. One independent ad salesman in Maryland would set a routine at his home office that was as regimented as any workplace. He entered his office at precisely 9 a.m. each morning, always dressed in a suit and tie, no matter whether he would ever leave the house that day or not.

165 — CHAPTER 9: STARTING YOUR OWN BUSINESS

However, if you have to meet with potential clients, you will need to use your home to do so if you do not have an office. It's hard for people to take a business seriously that is run out of your house, especially if you're a slob. If you have to stay at home because of a tight budget, get used to relative strangers viewing your living quarters.

Another problem is that using the home for business may simply prove too distracting. You may be tempted to spend too much time on break, watching television, playing computer games, or talking on the phone to relentless friends and family members, letting the business you've invested in suffer. You may get lonely, too, and miss those mindless water cooler conversations and bathroom gossip sessions that gave color to your workday.

Or your home may simply not be roomy enough to accommodate the equipment and storage you'll need for your business, whether it be merely a computer and filing cabinet, or a massage table, or a media outlet's worth of video, photography, and printing equipment.

AN OFFICE OF YOUR OWN

If this is the case, then you will probably have to rent some kind of office space. If you do so, the most important thing you'll need to consider is how important location is to your business, either for prestige or easy access to business services and clients.

CHAPTER 9: STARTING YOUR OWN BUSINESS

How much you should invest in getting the best possible location for yourself (the better the address, the pricier), and, just as when figuring out how to set up a business in your home, how much space will you need?

The place to start is by making a list of things you know you will require—a computer, a desk, a cabinet, chairs, a copier—and then use graph paper to map out your office for yourself, and see how many square feet you'll need to perform the operations necessary in your business without undue discomfort. Then start shopping around, and see what's available, and what might be made to fit your particular needs.

Tip: There are realtors who specialize in small commercial spaces. They are there for people like you. Check the yellow pages, and contact more than one.

EQUIPMENT

The equipment needed for any business will depend on what you're up to, but if it's heavily computer-oriented, take comfort that the longer you wait, the cheaper the equipment becomes (usually). If your endeavor is a little less high tech, you still need to

TOP-10
SIGNS YOUR COMPUTER HAS A VIRUS

10 Every time you double-click something, a message box asks, "Is that your final answer?"

9 Your motherboard keeps making chicken soup.

8 Every time you hit the delete key, a naked photo of Shelley Winters pops up.

7 Mucus is dripping out of the disk drive.

6 Before ejecting the CD, it makes a disgusting hocking noise.

5 It's having a helluva time getting a referral from the HMO's primary care tech support guy.

4 Your screen saver now shows Pamela Anderson at home with the flu.

3 Dell customer service recommends the "nighttime, freezing, rebooting up-locking, destroying, hosed-drive, deleted so you can buy a new PC medicine."

2 Your dancing hamsters are all dead.

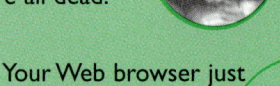

1 Your Web browser just tossed its cookies.

[Courtesy of The Top 5 List: www.topfive.com]

CHAPTER 9: STARTING YOUR OWN BUSINESS

plan and shop around. Your attention to detail at this stage will tell you something about your ability to focus with your financial future on the line.

Computers

You will need a computer of some kind, probably not just a laptop but a full personal computer with keyboard, screen, printer, and modem, along with a word processor for correspondence and memos, a spreadsheet program for doing your accounts, and perhaps a graphics program to help you design flyers, mailings, and advertising (most computers will come pre-equipped with these items and more).

How powerful a computer will depend on what you will need it to do. A fast machine may run you between $2,000-$3,000. You will also need to consider whether you want a separate phone line to use solely for Internet access or even a cable (like a television cable) for the latest in high-speed Internet access. There are pluses and minuses to these choices, including whether you need your own server and how it might function. Because so many vendors are entering the access market, there are literally dozens of deals you can make, and they can be both ill-suited to your needs and expensive. Remember that you are dealing with salespeople and demand that technical expertise be made available so you can understand what you're buying.

Phones

E-mail has taken much of the business communication burden from telephones and letters, but you can still expect to spend a substantial amount of time on the phone. Customer questions and complaints will require a prompt response.

If you want to get phone calls while on the move, you should consider a cell phone, or, minimally, a beeper, which will buzz or shake when you get a call and allow callers to display their numbers so you can call them back at your convenience.

Tip: A good way of enticing customers to make that all-important first call to your business may be setting up your own toll-free 800 number.

More Stuff!

Other things to consider are a fax machine, which helps when you need to meet strict deadlines, especially on a regular basis; a scanner, which will greatly increase your computer's graphics potential by letting you transfer images (and documents) directly into a computer file; and a small copier.

Tip: Business equipment (computers included) can be leased. This reduces start-up costs but leasing is always more expensive than buying.

CHAPTER 9: STARTING YOUR OWN BUSINESS

FINANCING YOUR BUSINESS

They say it takes money to make money, and like all such sayings, they get it about half right. It is best when starting a new business to use your own savings, rather than borrow money and add debt to your burdens.

And starting on a shoestring is not necessarily the worst way to go. In fact, the survival rate for businesses that start up with little capital is actually higher than those with more money available, partly because it forces the novice entrepreneur not to expand too quickly or set his or her sights too high at the outset. If you don't have much money, you avoid investing in mistakes that will be avoidable only with experience.

Also, it forces the novice entrepreneur to keep down overhead costs and to rely on the kind of can-do, make-shift spirit common to many of the world's most successful businesspeople.

Be that as it may, few if any businesses can be started without at least some money. Here are some of the choices:

Keep Your Day Job

Sorry for this perhaps deflating advice, but if you already have a good full-time job, keep it, even if it's at Toys "Я" Us. This may be the best way of financing yourself as you assert your independence to become your own full-time boss. You may have to start your own business slower than you otherwise might, and work at it initially only twenty rather than say forty or more hours a week. This may not only keep you from going into debt (or at least cut down on your debt) but it will help you in other ways as well, especially if the job you work has substantial benefits, like health insurance, not to mention a regular paycheck, so you know the rent or mortgage will still get paid, plus food will continue to grace your dinner table in the evening.

The drawback with keeping a full-time job is that it may compromise your new business, which admittedly may have a better chance of success if you can give it your full and undivided attention for those first few start-up weeks. If this is the case, you may want to use up your vacation time if you have any, or, finally, you may decide that the old job, for whatever reason, is simply not worth keeping with better prospects before you.

169 — CHAPTER 9: STARTING YOUR OWN BUSINESS

Friends and Family

Friends and family may be good for something other than long distance discounts. They could be a source of ready cash, if they have some and you can convince them to turn it over. Maybe they owe you a favor, whatever. The downside: You're known forever at holidays as the bum who didn't pay them back.

Banks

For a business loan from a bank, what you want is a commercial rather than a savings bank. Many bankers will, of course, be reluctant to simply hand over a large sum of money to someone who walks in off the street with an untested idea and no track record of successful business ventures to point to for reassurance. They may be simply unwilling to lend you money, period, at least at first. But don't take this personally. Ask them why, exactly, and what they need. And shop around. Some commercial lenders may be more amenable to your needs than others. What they will want to know is when they will get their money back, with interest. They will want to examine your personal credit history, and they will want collateral, stocks, bonds, and valuable assets, to have something to take from you should you fail to pay the loan back.

If you take this route, be sure to examine different loan options, balloon loans, working capital loans, lines of credit, etc., and decide which is best for you and your business. Also: Ask your commercial lender if they have any support in place for new businesses, like counseling, legal advice, etc. Some banks do provide these services, others you'll hear from precisely once a month: When you get their bill in your mailbox.

If you don't like the terms given for business loans from banks, or fail to get approval, there are some other places you might try. Check out, for starters, the Small

TOP-10 REASONS FOR BEING FIRED FROM TOYS "Я"US

10 A little too much joie de vivre while demonstrating the erector set, if you know what we mean.

9 Every time you're passed over for a promotion, you stick your head in an Easy Bake Oven and threaten to "end it all."

8 You got caught adding a garage to your house using embezzled Lego bricks.

7 Numerous parental complaints about your "Tickle Me Carl The Stockboy" display.

6 Cross-dressing the Ken and Barbie dolls and telling kids they're the new "Jerry Springer" edition.

5 The "My Little Taxidermy Kit" (with starter squirrel) is not selling.

4 Impromptu demonstrations of why Malibu Ken is not anatomically correct.

3 Got caught doing your Dolly Parton impression with basketballs again.

2 Your sales display, "Barbie's Struggle for Survival in Post-Nuclear Fallout Malibu" was not exactly an overwhelming success.

1 Regardless of the question, you answer, "Bite me, kid—I "Я" on break."

[Courtesy of The Top 5 List: www.topfive.com]

CHAPTER 9: STARTING YOUR OWN BUSINESS

Business Administration's Web site (www.sba.gov). This government office is there for people like yourself, and besides being a good source of technical information and advice, they do also help certain small businesses secure loans. They also have a group of investors called Angels with whom they match beginning entrepreneurs, kind of a venture capital deal for the novice set. (Venture capitalists may be people you'd want to get in touch with later, when your business is already established and needs money for expansion and growth.)

Grants and Awards

Look into government grants and foundation awards. There are such things out there, free money from institutions public and private that wish to support initiative and economic growth. The library should have books cataloguing places to which you might apply.

Many such grants and awards are either given to already established businesses that have a social mission attached to them, such as educating inner city youth or health care, or will, at the very least, be very specific about what type of businesses have the qualities they are interested in promoting. If such grants or awards are appropriate to your situation, remember also that there is a lot of competition out there, and the best way to get yourself some attention is to write up an interesting enough and convincing enough grant proposal (writing grant proposals is so important, in fact, that it has emerged as something of a profession unto itself).

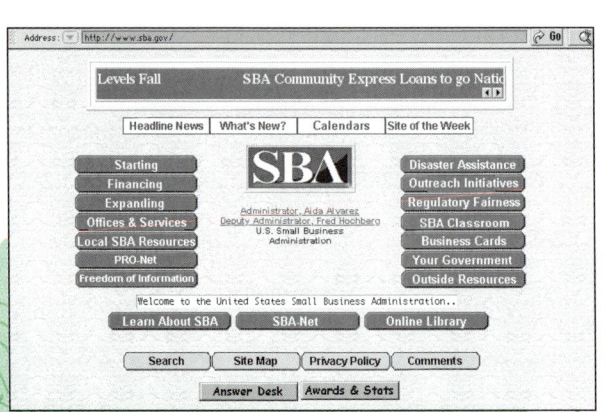

Other Loan Sources

You can also take loans out on your home (a home equity loan), life insurance policy, or retirement fund. As always, make sure to read the fine print and understand the risks involved before you sign on the dotted line. If you do take a loan out on your home, for example, you are putting your home at risk, and this may be more than you bargained for (then again, maybe not).

Personal Loans and Credit Cards

You may want to try getting a personal loan if you can't get a business loan, or simply sign up for a bunch of credit cards. Some people have been successful using these desperate measures, but the terms of such loans carry high-interest rates, so this is more of a last resort than anywhere near a reasonable way to finance your business venture.

Partnerships and Investors

If you are at the point where maxing out your credit cards seems the only solution, you might stop to consider taking on a partner instead, or enticing one or more people to invest in your business. These are good ways of increasing your capital and getting your business safely up and running. A partner might help you in a variety of ways, including increasing resources (space, for example, if your partner has a garage to store stuff in; or equipment, if your

CHAPTER 9: STARTING YOUR OWN BUSINESS

partner has a super computer; or know-how, if your partner already knows more about business than you or is more Internet savvy than you are). Another head to help make crucial decisions, all in exchange for an interest in the business itself, may be worth it. If you do take on a partner (or partners), it will be important to specify ahead of time (and draw up a contract to this effect), what the various contributions and roles will be, who will have the final say on what issues, and what the percentage of ownership will be, so as to avoid unnecessary and debilitating conflicts once the business is begun.

Nothing will split partners faster than profits.

Investors are not looking to help you run your business as they are to share in the wealth you presumably will be creating. They are looking to get more money out, substantially more, than they put in. They will give you a sum of money for a percentage of ownership. They'll want to be convinced that your business is a great idea and will be successful.

The big plus concerning investors (and partners) is that accepting their money is qualitatively different than accepting a loan from a bank. There is no collateral, there are no monthly payments. The investor or partner only wins if you yourself win, and loses along with you if you lose, as opposed to the bank, which may add insult to injury by repossessing your house or car after your business venture has gone belly-up.

To find investors or partners, what you may want to do is simply ask around. Office colleagues may want to try something new as much as you do and be happy to help build the widget you've had the initiative to design. Or they may know someone who does. Friends and family, again, might be more comfortable with helping you out (and you may be more comfortable with letting them) if that help is given such objective status as "investment" or "partnership." Lastly, you might just try putting an ad in the newspaper.

Tip: If none of the above solutions seem to fit the bill by itself, try a combination of two or three, a partner, an investor, a business loan, some of your own savings, as necessary and as they become available.

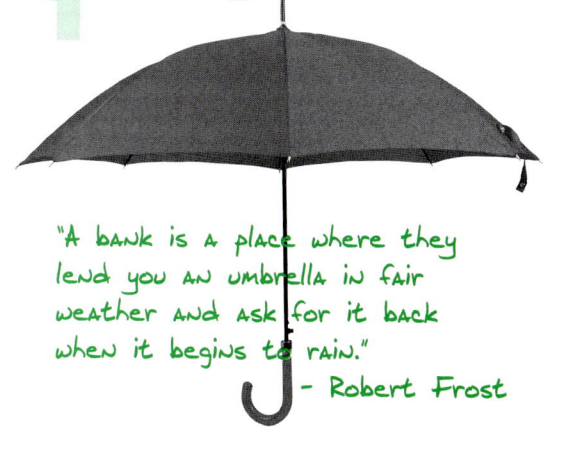

"A bank is a place where they lend you an umbrella in fair weather and ask for it back when it begins to rain."
— Robert Frost

CHAPTER 9: STARTING YOUR OWN BUSINESS

FINANCE DIARIES

BUSINESS CENTS
(OR, RISK & REWARD, INC.)

Being home (a lot) more than Marie, Bill had (a lot of) time to think. He thought about his future, thought about his past, thought about himself and Marie, but mostly he thought about his work situation. (Or lack of one.) Despite what he told Marie (that no one ever offered him a job), he had actually been offered several employment opportunities. However, they were either go nowhere, nothing jobs, or awesome jobs that paid peanuts.

He wasn't a proud guy, and he knew that his freeloader status wasn't exactly helping the situation with their combined finances, but he watched Marie sail off to work each morning, eager to start her day. Ready to de-bug or de-program or bug or program or whatever it was that she did all day. Naturally, she would have preferred to have been independently wealthy, but, barring that, she was doing what she went to school for, she was doing what she loved, and she was getting paid well to do it.

And that's what Bill wanted. He didn't want to start out in retail and wait for something better to come along. He didn't want to go back to school and get yet another degree he wouldn't be able to use. He didn't want to settle, yet he was eager to get started in the business world and make his mark. With the emphasis on *his*.

And so, seated with Scully around yet another coffee shop table, surrounded by crumpled sugar packets and steaming mugs of joe, Bill was discussing his financial frustrations when his friend pointed out the obvious: "Why don't you just start your own business?"

At first, Bill scoffed. Yeah, right, he grumbled. Oh, sure, he pooh-poohed. But as the morning wore on into the afternoon, he found himself believing Scully's confidence in him. After all, Bill had a great degree. Plenty of industry experience through his double internships, and practical experience in the real world workforce, thanks to good, old Scully.

CHAPTER 9: STARTING YOUR OWN BUSINESS

Why couldn't he start his own business? After all, he could simply run it out of the guest bedroom. All he'd need was a fax machine, a better computer, the Internet, e-mail, a separate business phone line, some fancy stationary, oh, and business cards. Of course, he'd have to register an Inc. or a Co. name, which would probably take some hefty legal fees, there would be the ad in the yellow pages, possibly the newspaper, and, of course, it might take a few months of overdue bills before he ever landed his first client.

"Where would I get the money?" grumbled Bill, signaling the friendly waitress for a free refill. "It costs tons to start a new business."

"That's what banks are for, my friend," said Scully enthusiastically, as if Bill was Donald Trump with a line of credit as long as the Atlantic City coastline. "They're practically begging to give tech guys like you money these days."

"Yeah, but that's for Web sites and stuff," Bill explained. "I'm just a lowly freelance programmer. No job, no savings, no collateral. I'd never get a loan." Scully was silent in the face of his friend's predicament. Then, as if a light bulb had gone off over his greasy forehead, but more than likely it was just another wave of his constant caffeine buzz, Scully's face brightened and he leaned over to whisper his brilliant new plan to his buddy.

"I have this friend," murmured Scully. "He plays the market."

"What?" asked Bill, uncomprehending and still waiting for his coffee refill. "Like—the fish market?"

"No, man," spat Scully. "The stock market. He plays it big. Reads all those financial magazines, checks out the money Web sites, reads the Business section, watches the market round-up on CNN, the whole bit. Anyway, he hears about these hot tips, checks into them, and if they're kosher, he sinks a few thousand bucks into them, buys up as many shares as he can, watches them rise, and rise, and rise, and the minute they start to level out for a day or two, he dumps them and walks away with two, three, sometimes even four to five times what he put into them."

"Yeah, right," scoffed Bill. "I think you've rented *Boiler Room* a few too many times."

"I'm serious, dude," urged Scully. "He's got the golden touch. If you were to work for me for a week, a full week, none of this work two days, take the next five off, I could pay you close to a grand, hook you up with this guy's phone number, and he could give you a hot tip that would quadruple your initial investment and turn it into something usable for your new business.

TOP 5 BUSINESS VENTURES GUARANTEED NOT TO GET A LOAN

5 Crack Heads, Inc.

4 Odor Eaters Brand Frozen Dinners

3 Pee Wee Brand Extra-Small Condoms

2 The Pauly Shore School of Drama

1 Campbell's Chicken Poop

CHAPTER 9: STARTING YOUR OWN BUSINESS — 174

Think about it. We've got a big apartment complex we're doing this week, I could sure use the help."

That night, in bed, Bill could hardly sleep with visions of fax machines and Office Depot credit cards running through his head. All the tossing and turning woke Marie up, and even though Bill had wanted to keep his stock market shenanigans a secret from his better half, the late hour and the excitement pushed it out of him.

When Marie picked her jaw up off of the queen size bed, she scolded Bill for being so unrealistic. "Don't you know the stock market is for suckers and grifters?" she asked. "For every 'guy with the golden touch' like you're friend's friend, there are five thousand suckers who lose every cent they sink into the market. Is that what you want to do? Lose what little money we have on your stock market scheme?"

"But it wouldn't cost us a cent" Bill explained. "I'll work for Scully, make the grand, and it's all gravy. I mean, if I didn't work for Scully and just sat around here reading the want ads, the thousand bucks wouldn't even be an issue."

"Sure," pointed out Marie. "Or, you could be sitting here when the perfect job opportunity came knocking, only you'd be missing it because you were whacking weeds with Spooky Scully."

"Well," spelled out Bill. "Nothing personal, honey, but it's my life and this is just something I have to do. Goodnight."

Marie, impressed with Bill's motivation, could only lie back down and try to sleep. It wasn't easy. Despite her admiration of Bill's gumption, she was still petrified of gaining, then losing, the amount of money he was talking about. She saw visions of Chapter 11 bankruptcy, handcuffs, and long prison terms for trading on insider information. Still, she had to trust Bill. After all, he was her man. For better or worse.

The next morning, Bill put on his battered, grass-stained sneakers and headed out the door before Marie was even awake. For five long days, he trimmed and he toiled, he sweated and weed whacked, and hoped and prayed that he was doing the right thing.

By Friday, he was five pounds lighter and one thousand dollars richer. Scully wrote the "golden boy's" phone number on the back of a LawnsCrafters, Inc. business card, and underneath, a specific time when to call.

"Call this number," warned Scully. "But only at the time it says on the card. That will tell the guy that you are who you say you are. Also, don't say anything. Just call, wait for him to pick up, listen to his tip, and then hang up."

"Wow," said Bill, unimpressed with all of the secrecy. "Should I take a Greyhound bus out of town and use a pay phone too?"

CHAPTER 9: STARTING YOUR OWN BUSINESS

"Would that be too inconvenient?" asked Scully in all seriousness.

Bill laughed and deposited his paycheck before his skittish friend could renege on the deal. That night, at precisely 11:15 p.m., just like it said on the back of Scully's business card, Bill called the mysterious phone number. Then, ten rings later, just as he was about to hang up and go on a thousand dollar CD spending spree, a voice answered the phone and said the following words: "Buy 100 shares of Technicom at 8 1/4 per share tomorrow morning when the market opens. That is all."

Of course, after Bill quit laughing at the "that is all," comment, he wrote down the golden boy's tips and told Marie about it the next morning at breakfast.

"Technicom?" said Marie over the top of her orange juice glass. "Never heard of it."

"That's the point," urged Bill. "If everybody knew about it, it wouldn't be a 'hot' tip. Come on, Marie. Let me do this."

"How, Bill?" asked Marie, thinking that she had suddenly found an out. "You don't even have a broker."

But Bill only smiled. "Scully's got an account over at Ameritrade," he pointed out. "He gets a few free trades if he signs up a new member. All I have to do is give him the go ahead and the savings account number and we're on."

"I don't really feel comfortable about them having our savings account number," said Marie, looking for any excuse to derail Bill's Technicom train.

"Why?" asked Bill. "All it has in it is my check from yesterday. It's not like they can scam us for anything."

"Just a thousand dollars," pointed out Marie. "That's all."

That is all ...

In protest over Marie's protestations, Bill sat silently while she tossed out every fearful argument she could muster: online scams, insider trading, Internet rip-offs, losing a thousand dollars, the whole works. Calmly, quietly, Bill disputed every fear with a rational explanation. He had the fever, and for possibly the first time in his life, had an opportunity to make some real money. Add to that, his theoretical new business venture was hanging in the balance. He understood Marie's concerns, but there was no way he was going to let them derail his vision. If it had been her money, he wouldn't even be considering it. But this was his deal, and he wanted to do it his way.

Eventually, Marie broke down and threw up her hands in mock defeat. She gave him her blessing, and a few more warnings to be careful, on her way out the door to work. Bill called Scully, gave him the information he needed, and then waited until an e-mail confirmation allowed him to make his very own, very first, online stock trade.

After the stocks were purchased, there was nothing to do but wait. He bookmarked the online trading Web site, and checked it throughout the day to see if this "golden boy" knew what he was talking about. Turned out, he did.

The stock rose, in small increments, throughout the afternoon and on through the evening. (Bill set his egg timer and checked it every hour!) By the next day, Bill had made a cool two hundred dollars on his investment. By that evening, it

CHAPTER 9: STARTING YOUR OWN BUSINESS

was up to three hundred. Bill tried to remain calm and keep things in perspective.

"Calm down," he told himself. "Calm down. It'll level off eventually. It can't keep climbing like it is. It just can't."

But it did. Bill's proudest moment in months, possibly years, was blindfolding Marie and leading her into the dimly lit den to show her the personalized growth chart of his earnings with Technicom only a short week later. Why, the cute little Ameritrade graphic looked like something off of an EKG!

It just went up and up and up.

"How much have you made by now, Bill?" she asked, hardly believing her eyes.

"Two thousand dollars," he crowed.

"No," Marie countered. "I mean, how much have you made without your initial investment?"

"I know what you meant, Marie," scolded Bill. "I'm familiar with a few economic terms myself by now. The difference between my 'initial investment' and my 'gross profit' is two thousand dollars. As in, I'm up two grand! For a total investment of three grand."

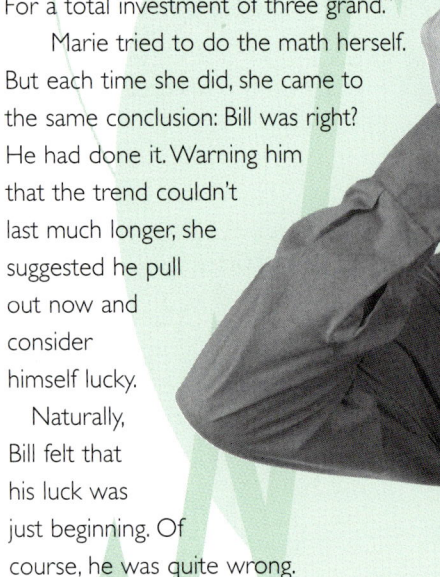

Marie tried to do the math herself. But each time she did, she came to the same conclusion: Bill was right? He had done it. Warning him that the trend couldn't last much longer, she suggested he pull out now and consider himself lucky.

Naturally, Bill felt that his luck was just beginning. Of course, he was quite wrong.

Throughout the week, the golden boy's golden stock continued to perform. Up and up it went, to the point that Bill was no longer considering starting his own business, but simply sitting back and watching his investment grow and grow and grow. Each night, Marie would drift into the den for a status report, and walk away impressed but insecure. She wanted Bill to feel proud of his accomplishments, but she wanted him to see them in perspective. She wasn't sure he could back out now. He'd become quite greedy.

In fact, when the news about a possible merger between two fast-growing telecommunication companies was leaked to the press, one of them being Technicom, the information had a negative effect. The stock plunged a good five points by the close of the market. Marie, practically hyperventilating as she listened to Marketplace on NPR on the way home from work, hoped against hope that Bill would finally wise up and dump the stock by the time she got upstairs. (If only to avoid another Technicom tirade!) But, alas, his greed wouldn't allow him to give up now.

She watched as he sat, slumped in his desk chair in front of his glowing laptop, day after day, night after night, while the stock rose and fell, fell, and fell some more, and finally rose one more time before falling all the way to Bill's "pull-out point."

177 —CHAPTER 9: STARTING YOUR OWN BUSINESS

Like a gambler feeding quarters to a ravenous slot machine that's destined to "hit" at any minute, she watched Bill hold on to Technicom in the vain hope that it would rise like a Phoenix from the ashes and return again to be his proud goose that laid the golden egg.

Marie wanted to scream. She wanted to shout. She wanted to cry. But mainly, she wanted Bill to learn his lesson. Therefore, she started avoiding the den. She simply paid the pizza guy each night, and slipped the skinny box under the door for her boyfriend to have sustenance through his long, dwindling days as a stock watcher.

She waited and waited, and, finally, Bill emerged from the den a broken man. They hugged, and Bill got his first good night's sleep in a week. Marie left him in bed and left for work. She wrote him a sweet note by the coffeemaker, congratulating him on his brief "success," avoiding any talk about his recent failure, and telling him to "hang in there."

"I'd give $1,000 to be a millionaire."

— Lewis Timberlake

She never actually asked him how long he waited before selling off whatever stock he had left, but she knew it must have been too long when he called later that afternoon to check in on her.

Just before hanging up, he asked her a simple question: "Do you think I can start up my allowance again? I'm a little short this week."

Marie smiled despite herself. It was nice to have the old Bill back.

TOP 10 SIGNS YOU'RE "SUFFERING" FROM SUDDEN WEALTH SYNDROME

10 MasterCard calls to find out why all of a sudden you're super-sizing every friggin' meal.

9 Instead of downloading the latest Stephen King novel from the Internet, you hire the author to read it to you. In person. While tap-dancing. In his underwear.

8 You before: Refuse to pay back student loans to "stick it to The Man." You now: The Man.

7 After your recent hospital procedure, you threw a wad of C-notes at the nurse and shouted, "Free enemas for everyone!"

6 George W. Bush slobbers as he kisses your butt.

5 The spectacularly sharp image of Alan Greenspan on your new 200-inch HDTV is obscured by globs of flung-across-the-room caviar.

4 Before: Bought stuff at Old Navy. Now: Bought an old navy.

3 You hire lackeys just to smack around your other lackeys.

2 You can't decide whether the supermodels just love you for your money or whether or not you care.

1 After the 17th Rolex, you decide to purchase a third wrist.

[Courtesy of The Top 5 List: www.topfive.com]

CHAPTER 9: STARTING YOUR OWN BUSINESS

LEGAL MATTERS

As you are probably aware, every aspect of our lives, from birth to marriage to death, is in one way or another regulated by the government, and starting a business is no exception to this rule. Much of the regulations you will have to concern yourself with occur at the state rather than the federal level, and may vary widely not only from one type of business to another, but also for different types of business in different states, so much so that in certain areas you may not be legally allowed to start and run any business out of your home.

To find out what the rules are, you should contact both your local chamber of commerce and the nearest office of the Small Business Administration. You may have to get a license, undergo training, or fulfill certain safety requirements, and such things, because they more than likely will cost money, may play a significant role in your venture, and should serve as footnotes on your business plan and priority items on to-do lists.

The Taxman Cometh

There will also be federal regulations that apply to all businesses, particularly with regard to that much-maligned department of state, the Internal Revenue Service. You will have to pay a tax on whatever profits you make. But remember, there are many incentives built into the wildly complex and ever-changing United States tax code, and much of your start-up costs and even day-to-day operating costs may be used as tax deductions. If you are working from home, for example, a percentage of your rent or mortgage payments may be deducted from your tax. Interest on business loans is also deductible. Depending on your facility with numbers, it may be cost-effective to hire an accountant to make sure you get all the deductions coming to you and that you don't get tripped up by the often tricky task of figuring taxes, which will depend on how you structure your business legally.

Some Legal Business Structures

Ways to legally structure your business include a sole proprietorship, a C corporation, an S corporation, or a limited liability company. A sole proprietorship is the simplest and easiest way to go, and most common for small businesses with a single owner and little or no debt. It is your default status, and will require no professional assistance. If you have partners, then you must use a general partnership. In either of these cases, the business's proprietor(s) can simply file personal tax returns with profits from the business as part of their income, but remain personally liable for any debts incurred by the business.

If you want to separate your business and personal debts, you need to incorporate. If you become a C corporation, you will be taxed twice, as a corporation and as an owner profiting from the corporation. You will only get taxed once, as an owner, however, if you choose to be an S corporation.

Consulting an attorney is probably a good idea for deciding which path you want to take, since for all but sole proprietorship, you will need to use an attorney to get properly set up anyway (although you can do it yourself with a little study and the correct forms).

Limited liability company status is handled at the state level. A limited liability company will be treated as a partnership at tax time, but its owners will be freed from personal liability.

You Must Keep Records!

For tax purposes you will need in any of the above cases to keep careful records of your business dealings, with at minimum a balance sheet and an income statement, in case you are audited. One way to get audited, by the by, is to show no profits over a five year period. This will make the IRS suspect that you are exploiting a hobby as a way of cutting down your tax bill, and they may want to make sure that you really are an unsuccessful-as-yet business owner rather than a scam artist.

What's in a Name?

When you set up your business's legal structure you will also need to name your business, which could be a lot of fun. The name should be memorable and descriptive without being too limiting, since your business may well change over time to include more services/products than originally envisioned. A business can be made by a name that gives it character and enables a successful marketing and advertising strategy. Some names may be taken, which you will learn when you apply to become a business with your state. So have some alternatives in mind.

Insurance

You should probably look into business insurance as well, including insurance against theft, fires, and even lawsuits. Then again, if you are doing this on the seat of your pants,

CHAPTER 9: STARTING YOUR OWN BUSINESS

you might just prefer to go without insurance except that minimum which is legally mandated (if you have employees, for example, you must have unemployment coverage, and certain businesses will require certain types of insurance). If you have an at-home business, you could most simply and cheaply attach what's called a "rider" to your homeowner's insurance.

PAYMENT

The best payment to get from your customers is good old cash money. It doesn't bounce, and it is accepted everywhere, from bank to bistro to bum. Money orders don't bounce either. Checks can be more problematic. They can bounce and they can be forged and sometimes are. If you do accept checks (and it's best to accept as many forms of payment as you can), it is smart to check the signature against the customer's signature on a driver's license or other form of ID, and check the photo on the ID against the face of the customer, with a brief, polite glance, of course.

Credit cards eliminate much of the hassle of receiving payment from customers, for a fee, usually two to five cents on every dollar you receive on credit, a set-up fee, and an equipment rental fee, for the software and modem you'll need to authorize credit cards, all of which makes them a potentially burdensome expense. A small business also may have trouble getting a credit card company's merchant authorization in the first place (small businesses are too high risk and low volume for them to deal with, for the most part). If you can get merchant authorization (hint: try American Express),

there are certain benefits to accepting credit cards. They are used extensively. A bookstore can do more than 60 percent of its business with credit cards. People are often more willing to use credit cards than cash, especially with large purchases, and credit cards make impulse buying seem guilt-free.

And credit card companies guarantee you get paid by taking the debt themselves, so you won't have to worry about collecting fees from recalcitrant customers who take your service or product then are suddenly very difficult to get a hold of. That becomes the MasterCard people's problem.

Collecting Debts

Even if you accept credit cards and certainly if you don't, there will be times when you have done everything right, given a quality product to your customer, who has then proceeded to ignore your bill or given you a bad check. This may not be so bad if it happens once in a great while, but if you let such things go in the nail-biting world of small business, it could ultimately drain your resources. Besides which, there's the principle of the thing. So what do you do? What you do is wait a week then send them a letter, with a copy of the invoice, on stationary with your business's name and address at the top, asking for payment, in a curt manner. This will as often as not prompt a reasonably quick response. If it doesn't within a couple of weeks, you might send out another letter that mentions potential legal action. After this you may have to take your customer to small claims court or turn the account over to a collection agency, who will do the threatening and harassment for you for a percentage of what they recover, from 30 to 45%. This is a lot, but at least you'll recover some of your money and, perhaps most importantly, keep the integrity of your business intact.

EMPLOYEES

Novice business owners tend to be a willful lot and will do what they can and what they must to get themselves started, using whatever materials are at hand and using whatever people become available to help them as well. Sometimes at first they will hire friends and family members. This does not create exactly the same tensions that combining home and business or asking family members for start-up money might, since the commitment need only last as long as it remains amiable and since you are presumably paying them.

At some point you may have to have other people do work for you, either by paying independent contractors (freelancers) for services on a job by job basis, or, if you know you will require more regular attendance, by hiring employees.

What you need to do first is get definite about what you will want a prospective employee to do for you, and how many hours a week of work you will need from your prospective employee.

Good Men and Women Wanted

How do you find qualified employees? The most oft-used method is advertising in the paper (and on the Web—most newspapers will list their ads both in print and in cyberspace). Ask for résumés, if you want to get the most qualified applicants (and remember that résumés can lie too). Ask a few pertinent questions to make sure you're not about to waste your time, then schedule an interview.

CHAPTER 9: STARTING YOUR OWN BUSINESS 182

There are standard interview questions that can be found in books, questions like "Where do you see yourself in five years?" But it may be better just to find out what experience they've had, what they expect from the job, what their situation is (in college, already working a full-time job an hour and a half away, etc.), ask for references, check them, and, if you like the person and everything seems in order, make them an offer.

There is a federal minimum wage you must meet for most jobs, but for many jobs this will not be competitive enough, and you may want to check with a local trade association or simply skim the want ads to find out what the going wage for a particular job is. You can expect some give and take.

To Be a Boss

As an employer you must fulfill certain legal duties and must also be aware of your employee's extra-legal needs. Your legal duties include withholding federal and state income taxes, contributing to unemployment and worker's compensation systems, and matching social security holdings.

The first thing you'll need to do is fill out an "Application for Employer Identification Number" with the IRS, and the IRS will, in return, send you deposit slips you will use on a monthly basis to deposit your employee's taxes in the bank. There will be more paperwork as well, W-4 and W-2 forms for both your employee and the Social Security Administration. There are payroll services that will do these duties for a relatively small fee.

This is all part of the responsibility you take on when you hire someone to work for you. You might also want to get employee life insurance and disability insurance. The laws on these matters, like the zoning and licensing laws, vary from state to state, so you'll want again to check with appropriate offices (chamber of commerce, small business administration) or lawyers and accountants, to make sure you're doing what you must to remain within the limits of the law.

Warning: You must make certain that your prospective employee *is legally allowed to work in this country, either from citizenship or some other legal status (work visa, green card, etc.). Otherwise, you may face a hefty fine.*

"I owe the government $3,400 in taxes. So I sent them two hammers and a toilet seat."

— Michael McShane

CHAPTER 9: STARTING YOUR OWN BUSINESS

MARKETING

Marketing is the whole deal, from researching your potential customer base to coming up with a jingle and a slogan to advertising and promoting your business to finally (if it works) actually having a customer pay you for your product or service. The basic question behind marketing is: How do you get customers for your business? And the question that has to be answered before you even get started is: Are there any potential customers for your business?

If there is a customer base available, you still need to get to them, let them know that you are available. You need, that is, to advertise, send out mailings, take out a classified ad, staple fliers to telephone poles, call people up, or simply go from door to door. Perhaps you'll want to set up and maintain a Web page that will reach a global audience. All of these methods will cost you time and money, your two most valuable resources, so you must think about which one will be most effective in reaching the audience you seek. You must also be patient (advertising is a slow process of repetition and growing familiarity, not a thunderclap with immediate response), and be willing to alter your strategies as results and experience teach you what is and what is not working.

PRICE

The image you put forth and the prices you set are also important aspects of getting your product or service on a customer's shopping list. Your price must of course provide you with a profit, but must also be competitive. Check out the competition, see how their prices stack up with the quality of what they're selling. If you know your quality will be substantially higher than theirs, you may want your asking price to be higher as well (a good way of letting the customer, who expects to pay more for better, know that your product or service is of a substantially higher quality). Another good way to get customers is to convince them you can provide essentially the same thing as your competition at a lower price. You might also, as an unknown company in the beginning, consider giveaways, coupons, free consultations, or samples.

CUSTOMER SATISFACTION

The best thing you can do to get your business going and keep it running is leave your customers feeling satisfied, by making their experience a hassle-free and pleasant one, so not only will they return to you in the future but they will tell their friends about you. This is the easiest, cheapest, and most effective way of expanding your customer base. No amount of clever advertising can beat an honest, unpaid testimonial, and no amount of public relations and spin can do for your image among the people you want as customers than having earned their patronage with a solid job well done.

CHAPTER 9: STARTING YOUR OWN BUSINESS

Internet Sources

An especially relevant resource these days is, of course, the Web. But the number of sites dedicated to small businesses is formidable, and many of them may be useless or worse. So to get you started, you might want to try the following (and don't neglect their links, either):

For a "seven step start-up program for entrepreneurs," try **www.startupbiz.com/Doit/seven.htm**.

The American Chamber of Commerce has a site "for executives," at **www.acce.org**, which includes a link to ChamberBiz, "the Ultimate Small Business Resource."

For "a fun approach to serious business," take a look at **www.ideacafe.com**, which includes profiles, advice, and something called "Biz Horoscope."

The public television series, "Small Business 2000," has a Web site at **www.sb2000.com**, with online classes, stories about small businesses, and ideas about how to combine business with social ethics.

One of many summer internship programs can be found at The Iacocca Institute at Lehigh University's Global Village of Future Leaders of Business and Industry Web site at **www./lhigh.edu/~village**.

Meanwhile, **www.noboss.com** proclaims itself "the Web's richest database of detailed information on biz-ops you can launch for under $5,000."

And one of many places where you can purchase software and hardware online with the small business start-up in mind, is **www.Quicken.com/small_business**. (Check Microsoft and IBM for similar sites.)

Resources

Starting a small business is and will always be the province of people who are willing to "go it alone," but there is no reason the business novice should not exploit those communities and resources that are available to keep an admirable self-reliance from turning into a lonely solitude. Whatever type of business you are venturing into, from record producing to selling seeds to designing handkerchiefs, there is more than likely a trade association eager to have you join. And every trade will have at least one (and probably more than one) magazine, newspaper, or Web site available to members. Search these out and when you find one you like, subscribe to it. Keep up with the latest news, technology, and strategies of your new field.

FRANCHISES & TURNKEY BUSINESSES

Alternative possibilities, which may be better for you if you would like at least the ground to be broken before you start building, and are willing to accommodate a pre-existing set of business and brand fundamentals, include franchising and buying an existing business.

Franchising

When you buy a franchise what you buy is the rights for a given brand-name business, like Subway, for a given territory. If you buy into a franchise, you should get brand recognition, company-paid training, an explicit guide on how to run the business in question, quality advertising (for which you will most likely pay a fee), and most important, a regular, dependable supply of the franchiser's (hopefully proven) product, which it is your job to sell.

You are, as franchisee, in a sense, the franchiser's customer, and it is your job to satisfy another level of customers, the end-product users, that is, the people who actually eat at Pizza Hut, or Dunkin' Donuts, or even Ping's Take Out. This is a good way to make your business a more systematic, paint-by-numbers venture, if you feel more comfortable, as many painters do, as a copyist rather than the creator of original masterpieces.

There are cons, however. Buying a franchise does not guarantee success (nothing does), you will still have to work hard and assume much responsibility for the success or failure of the enterprise, you will still need to learn much about how to run a business, and you will be responsible to the business practices and accountants of your franchise's head office, to which you will pay an annual fee for the privilege. Still, for those for whom the idea of running a business is attractive, but who aren't quite ready to do so on their own authority only, a franchise might be the perfect option.

Turnkey Businesses

Another way to avoid much of the legwork involved in starting your own business is to buy an already existing business. People move, retire, get restless, change careers, or decide to spend more time with their children, and if they have a bookstore or a home-based daycare center they are no longer interested in running, will place an ad in the business opportunity section of the paper, list it on the Web or with a "business broker" (see your local yellow pages). If done correctly and carefully, buying a sound business for a fair price can deliver a fully equipped operation with an already established customer base. And unlike buying into a franchise, you may, over time, be freer to give this business your own personal stamp (though one must tread lightly so as to not alienate customers of the old regime).

With both the franchising and turnkey business options, make sure to investigate your purchase thoroughly, and get a franchise or turnkey business that feels right for you, that you will be willing to give the required effort and time and resources to without regretting your commitment six months or a year later (find out, for example, what your daily routine will look like, and how many hours you can expect to spend doing various chores after you've settled into a routine).

And remember, franchises aren't just fast-food restaurants, but include such things as pet care, résumé writing, or bookkeeping. And, if you're lucky, or patient, a turnkey business might include anything you think you'd be good at doing.

CHAPTER 9: STARTING YOUR OWN BUSINESS — 186

APPENDIX

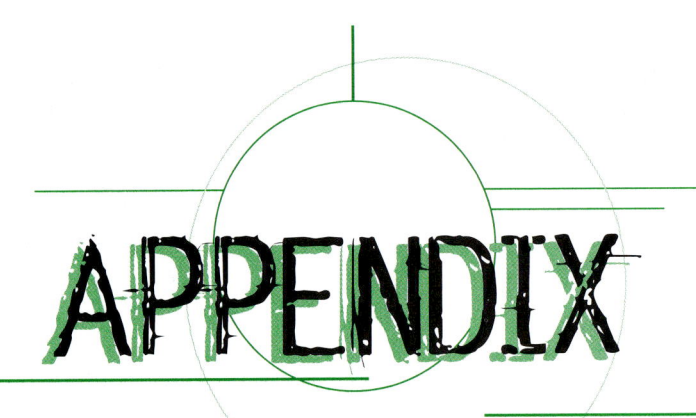

SECURITIES REGULATORY AGENCIES BY STATE

Alabama - Alabama Securities Commission

Alabama Securities Commission
RSA Plaza
770 Washington Ave., Suite 570
Montgomery, AL 36130-4700
(334) 242-2984

Alaska - Securities Section - Alaska Division of Banking, Securities and Corporations

The Division of Banking, Securities and Corporations
Department of Commerce and Economic Development
P.O Box 110807
Juneau, AK 99811-0807

Arizona - Arizona Corporation Commission Securities Division

Arizona Corporation Commission
Securities Division
1300 West Washington St., 3rd Floor
Phoenix, AZ 85007
(602) 542-4242

Arkansas - Securities Department

Securities Department
Heritage West Building
201 East Markham, 3rd Floor
Little Rock, AR 72201
(501) 324-9260

California - Department of Corporations, Securities Regulation Division

Securities Regulation Division
Department of Corporations
320 West 4th St.
Suite 750
Los Angeles, CA 90013
(213) 576-7505

Colorado - Division of Securities

Division of Securities
1580 Lincoln St., Suite 420
Denver, CO 80203-1508
(303) 894-2320

Connecticut - Department of Banking - Securities and Business Investments Division

Department of Banking
Securities Division
260 Constitution Plaza
Hartford, CT 06103
(860) 240-8230 or (800) 831-7225
(860) 240-8295 (fax)

Delaware - Delaware Department of Justice, Division of Securities

Division of Securities
State Office Building
820 North French St., 5th Floor
Wilmington, DE 19801
(302) 577-8424
(302) 577-6987 (fax)

District of Columbia - Securities Division of the District of Columbia

Securities Division of the District of Columbia
450 Fifth Street, N.W.
Suite 821
Washington, D.C. 20001
(202) 626-5105

Florida - Division of Securities and Investor Protection

Division of Securities
101 East Gaines St.
Tallahassee, FL 32399
(850) 410-9805 or (800) 848-3792

Georgia - Division of Securities and Business Regulation

Securities and Business
Regulation Division
West Tower, Suite 802
2 Martin Luther King Jr. Dr. SE
Atlanta, GA 30334
(404) 656-2894
(404) 657-8410 (fax)

Hawaii - Department of Commerce & Consumer Affairs, Securities Commission

Securities Commission
P.O. Box 40
Honolulu, HI 96810
(808) 586-2730

Idaho - Idaho Securities Bureau

Idaho Securities Bureau
700 West State Street, 2nd Floor
P.O. Box 83720
Boise, ID 83720-0031
(208) 332-8004
(208) 332-8099 (fax)

Illinois - Illinois Securities Department

Illinois Securities Department
Lincoln Tower
520 South Second St., Suite 200
Springfield, IL 62701-1722
(217) 782-2256 or (800) 628-7937
(within Illinois)

Indiana - Securities Division

Securities Division
302 West Washington St.
Room E-111
Indianapolis, IN 46204
(317) 232-6681 or (800) 223-8791

Iowa - Iowa Insurance Division - Securities

Securities Bureau
340 Maple Street
Des Moines, IA 50319-0066
(515) 281-4441

Kansas - Kansas Securities Commissioner

Kansas Securities Commission
618 S. Kansas Ave., 2nd Floor
Topeka, KS 66603-3804
(785) 296-3307

Kentucky - Kentucky Department of Financial Institutions, Division of Securities

Division of Securities
1025 Capital Center Dr.
Suite 200
Frankfort, KY 40601
(502) 573-3390

Louisiana - Louisiana Securities Commission

Louisiana Securities Commission
1100 Poydras St., Suite 2250
New Orleans, LA 70163
(504) 568-5515

Maine - Securities Division - Professional and Financial Regulation

State of Maine Securities Division
121 State House Station
Augusta, ME 04333-0121
(207) 624-8551

Maryland - Maryland Division of Securities

Maryland Division of Securities
Office of the Attorney General
200 St. Paul Place, 20th Floor
Baltimore, MD 21202-2020
(410) 576-6360
(410) 576-6532 (fax)

Massachusetts - Massachusetts Securities Division

Massachusetts Securities Division
One Ashburton Place, Room 1701
Boston, MA 02108
(617) 727-3548 or (800) 269-5428
(617) 248-0177 (fax)

Michigan - Corporation and Securities Bureau

Department of Consumer and
Industries Services
Corporation, Securities, and Land
Development Bureau
7150 Harris Dr.
Lansing, MI 48909-8145
(517) 241-6470

Minnesota - Division of Securities

Department of Commerce
Securities Division
133 East Seventh St., 2nd Floor
St. Paul, MN 55101
(651) 296-2284

Mississippi - Securities Division

Securities Division
P.O. Box 136
Jackson, MS 39205-0136
(601) 359-6364 or (800) 804-6364

APPENDIX

Missouri - Securities - Missouri Secretary of State

Securities Division
Missouri State Information Center
600 W. Main St. Room 229
Jefferson City, MO 65101
(573) 751-4136 or (800) 721-7996

Montana - Office of the State Auditor, Securities Department
Securities Department
P. O. Box 4009
Helena, MT 59604-4009
(406) 444-2040 or (800) 332-6148

Nebraska - Nebraska Securities Bureau

Nebraska Securities Bureau
Department of Banking & Finance
P.O. Box 95006
Lincoln, NE 68509-5006
(402) 471-3445

Nevada - Nevada Securities Division

Nevada Securities Division
555 E. Washington Ave., Suite 5200
Las Vegas, NV 89101
(702) 486-2440 or (800) 758-6440

New Hampshire - Bureau of Securities Regulation

New Hampshire Bureau of Securities
State House Room 204
107 N Main Street.
Concord, NH, 03301-4989
(603) 271-1463

New Jersey - Bureau of Securities

Bureau of Securities
Gibraltar Building
153 Halsey St., 6th Floor
P.O. Box 47029
Newark, NJ 07101
(973) 504-3600

New Mexico - New Mexico Securities Division

New Mexico Securities Division
P.O. Box 25101
Santa Fe, NM 87504-5101
(505) 827-7140
(800) 704-5533

New York - New York Bureau of Investment

Protection and Securities
NY State Department of Law
Office of the Attorney General
Bureau of the Investor Protection
and Securities
120 Broadway, 23rd Floor
New York, NY, 10271

North Carolina - Securities Division

Securities Division
Department of the Secretary of State
300 North Salisbury St.
Raleigh, NC 27603-5909
(919) 733-3924 or (800) 688-4507

North Dakota - North Dakota Securities Commission

North Dakota Securities Commission
State Capitol Building, 5th Floor
600 East Boulevard Ave.
Bismarck, ND 58505
(701) 328-2910 or
(800) 297-5124 (in state)

Ohio - Ohio Division of Securities

Ohio Securities Commission
77 South High St., 22nd Floor
Columbus, OH 43215
(614) 644-7381 or (800) 788-1194

Oklahoma - Oklahoma Securities Commission

Oklahoma Department of Securities
Suite 860, First National Center
120 North Robinson
Oklahoma City, OK 73102
(405) 280-7700
(405) 280-7742 (fax)

Oregon - Oregon Division of Finance and Corporate Securities

Oregon Securities Commission
350 Winter St. NE
Room 410
Salem, OR 97301
(503) 378-4387

Pennsylvania - Pennsylvania Securities Commission

Pennsylvania Securities Commission
1010 N. 7th St., 2nd Floor
Eastgate Office Building
Harrisburg, PA 17102-1410
(717) 787-8061 or
(800) 600-0007 (in state)

Puerto Rico - Commonwealth of Puerto Rico

Commonwealth of Puerto Rico
Office of the Commissioner of
Financial Institutions
Securities Division
PO Box 11855
Fernandez Juncos Station
San Juan, PR 00910-3855
(787) 723-3131

Rhode Island - Department of Business Regulation

Department of Business Regulation
Securities Division
233 Richmond St., Suite 232
Providence, RI 02903-4232
(401) 222-3048

South Carolina - Office of the Attorney General, Securities Section

Office of the Attorney General
Securities Section
P.O Box 11549
Columbia, SC 29211
(803) 734-9916

South Dakota - South Dakota Securities Commission

South Dakota Securities Commission
Division of Securities
Capitol Building
118 W. Capitol Ave.
Pierre, SD 57501
(605) 773-4823

Tennessee - Tennessee Securities Division

Tennessee Securities Division
Davey Crockett Tower, Suite 680
500 James Robertson Parkway
Nashville, TN 37243-0583
(615) 741-3187 (800) 863-9117

Texas - Texas State Securities Board

State Securities Board
P.O. Box 13167
Austin, TX 78711-3167
(512) 305-8302

Utah - Utah Division of Securities

Utah Division of Securities
P.O. Box 146760
Salt Lake City, UT 84114-6760
(801) 530-6600
(801) 530-6980 (fax)

Vermont - Department of Banking, Insurance & Securities

Department of Banking, Insurance
& Securities
Securities Division
89 Main St., Drawer 20
Montpelier, VT 05620-3101
(802) 828-3420

Virginia - Virginia Division of Securities and Retail Franchising

Division of Securities and
Retail Franchising
P.O. Box 23218
Richmond, VA 23218
(804) 371-9051
or (800) 552-7945 (in state)

Washington - Department of Financial Institutions, Securities Division

Department of Financial Institutions
Securities Division
P.O. Box 41200
Olympia, WA 98504-1200
(360) 902-8760

West Virginia - Securities Division - West Virginia State Auditor's Office

Office of State Auditor
Securities Division
Building 1 Room W100
Charleston, WV 25305-0230
(304) 558-2257

Wisconsin - Division of Securities

Division of Securities
P.O. Box 1768
Madison, WI 53701-1768
(608) 261-9555
or (800) 472-4325 (in state)

Wyoming - Securities Division

Securities Division
Secretary of State
200 West 24th Street
Cheyenne, WY 82002-0020
(307) 777-7370
(307) 777-5339 (fax)

GLOSSARY

A

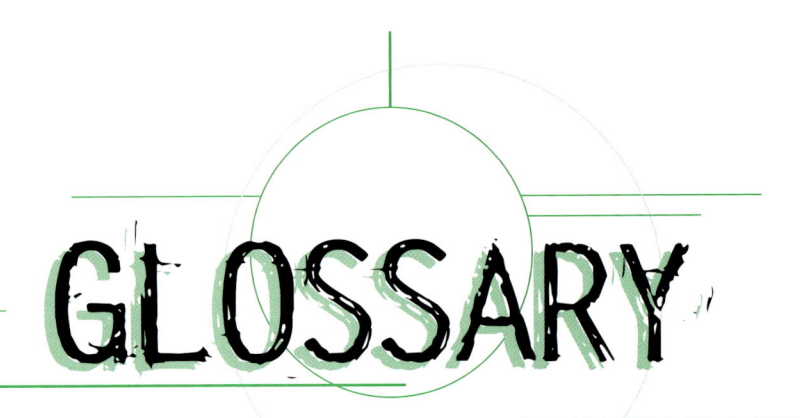

Accrued interest: The accumulated interest that is earned but not yet paid.

AIBD: Association of International Bond Dealers.

American Depository Receipts: Certificates issued by a U.S. financial institution, representing foreign shares held by the institution. One ADR may represent a portion of a foreign share, one share or a number of shares of a foreign corporation. If the ADRs are "sponsored," the corporation provides financial information and other assistance to the bank and may subsidize the administration of the ADRs.

American Stock Exchange (AMEX): One of the larger exchanges in the United States. It trades mostly in small- to medium-sized companies.

Amortization: The repayment of a loan by installments.

Analyst: Employee of a brokerage or other financial company who studies companies and makes buy-and-sell recommendations on their stocks or other financial instruments. Most specialize in a specific industry.

Annual percentage rate (APR): The periodic rate times the number of periods in a year. For example, a 1 percent monthly return has an APR of 12 percent.

Annual percentage yield (APY): The effective, or true, annual rate of return. The APY is the rate actually earned or paid in one year, taking into account the effect of compounding. The APY is calculated by taking one plus the periodic rate and raising it to the number of periods in a year. For example, a 1 percent per month rate has an APY of 12.68 percent (1.0112).

Annual rate of return: There are many ways of calculating the annual rate of return. If the rate of return is calculated on a monthly basis, you can multiply this by twelve to express an annual rate of return. This is often called the annual percentage rate. You can also compound it and this is called the annual percentage yield.

Annual report: Yearly record of a publicly held company's financial condition. It includes a description of the firm's operations, its balance sheet, and income statement. SEC rules require that it be distributed to all shareholders. A more detailed version is called a 10-K.

Annuity: A regular periodic payment made by an insurance company to a policyholder for a specified period of time.

Arbitrage: The simultaneous buying and selling of a security at two different prices in two different markets, resulting in profits and lowering the risks.

ARM (Adjustable rate mortgage): A mortgage that features predetermined adjustments of the loan interest rate at regular intervals based on an established index. The interest rate is adjusted at each interval to a rate equivalent to the index value plus a predetermined spread, or margin, over the index, usually subject to payment rate caps.

Articles of incorporation: Legal document establishing a corporation and its structure and purpose.

Ask: This is the quoted ask, or the lowest price an investor will accept to sell a stock. This is the quoted offer at which an investor can buy shares of stocks; also called the offer price.

Asset: Any possession that has value in an exchange.

Asset/equity ratio: The ratio of total assets to stockholder equity.

B

Back-end load fund: A mutual fund that charges investors a fee to sell (redeem) shares, often ranging from 4 to 6 percent. Some back-end load funds impose a full commission if the shares are redeemed within a designated time, such as one year. The commission decreases the longer the investor holds the shares.

Balanced mutual fund: This is a fund that buys common stock, preferred stock, and bonds. The same as a balanced fund.

Balance sheet: It is a summary of the assets, liabilities, and owners' or stockholder's equity.

Balloon maturity: Any large principal payment due at maturity for a bond or loan with or without a sinking fund requirement.

GLOSSARY 194

Bankruptcy: State of being unable to pay debts.

Bear: An investor who believes a stock or the overall market will decline. A bear market is a prolonged period of falling stock prices, usually by 20 percent or more. The period of 1929-32 was the worst bear market in U.S. history.

Bid price: This is the quoted bid, or the highest price an investor is willing to pay to buy a security. Practically speaking, this is the available price at which an investor can sell shares of stock.

Big Board: A nickname for the New York Stock Exchange. Also known as The Exchange. More than 2,000 common and preferred stocks are traded. Founded in 1792, the NYSE is the oldest exchange in the United States, and the largest. It is located on Wall Street in New York City.

Black market: An illegal market.

Block trade: A large trading order, defined on the NYSE as an order that consists of 10,000 shares of a given stock or a total market value of $200,000 or more.

Blue-chip company: Large and creditworthy company. Named after the most expensive poker chip.

Bond: Bonds are debt and are issued for a period of more than one year. The U.S. government, local governments, companies, and many other types of institutions sell bonds. When an investor buys bonds, he or she is lending money. The seller of the bond agrees to repay the principal amount of the loan at a specified time. Interest-bearing bonds pay interest periodically.

Book value: A company's book value is its total assets minus intangible assets and liabilities, such as debt. A company's book value might be more or less than its market value.

Broker: An individual who is paid a commission for executing customer orders. Either a floor broker who executes orders on the floor of the exchange, or an upstairs broker who handles retail customers and their orders.

Bull: An investor who thinks the market will rise.

Bulldog market: The foreign market in the United Kingdom.

Bull market: Any market in which prices are in an upward trend.

Buydowns: Mortgages in which monthly payments consist of principal and interest, with portions of these payments during the early period of the loan being provided by a third party to reduce the borrower's monthly payments.

GLOSSARY

C

Capital gain: When a stock is sold for a profit, it's the difference between the net sales price of securities and their net cost, or original basis. If a stock is sold below cost, the difference is a capital loss.

Cash cow: A company or division of a company that generates a steady and significant amount of cash flow.

Certificate of deposit (CD): This is a certificate issued by a bank or thrift that indicates a specified sum of money has been deposited. A CD bears a maturity date and a specified interest rate, and can be issued in any denomination. The duration can be up to five years.

Chicago Mercantile Exchange (CME): A not-for-profit corporation owned by its members. Its primary functions are to provide a location for trading futures and options, collect and disseminate market information, maintain a clearing mechanism, and enforce trading rules.

Churning: Excessive trading of a client's account in order to increase the broker's commissions.

Closed-end mortgage: Mortgage against which no additional debt may be issued.

Commission: The fee paid to a broker to execute a trade, based on number of shares, bonds, options, and/or their dollar value. In 1975, deregulation led to the creation of discount brokers, who charge lower commissions than full service brokers. Full service brokers offer advice and usually have a full staff of analysts who follow specific industries. Discount brokers simply execute a client's order—and usually do not offer an opinion on a stock.

Commodity: A commodity is food, metal, or another physical substance that investors buy or sell, usually via futures contracts.

Compounding: The process of accumulating the time value of money forward in time. For example, interest earned in one period earns additional interest during each subsequent time period.

GLOSSARY — 196

Compound interest: Interest paid on previously earned interest as well as on the principal.

Consolidation: The combining of two or more firms to form an entirely new entity.

Cushion bonds: High-coupon bonds that sell only at a moderate premium because they are callable at a price below that at which a comparable non-callable bond would sell. Cushion bonds offer considerable downside protection in a falling market.

D

Day trading: Refers to establishing and liquidating the same position or positions within one day's trading.

Debt/equity ratio: Indicator of financial leverage. Compares assets provided by creditors to assets provided by shareholders. Determined by dividing long-term debt by common stockholder equity.

Deep-discount bond: A bond issued with a very low coupon or no coupon and selling at a price far below par value. When the bond has no coupon, it's called a zero coupon bond.

Default: Failure to make timely payment of interest or principal on a debt security or to otherwise comply with the provisions of a bond indenture.

Direct stock-purchase programs: The purchase by investors of securities directly from the issuer.

Diversification: Dividing investment funds among a variety of securities with different risk, reward, and correlation statistics so as to minimize unsystematic risk.

Dividend: A dividend is a portion of a company's profit paid to common and preferred shareholders. A stock selling for $20 a share with an annual dividend of $1 a share yields the investor 5 percent.

Dividend reinvestment plan (DRP): Automatic reinvestment of shareholder dividends in more shares of a company's stock, often without commissions. Some plans provide for the purchase of additional shares at a discount to market price. Dividend reinvestment plans allow shareholders to accumulate stock over the long term using dollar cost averaging. The DRP is usually administered by the company without charges to the holder.

Dow Jones industrial average: This is the best known U.S. index of stocks. It contains 30 stocks that trade on the New York Stock Exchange. The Dow, as it is called, is a barometer of how shares of the largest U.S. companies are performing. There are thousands of investment indexes around the world for stocks, bonds, currencies, and commodities.

E

Earnings: Net income for the company during the period.

Earnings before interest and taxes (EBIT): A financial measure defined as revenues less cost of goods sold and selling, general, and administrative expenses. In other words, operating and non-operating profit before the deduction of interest and income taxes.

Earnings per share (EPS): EPS, as it is called, is a company's profit divided by its number of outstanding shares. If a company earned $2 million in one year and had 2 million shares of stock outstanding, its EPS would be $1 per share. The company often uses a weighted average of shares outstanding over the reporting term.

Efficient portfolio: A portfolio that provides the greatest expected return for a given level of risk (i.e. standard deviation), or equivalently, the lowest risk for a given expected return.

Extendable bond: Bond whose maturity can be extended at the option of the lender or issuer.

F

Five Cs of credit: Five characteristics that are used to form a judgment about a customer's creditworthiness: character, capacity, capital, collateral, and conditions.

Freddie Mac (Federal Home Loan Mortgage Corporation): A Congressionally chartered corporation that purchases residential mortgages in the secondary market from S&Ls, banks, and mortgage bankers and packages these mortgages for sale into the capital markets.

G

Global bonds: Bonds that are designed so as to qualify for immediate trading in any domestic capital market and in the Euromarket.

Government National Mortgage Association (Ginnie Mae): A wholly owned U.S. government corporation within the Department of Housing & Urban Development. Ginnie Mae guarantees the timely payment of principal and interest on securities issued by approved servicers that are collateralized by FHA-issued, VA-guaranteed, or Farmers Home Administration (FmHA)-guaranteed mortgages.

Graduated-payment mortgages (GPMs): A type of stepped-payment loan in which the borrower's payments are initially lower than those on a comparable level-rate mortgage. The payments are gradually increased over a predetermined period (usually 3, 5, or

GLOSSARY 198

7 years) and then are fixed at a level-pay schedule that will be higher than the level-pay amortization of a level-pay mortgage originated at the same time. The difference between what the borrower actually pays and the amount required to fully amortize the mortgage is added to the unpaid principal balance.

I

Income bond: A bond on which the payment of interest is contingent on sufficient earnings. These bonds are commonly used during the reorganization of a failed or failing business.

Index fund: Investment fund designed to match the returns on a stockmarket index.

Initial public offering (IPO): A company's first sale of stock to the public. Securities offered in an IPO are often, but not always, those of young, small companies seeking outside equity capital and a public market for their stock. Investors purchasing stock in IPOs generally must be prepared to accept very large risks for the possibility of large gains. IPOs by investment companies (closed-end funds) usually contain underwriting fees, which represent a load to buyers.

Insured bond: A municipal bond backed both by the credit of the municipal issuer and by commercial insurance policies.

Interest: The price paid for borrowing money. It is expressed as a percentage rate over a period of time and reflects the rate of exchange of present consumption for future consumption. Also, a share or title in property.

IRA/Keogh accounts: Special accounts where you can save and invest, and the taxes are deferred until money is withdrawn. These plans are subject to frequent changes in law with respect to the deductibility of contributions. Withdrawals of tax deferred contributions are taxed as income, including the capital gains from such accounts.

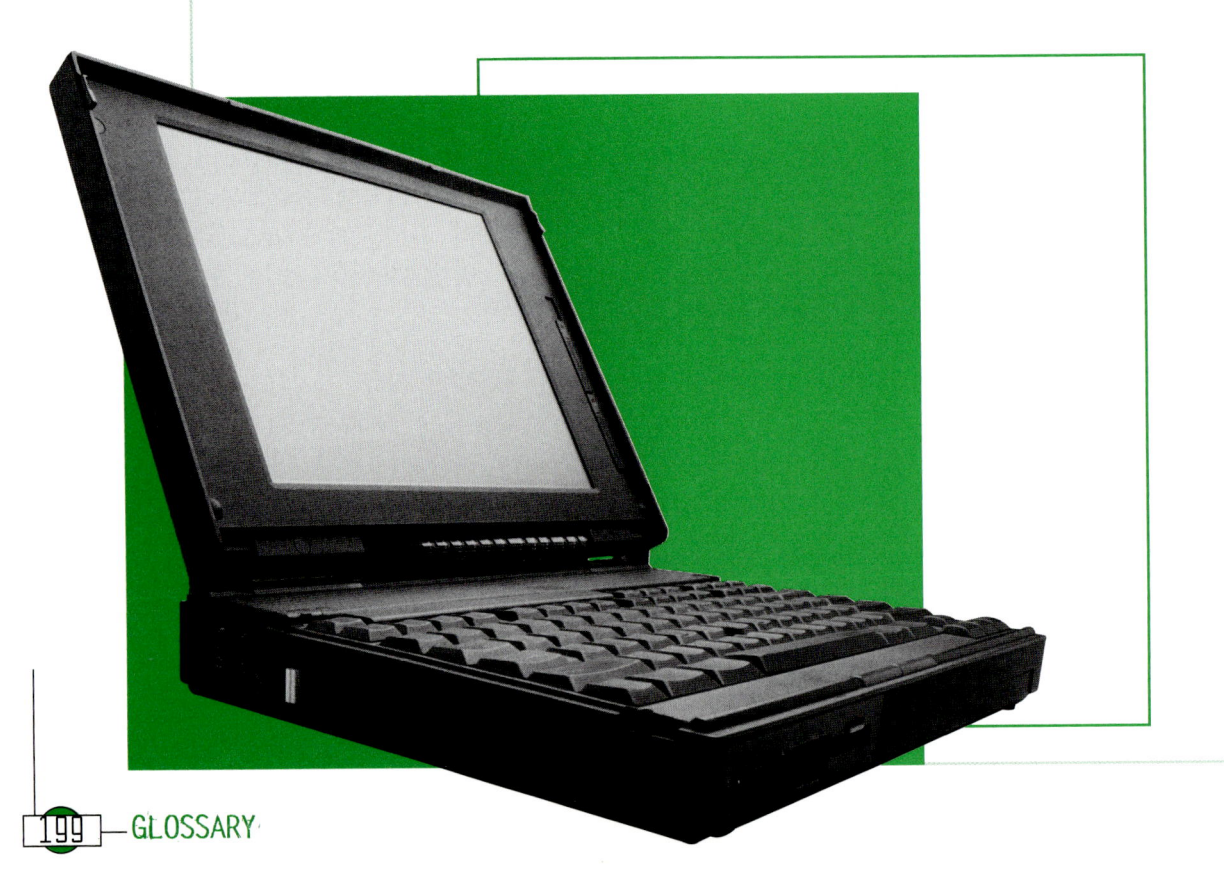

GLOSSARY

J

Junk bond: A bond with a speculative credit rating of BB (S&P) or BA (Moody's) or lower is a junk or high yield bond. Such bonds offer investors higher yields than bonds of financially sound companies. Two agencies, Standard & Poor's and Moody's Investor Services, provide the rating systems for companies' credit.

L

Line of credit: An informal arrangement between a bank and a customer establishing a maximum loan balance that the bank will permit the borrower to maintain.

Long bonds: Bonds with a long current maturity. The "long bond" is the 30-year U.S. government bond.

M

Money market fund: A mutual fund that invests only in short term securities, such as bankers' acceptances, commercial paper, repurchase agreements, and government bills. The net asset value per share is maintained at $1.00. Such funds are not federally insured, although the portfolio may consist of guaranteed securities and/or the fund may have private insurance protection.

Mutual fund: Mutual funds are pools of money that are managed by an investment company. They offer investors a variety of goals, depending on the fund and its investment charter. Some funds, for example, seek to generate income on a regular basis. Others seek to preserve an investor's money. Still others seek to invest in companies that are growing at a rapid pace. Funds can impose a sales charge, or load, on investors when they buy or sell shares. Many funds these days are no-load and impose no sales charge. Mutual funds are investment companies regulated by the Investment Company Act of 1940.

N

NASDAQ: National Association of Securities Dealers Automatic Quotation System. An electronic quotation system that provides price quotations to market participants about the more actively traded common stock issues in the OTC market. About 4,000 common stock issues are included in the NASDAQ system.

New York Stock Exchange (NYSE): Also known as the Big Board or The Exchange. More than 2,000 common and preferred stocks are traded. The exchange is the oldest in the United States, founded in 1792, and the largest. It is located on Wall Street in New York City.

No-load fund: A mutual fund that does not impose a sales commission.

No-load mutual fund: An open-end investment company, shares of which are sold without a sales charge. There can be other distribution charges. A true "no-load" fund will have neither a sales charge nor a distribution fee.

P

Portfolio: A collection of investments, real and/or financial.

Premium bond: A bond that is selling for more than its par value.

Prime rate: The interest rate at which banks lend to their best (prime) customers. Much more often than not, a bank's most creditworthy customers borrow at rates below the prime rate.

R

Return on assets (ROA): Indicator of profitability. Determined by dividing net income for the past 12 months by total average assets. Result is shown as a percentage. ROA can be decomposed into return on sales (net income/sales) multiplied by asset utilization (sales/assets).

Return on equity (ROE): Indicator of profitability. Determined by dividing net income for the past 12 months by common stockholder equity (adjusted for stock splits). Result is shown as a percentage. Investors use ROE as a measure of how a company is using its money.

T

Trade: A verbal (or electronic) transaction involving one party buying a security from another party. Once a trade is consummated, it is considered "done" or final. Settlement occurs one to five business days later.

Traders: Persons who take positions in securities and their derivatives with the objective of making profits. Traders can make markets by trading the flow. When they do that, their objective is to earn the bid/ask spread. Traders can also be of the sort who take proprietary positions whereby they seek to profit from the directional movement of prices or spread positions.

Treasury bills: Debt obligations of the U.S. Treasury that have maturities of one year or less. Maturities for T-bills are usually 91 days, 182 days, or 52 weeks.

Treasury bonds: Debt obligations of the U.S. Treasury that have maturities of ten years or more.

Treasury notes: Debt obligations of the U.S. Treasury that have maturities of more than two years but less than ten years.

U

Underfunded pension plan: On occasion a company's pension plan can run into financial trouble and will become underfunded. Some run into difficulty after a company is purchased and excess pension money is repurposed.

Underwriter: A firm, usually an investment bank, that buys an issue of securities from a company and resells it to investors.

Underwriting fee: The portion of the underwriting money that compensates the securities firms that underwrite a public offering.

Unsecured debt: Debt that does not identify specific assets that can be taken over by the lender in case of default.

V

Value-added tax: Method of taxation in which a tax is levied at each stage of production on the value added at that specific stage. Sometimes called a "hidden tax."

Variable rate loan: The interest rate on the loan fluctuates based on a base interest rate such as the prime rate. If the prime rate falls, so does the loan rate.

Venture capital: An investment in a start-up business. Type of financing sought by early-stage companies seeking to grow rapidly and often used by Internet startups.

W

Waiting period: Time during which the SEC examines a firm's registration statement. During this time the firm may distribute a preliminary prospectus.

Warrant: A security entitling the holder to buy stock at some specified future date at a specified price, usually one higher than current market. This "warrant" is then traded as a security, the price of which reflects the value of the stock. Warrants are like call options, but with much longer time spans—sometimes years.

Well diversified portfolio: A portfolio spread out over many securities in such a way that the weight in any security is small. The risk of a well-diversified portfolio closely approximates the systemic risk of the overall market, the unsystematic risk of each security having been diversified out of the portfolio.

White knight: A friendly potential acquirer of a firm sought out by a target firm that is threatened by a less welcome suitor.

Workout: Arrangement between a borrower and creditors.

Write-down: Decreasing the book value of an asset if its book value is overstated compared to current market values.

Y

Yield: The percentage rate of return paid on a stock in the form of dividends, or the effective rate of interest paid on a bond.

Yield to maturity: The percentage rate of return paid on investments such as bonds if you buy and hold it to its maturity date.

Z

Zero-coupon bond: A bond in which no coupon is paid over the life of the contract. Instead, both the principal and the interest are paid at the maturity date.

GLOSSARY 202

A

A.B. Watley, Inc., 48
Accutrade, 48
Ace Hardware, 89
adjustable rate mortgage (ARM), 133
adult (Web) sites, 152
Affleck, Ben, 90
aggressive growth stocks, 88
Alabama Securities Commission, 187
Alaska Division of Banking, Securities, and Corporations, 187
Alcoa Aluminum, 39
Allen, Woody, 71
All or None (AON), 50
Amazon.com, 37, 79, 88
America Online, 22, 88
American Airlines, 160
American Demographics, 6
American Express Brokerage, 48
American Savings Education Council, 18
Ameritrade, 46, 48, 176-177
annual reports, 73
AP Business and Finance wires, 60
Arizona Corporation Commission, Securities Division, 187
Arkin, Alan, 145

123Jump.com, 77
401(k), 17, 18

asbestos, 141
assets, 8
Aykroyd, Dan, 122

B

balloon loans, 135
bankruptcy, 16
bargain stocks, 88
Barnes & Noble, 88
Barton, Ron, 153
Barton, Mark, 82
Beanie Babies, 33-34
bear, 20
Beatles, The, 120
Bell, Alexander Graham, 159
Beverly Hillbillies, The, 141
Bidwell & Company, 48
Bilzerian, Paul, 21
blue chip stocks, 67
Boiler Room, 2, 90, 174
bond funds, 97
bond listings, 111
bond maturity, 111
bonds, 13, 43, 46, 109-112
book value, 21
Bowerman, Bill, 159
brokerage firms, 11, 43-52
Brooklyn, 125
Brown & Co., 48
Buchanan, Pat, 99
Buffett, Warren, 39

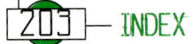

bulk e-mailing scams, 152
bull, 20
Bull & Bear, 20
Bull & Bear Securities, 48
Bush, George W., 178
business bonds, 116
business consulting, 164
business opportunity scams, 152
Businesswire, 60
Buy.com, 37
buyer's broker, 143
buying (vs. renting), 126

C

C corporation, 179
cable descrambler kits, 151
California, 148
California Department of Corporations, Securities Regulation Division, 187
call, 12
capital gains distributions, 100
Carter, Nell, 64
cash account, 49, 53
cash flow, 71
CBS, 38
CDNow.com, 79, 120

Certificate of Deposit (CD), 11-13
chain letters, 152
Chapter 11 bankruptcy, 175
Charles Schwab, 46, 47, 48
Chicago Board of Trade (CBOT), 124
Chicago Mercantile Exchange, The, 122
Chicago Stock Exchange, The, (CHX), 58
Cisco, 88
cleaning services, 164
close, 67, 112
Clouseau, Inspector, 39
CMGI, 88
Coca-Cola, 39
Coffee, Sugar, and Cocoa Exchange, Inc., 124
Colorado Division of Securities, 187
commercial lenders, 170

commercial real estate, 146

commission, 142

commodities, 34-35

common stock, 70

Commonwealth of Puerto Rico,
 Office of the Commissioner of
 Financial Institutions, 191

computer services, 164

Connecticut Department of Banking, 188

consolidate financial statement, 74

construction, 164

Corleone, Don, 3

Corleone, Sonny, 3

corporate concierge, 158

coupon, 111

credit cards, 14-15

credit repair scams, 151

credit reports, 15-16

Crimes and Misdemeanors, 71

current yield, 112

Curtis, Jamie Lee, 122
customer satisfaction, 184
Cyberinvest, 59
cyclical stocks, 68

D

Dark Ages, 28, 41
DATEK, 46, 48
day order, 49
day trader, 6
day trading, 82
Dean, James, 141
debt to equity ratio, 20
deed of ownership, 132
Deep Space Nine, 154
Delaware Department of Justice, Division of Securities, 188
Delta Airlines, 69
deposit brokers, 11
Diesel, Vin, 90
Dilbert, 155
Discover, 47
Disney, Walt, 42
Disney Co., The, 39
Disney World, 42
div, 67
dividend stock, 68
dividend yield, 21
dividends, 13, 14, 17, 21, 100
DLJ Direct, 46, 48, 59
DMN Capital, 149
dot-coms, 68

Douglas, Michael, 85
Dow Jones Industrial Average, 30, 38
Dowjones.com, 60
down payment, 128
downside stocks, 68
Dreyfus, 48
Dun and Bradstreet, 150

E

E*TRADE, 46, 48
earnings per share (EPS), 21, 71
easy money scam, 152
eBay, 88
economic indicators, 21

economics, 27
EDGAR database, 74-75
Edwards, A. G., 32
Eel farming, 148
Egroup, 88
Elaine's (restaurant), 82
electronic communications network (ECN), 59
Emusic.com, 87
E-Pawn, 149
Equinox, 15
equity funds, 97
escrow, 129
Europe, 126
Excite, 88
Excite.com/money, 60

F

Fazier, Bill, 32
Federal Bureau of
    Investigation (FBI), 149
Federal Deposit Insurance Corp.
    (FDIC), 11, 14, 150
Federal Home Loan Mortgage Corp.
    (Freddie Mac), 115
Federal Housing Authority, 136
Federal National Mortgage Association
    (Fannie Mae), 115
Federal Trade Commission, 16
FedEx, 159
fee-exempt securities, 52
Ferengi Rules of Acquisition, 154
Fidelity, 46

Fidelity Power Street, 48
Fiedler, R., 41
Fill-or-Kill, 50
finance.yahoo.com, 60
FinanCenter, 8
financial highlights, 73

financial stocks, 68
financing your business
    friends and family, 170
    banks, 170
    grants and awards, 171
    personal loans and credit cards, 171
    partnerships and investors, 171
financing your home, 128
fixed-rate mortgage, 134
Florida, 147
Florida Division of Securities and Investor Protection, 188
Fogdog, 40
For Sale By Owner (FSBO), 142
Forbes, 2
Ford, 22
Fox, Bud, 85
franchising, 185
frauds (and scams), 147-156
Frost, Robert, 31, 172
funds of funds, 98

G

"Getting Back in the Black," 16
Ganas, Spyridon, 37
Gap, The, 39
Gates, Bill, 38, 157
Gekko, Gordon, 85
General Accounting Office, 50
general contracting, 164
General Electric, 33
General Motors, 22, 37
general obligation bonds, 116
Geoffrey the Giraffe, 170
Georgia Division of Securities and Business Regulation, 188
get something free scam, 151
Giant, 141
Gifford, Kathie Lee, 27
Gillette, 39
Glengarry, Glen Ross, 2, 145
Godfather, The, 3
Golden Waters Production, 148
Good Till Canceled (GTC), 50
good value stocks, 88
Government National Mortgage Association (Ginnie Mae), 115
government regulations, 146
government reports, 74

INDEX 208

Great Depression, the, 28
Greenspan, Alan, 178
Greyhound bus, 175
growth funds, 101
growth stocks, 68, 88
guaranteed credit (scams), 151
guaranteed loan (scams), 151

H

Harris, Ed, 145
Hawaii Department of Commerce and Consumer Affairs, 188
health and diet scams, 151
Hi, 66
High tech public relations, 158
Holmgren, David, 47
home (as an asset), 127
home based startups (list of), 164
Home Depot, 39
Home Shopping Network, The, 160
hot startup businesses (list of), 158
Housing & Urban Development (HUD), 136
housing inspectors, 144
How the World Works, 27
Hudson, Rock, 141
hybrid funds, 98

I

I bonds, 113
IBM, 38
Idaho Securities Bureau, 188
Illinois Securities Department, 188
independent auditor's report, 73
index funds, 97
Indiana Securities Division, 188
Individual Retirement Account (IRA), 17-18, 45, 49
Industrial revenue bonds, 116
industry funds, 98
inflation, 31
inflation-indexed Treasuries, 115
Initial Public Offerings, (IPOs), 40, 68
Interactive Products & Services, 148

209 — INDEX

interest rate, 11, 12, 46, 70, 111
Internal Revenue Service (IRS), 179
international stocks, 68
Internet Stocks News, 79
investment categories (list of), 67
Iowa Insurance Division, 189
Iqnet.com, 82
IRS, 10

J

J.C. Penney, 22
JB Oxford, 48
Jetsons, The, 42
John Deere, 85
Jordan, Michael, 22
Juice bars, 158

K

Kabler, Sophia, 162
Kansas Securities Commissioner, 189
Karan, Donna, 69
Katt, Nicky, 90
Kellner, Dr. Irwin, 38
Kentucky Department of Financial Institutions, 189
Kerr, Branden, 129
King, Stephen, 178
Kmart, 22
Knotts, Don, 64
Kournikova, Anna, 69

L

lead, 141
legal fees (when buying a house), 129
Lemmon, Jack, 145
lender fees, 31
length (or a mortgage), 134
Leno, Jay, 33
leveraged buyout, 21
liabilities, 8
limit order, 49, 52
lo, 66
loads, 102
Long, Nia, 90

Louisiana Securities Commission, 189
Love, Courtney, 42
Lycos, 88

M

Maine Securities Division, 189
margin account, 49, 53
margin calls, 51-52
market capitalization, 22
market maker, 58
market order, 49
marketing, 184
Market Watch, 38
marketing services, 164
Maryland Division of Securities, 189
Massachusetts Securities Division, 189
massage service, 158
MasterCard, 178
match making service, 158
Matrix, The, 4
maturity (in bonds), 111
Mawn, Barry, 149
McShane, Michael, 183
Merrill Lynch, 44, 47, 59
message from the chief executive officer (or president), 73

Metropolitan Financial Management, 10
Mexico, 136
Michigan Corporation and Securities Bureau, 189
Microsoft, 33, 69, 81, 88
MidAmerica Commodity Exchange, The, 123
Milken, Michael, 21
Minnesota Division of Securities, 189
Mississippi Securities Division, 190
Missouri Secretary of State, 190
mobsters (in investing), 149
money market deposit account, 13
money market funds, 13-14, 98
monthly income and expenses, 9
Morgan Stanley Dean Witter, 47, 48
mortgage-backed bonds, 115
mortgage brokers, 135
mortgage payment, 128
Motley Fool, The, 60
Msn.com, 82
MSNBC, 67
Multiple Listing Service (MLS), 143
municipal bonds, 115
Murphy, Eddie, 43, 122
mutual funds, 13, 43, 45, 96-105

N

name (of the bond), 112
Napa Valley, 126

NASDAQ, 56
National Association of Securities Dealers, Inc., 55
NBC, 33
Nebraska Securities Bureau, 190
negative amortization, 135
Neiman Marcus Group, 22
net chg., 67, 112
net income, 22
net worth, 7-8
Nevada Securities Division, 190
New Economy, 3
New Hampshire Bureau of Securities Regulation, 190
New Jersey Bureau of Securities, 190
New Mexico Securities Division, 190
New York Bureau of Investment, 190
New York Mercantile Exchange, The, 121
New York Stock and Exchange Board, The, 57
New York Stock Exchange, The, (NYSE), 23, 56-57, 59
New York Times, The, 37
NFO Interactive, 46, 88
niche label clothing, 158
Nightmare on Elm Street, 119
Nikkei stock index, 99
Nike, 47, 159
no-loads, 102
North Carolina Securities Division, 191
North Dakota Securities Commission, 191

O

off-shore frauds, 152
Ohio Division of Securities, 191
Ohio State University, 8
Oklahoma City, 125
Oklahoma Securities Commission, 191
Old Economy, 3
Old Navy, 178
On-Line Broker 2000 Survey, 47
Online Brokerage Market: Consumers, Web Sites, & Competition, Third Edition, 46
online education, 158
online file storage, 158
online film distribution, 158
On-Line Investor, 60
Orben, Robert, 2
Oregon Division of Finance and Corporate Securities, 191
outstanding shares, 22

P

"pump and dump" scam, the, 148
P/E growth ratio (PEG), 71
P/E ratio, 22, 67
Pacino, Al, 145
PaineWebber, 47
painting, 164
Pennsylvania Securities Commission, 191
pension, 20

INDEX 212

Q

Qualcomm, 1
Quicken.com, 60

R

radon, 141
rate of return, 29-31
Reagan, Ronald and Nancy, 79
real estate, 31, 164
real estate agents, 142
RealTickIII, 59
Reeves, Keanu, 4, 130
refinancing (your mortgage), 145
rental properties, 146
renting (vs. buying), 126
report on operations, 74
Responsibility Research Center, The, 87
retirement, 7, 16-19
Reuters' Instinet, 59, 60
Revenue bonds, 116
revenues, 22
Rhode Island Department of Business regulation, 191
Rhodes, Jim, 10
Ribisi, Giovanni, 90
risk, 54
risk tolerance, 32-33
Rocker, John, 40-41
Rolex, 178
Romer, Paul, 28

Perkins loans, 15
Peter, Laurence J., 23
Philidelphia Stock Exchange (PHLX), 57
Philip Morris, 69
points (on a mortgage), 134
Ponzi, Charles, 147
preferred stock, 70
prepayment penalties, 135
price/sales ratio (PSR), 71
property tax, 128
prorated payments, 137
Providence Foundation Fund, The, 153
Prudential, 47
pyramid approach (to investing), 36
pyramid schemes, 147

Roth IRA, 17-18
Ryder Moving Services, 162

S

S & P 500, 81
S corporation, 179
Saks, 22
savings, 7, 10
savings account, 11
savings banks, 170
Scottrade, 59
Scrooge McDuck, 119
Sears, 22, 89
securities, 23
Securities and Exchange Commission, (SEC),11, 74, 14, 43, 50, 52-53, 148
Securities Division of the District of Columbia, 188
Securities Investor Protection Corporation, 54-55
Series E/EE bonds, 113
Series HH bonds, 114
share appreciation, 100
Sheen, Charlie, 85
Shore, Pauly, 174
Singer Co., 21
Small Business Administration, The, 171, 179
Smith, Fred, 158
Smith, Lee, 88
social security, 6, 18
socially responsible, 98
sole proprietorship, 179
South Carolina Office of the Attorney General, Securities Section, 191
South Dakota Securities commission, 192
spam (e-mail), 150-152
Spectrem Group, The, 46, 88
Springstreet.com, 161
Stafford loans, 15
Standardandpoors.com, 76
Star Trek, 154
Starr, Ringo, 1
starting your own business, 157
start-up fees, 153
stock exchange, 23
stock listings, 111

stock split, 23
Stockpoint.com, 77
stocks, 13, 43, 65, 67
Stockscreener.com, 81
Stocksniffer.com, 78
Stone, Oliver, 85
stop order, 50
street name, 23
Subway, 185
supply and demand, 27
Survivor, 42

T

taxes, 10
Taxpayers Relief Act, 16
Taylor, Liz, 141
technology/internet stocks, 88
Templeton, John, 39, 65
Tennessee Securities Division, 192
Terminator 2, 4
Texas State Securities Board, 192
TheStreet.com, 47, 86
Tiger Management LLC, 40
Timberlake, Lewis, 178
Times Square, 136
title insurance, 129
Tomorrowland, 42
tot tech, 158
Toys "Я" Us, 169
Trading Places, 2, 43, 122
Trans Union, 15
Treasury bills, 115
Treasury bonds, 115
Treasury notes, 115
trucking, 164
Trump, Donald, 64
turnkey businesses, 186
Tyler, Troy, 158

U

U. S. Treasury bonds, 34
U. S. Treasury Department, The, 112
USA Today, 87
Utah Division of Consumer Protection, 153

215 — INDEX

Utah Division of Consumer Protection, 153
Utah Division of Securities, 192

V

vacation prize promotions, 151
Value America, 40, 87
Value Line, 75
value funds, 101
value stocks, 68

variable-rate CD, 12
VeriSign, 22
Vermont Department of Banking, Insurance, and Securities, 192
Veteran's Administration (VA), 136
Virginia Division of Securities and Retail Franchising, 192
Visa, 162
VOL 100s, 67
volume, 112

W

Wall Street, 43, 47
Wall Street, 2, 85, 90
Wall Street Journal, The, 60, 32, 42, 148
Wal-Mart, 39, 69
Washington Department of Financial Institutions, 192
Waterhouse, 46
Weather Channel, The, 21
West Virginia Securities Division, 192
WhisperNumber.com, 78
Wilshire 500, 81
Wisconsin Division of Securities, 192
work-at-home schemes, 152
working from home, 153
World War II, 69
www.ag.ohio-state.edu, 8
www.finacenter.com, 8
Wyoming Securities Division, 192

Y

Yahoo!, 88,
yield %, 67
Yoakam, Dwight, 141